MySQL 5.1 Plugin Development

Extend MySQL to suit your needs with this unique guide
into the world of MySQL plugins

Sergei Golubchik

Andrew Hutchings

open source
community experience distilled

PACKT
PUBLISHING

BIRMINGHAM - MUMBAI

MySQL 5.1 Plugin Development

First published: August 2010

Production Reference: 1190810

Published by Packt Publishing Ltd.
32 Lincoln Road
Olton
Birmingham, B27 6PA, UK.

ISBN 978-1-849510-60-8

www.packtpub.com

Cover Image by Asher Wishkerman (a.wishkerman@mpic.de)

Credits

Authors

Sergei Golubchik

Andrew Hutchings

Reviewer

Giuseppe Maxia

Acquisition Editor

Sarah Cullington

Development Editor

Swapna Verlekar

Technical Editors

Priya Darwani

Chris Rodrigues

Indexer

Monica Ajmera Mehta

Editorial Team Leader

Akshara Aware

Project Team Leader

Ashwin Shetty

Project Coordinator

Zainab Bagasrawala

Proofreader

Kevin McGowan

Graphics

Geetanjali Sawant

Production Coordinator

Arvindkumar Gupta

Cover Work

Arvindkumar Gupta

About the Authors

Sergei Golubchik started modifying MySQL source code in 1998, and has continued as a MySQL AB employee since 2000. Working professionally with MySQL sources, he has had the opportunity to get to know and extend almost every part of the server code—from the SQL core to the utility functions. He was one of the primary architects of the Plugin API. After working for ten years in the ever-growing MySQL AB, and later in Sun Microsystems as a Principal Software Developer, he resigned to join a small startup company that works on a MariaDB—an extended version of the MySQL server, where he continues to do what he likes most—hack on MySQL, architecting, and developing MySQL/MariaDB Plugin API, making it even more powerful, safe, and easy to use.

He works and lives in Germany, near Cologne, with his lovely wife and two kids.

Andrew Hutchings is currently one of the top MySQL Support Engineers working at Oracle. He came from failing Computer Science at A-Level (British exams for 17-18 year olds) to working on, pretty much, every field of computing. His first development job was as an 8-bit assembly firmware developer for an environment monitoring company. He then went on to become a senior PHP and C/C++ developer as well as a DBA and system administrator for a large UK magazine chain. From there he was snapped up by Sun Microsystems as a MySQL Support Engineer specializing in MySQL Cluster and C/C++ APIs, much of this work involving deep analysis of the MySQL source code. Sun has since been bought by Oracle and Andrew is continuing his role there and was a tutorial speaker at the 2010 O'Reilly MySQL Conference & Expo. In his spare time Andrew is an active community developer of MySQL, MySQL Cluster, Drizzle, and MySQL Data Dumper (mydumper for short) as well as other small, related projects.

I'd like to thank my wife, Natalie, and my children, Tomos and Oliver, for putting up with me while I was writing this book. I also wish to thank my colleagues, ex-colleagues, and others in the MySQL community (you know who you are) for their help and support in getting started with writing a book. And, of course, my co-author Sergei, without whom this whole book would not have been possible.

About the Reviewer

Giuseppe Maxia, a.k.a. *The Data Charmer*, is the MySQL Community Team Lead at Sun Microsystems. He is an active member of the MySQL community and a long time open source enthusiast. For the past 23 years he has worked in various IT related fields, with focus on databases, object-oriented programming, and system administration. He is fluent in Italian, English, Perl, SQL, Lua, C, Bash, and a good speaker of C++, French, Spanish, and Java.

He works in cyberspace, with a virtual team.

Table of Contents

Preface

Plugin based architecture is not something new, many popular software products use it. It is good both for the software product itself—if done properly it forces developers to structure the code and think about clean interfaces, which helps to keep the code maintainable over years—and for the users—as they can extend it without waiting for the vendor or choose from numerous third-party extensions.

History of the Plugin API

MySQL used to have "pluggable" extensions in a form of dynamically loaded functions since version 3.21.24 released in February 1998. Despite being quite limited in functionality, they were useful and people were using them. In early 2005, one of the authors of this book together with another MySQL developer, Sergey Vojtovich, were working on loadable parsers for MySQL full-text search, to be able to load a very specialized parser that one of their customers wanted. And Brian Aker, who was MySQL Director of Architecture at that time, suggested creating a unified interface for loadable "modules". Based on this idea we developed the *MySQL Plugin API*—a generic framework that allowed loading of any functionality in the server—and *Full-text Parser plugins* were the first plugin type.

Storage Engine API already existed in MySQL at that time—Michael "Monty" Widenius, the original author of MySQL, had it since the very first MySQL version, although he only added the `handler` class few years later, in 1999. This made *Storage Engine plugins* an easy target, and we added them as the next plugin type. Soon after that I, and another MySQL developer, Antony Curtis, extended Plugin API with the *autotools* support, the infamous `plug.in` file and `MYSQL_PLUGIN_*` macros that go in it, and implemented support for server variables, `MYSQL_SYSVAR_*` and `MYSQL_THDVAR_*` macros. Brian Aker added two more plugin types—*Information Schema Table plugins* and *Daemon plugins*.

Life was going on even after MySQL 5.1 was released — Antony Curtis and I have developed *Audit plugins*. And very recently I and an external contributor, MIT student R.J. Silk, have completed the work on pluggable authentication and *Authentication plugins* were born.

Meanwhile, Michael "Monty" Widenius had left MySQL and started a new company to work on MySQL fork, that he named MariaDB. Another former MySQL developer, Sanja Byelkin, and I have implemented the latest (at the time of writing) feature in the Storage Engine API, the engine defined attributes in the CREATE TABLE statement.

Idea of this book

Today, the MySQL Plugin API is a robust and proven feature. There are many third-party plugins both open and closed source, the most popular being Storage Engines, often accompanied by Information Schema tables, and Full-text parsers.

However, the API documentation is not very helpful. If you are anything like me, you prefer fiction to a dictionary and a few good examples to a grammar description in the Backus-Naur form. The Plugin API documentation describes the functions and the structures but does not show how to use them. Tutorials, on the other hand, help the reader to understand how to use the API. Examples are important to illustrate the concepts and to bootstrap a new plugin project easily.

This is where the idea of this book came from. We wanted to create a book that would allow readers to start writing plugins right away. With detailed tutorials and practical plugin examples, thoroughly explained line by line, highlighted common mistakes and clarified design decisions. And with code samples that you can start using in your projects. Not just the code you can copy, but more importantly, the code you understand — every line, every variable — as if you had written it yourself.

But this book is not a reference manual. It does not contain an exhaustive list of all functions, classes, and macros of the MySQL Plugin API. The API is documented in the header files and in the MySQL manual. But to use it, you need to know what to look for. It is often said that asking the right question is half the right answer. This book teaches you to ask right questions. It gives detailed *understanding* — not just *knowledge* — of the MySQL Plugin API, and even if you will not have every piece of the puzzle, you will have most of them, you will know how they fit together, and you will be able to see the whole picture.

What this book covers

The book encourages consecutive reading, but chapters can be read in any order too. They are mostly independent, and, if needed, you can start reading from, for example, storage engine chapters without reading about full-text search parsers or UDFs. The book is structured as follows.

Chapter 1, Compiling and Using MySQL Plugins lays the necessary foundation for the rest of the book, you will need it in all of the following chapters. It describes how to compile, link, and install UDFs and plugins. Even if you are only interested in, say, full-text parsers or storage engines, you may want to read this chapter first. It is not called *Read Me First!!!* only because we suspected that the editor may not have wanted a lot of exclamation marks in the chapter title.

Chapter 2, User Defined Functions deals with UDFs - these dynamically loaded server extensions that first appeared in the server in 3.21.24, the great-grandparents of the MySQL Plugin API. Although, strictly speaking, UDFs are not MySQL Plugins — not part of the MySQL Plugin API — they are still used to load functionality in the server at runtime, just like plugins are, and sometimes they are used to complement the plugin functionality.

Chapter 3, Daemon Plugins introduces the reader to the MySQL Plugin API. It talks about the most simple plugin type — Daemon plugins. It starts with the basic structure of a plugin — what a plugin declaration should look like, what plugin types are, and so on. Then it describes features common to all plugin types — initialization and de-initialization callbacks, status variables, and configuration system variables. After that it describes and analyzes line by line four Daemon plugin examples — from a simple plugin that prints *Hello World!* when loaded, to a system monitoring plugin that periodically logs the number of connections, to a system usage status plugin that displays the memory and I/O usage of the MySQL server.

Chapter 4, Information Schema Plugins is dedicated to plugins that add tables to INFORMATION_SCHEMA. It describes all of the necessary data structures and ends with two plugin examples — a simple INFORMATION_SCHEMA table with versions of different MySQL subsystems and system usage statistics presented as an INFORMATION_SCHEMA table.

Chapter 5, Advanced Information Schema Plugins delves more into the topic started in the previous chapter. It explains how to use condition pushdown and how to extract and display information from the server internal data structures. It presents three plugins that demonstrate condition pushdown, list all user variables, and all binary log files.

Chapter 6, Full-text Parser Plugins is about plugins that extend the MySQL built-in full-text search. It describes all of the data structures and the code execution flow and illustrates all that with an example plugin that can parse PHP scripts.

Chapter 7, Practical Full-text Parsers is devoted to the advanced applications of the plugins of this type. It explains how the search in Boolean mode works and contains more plugin examples — an Exif parser that allows users to search within embedded comments in image files, a Soundex parser that post-processes all words with a Soundex algorithm making the search invulnerable to typos and misspelled words, and a Boolean search parser plugin that supports AND and OR operators.

Chapter 8, Storage Engine Plugins starts the discussion about the most complex and versatile plugin type in MySQL. It gives an overview of the main concepts of the Storage Engine API and thoroughly analyzes sources of the very simple read-only storage engine.

Chapter 9, HTML Storage Engine - Reads and Writes continues the Storage Engine series. It presents a storage engine plugin that keeps table data in HTML tables and uses it to explain how to implement an updatable data stores.

Chapter 10, TOCAB Storage Engine - Implementing Indexes concludes the Storage Engine part of the book. In this chapter, we develop a storage engine that supports indexes, using it to explain how the indexing part of the MySQL Storage Engine API works, how to build an engine that uses an external indexing library, and how to work around the incompatibilities of their APIs.

Appendix talks about new MySQL Plugin API features, those that did not make it into MySQL 5.1. It describes Server Services, what they are and why they were introduced, the Audit plugins, the example of a plugin that audits security violations, Authentication plugins, with a plugin that uses USB devices to identify users, and engine attributes in the CREATE TABLE, demonstrating the feature with the help of the storage engine from *Chapter 10*.

What you need for this book

The book assumes basic knowledge of SQL and MySQL in particular, and until MySQL developers implement support for plugins in scripting languages, which would be great but can hardly happen any time soon, a certain level of familiarity with C, and for storage engines C++, will be required.

Who this book is for

We wrote this book for people who want to create MySQL plugins. They could be developers with a great idea for a new storage engine. But more often than not they will be application developers that need to solve a specific problem, whether it is searching text within Microsoft Word or Open Office documents, monitoring the database server with their company-wide monitoring framework, querying with SQL the multi-gigabyte files created with a 20 year old custom data storage library and joining them with new relational data, or adding MySQL to the company-wide single sign-on setup. All this and much more can be done with MySQL plugins.

Conventions

In this book, you will find a number of styles of text that distinguish between different kinds of information. Here are some examples of these styles, and an explanation of their meaning.

Code words in text are shown as follows: "The second argument of the `name_init()` function is a pointer to the `UDF_ARGS` structure."

A block of code is set as follows:

```
typedef struct st_field_info
{
  const char* field_name;
  uint field_length;
  enum enum_field_types field_type;
  int value;
  uint field_flags;
  const char* old_name;
  uint open_method;
} ST_FIELD_INFO;
```

When we wish to draw your attention to a particular part of a code block, the relevant lines or items are set in bold:

```
static int tocab_init(void *p)
{
  handlerton *tocab_hton = (handlerton *)p;
  tocab_hton->create = tocab_create_handler;
  tocab_hton->table_options = table_option_list;
  return 0;
}
```

Any command-line input or output is written as follows:

```
shell$ mysql_config --cflags
```

New terms and important words are shown in italics. Words that you see on the screen, in menus or dialog boxes for example, appear in the text like this: "Then in the **C/C++** section we need to add the MySQL include path to **Additional Include Directories**".

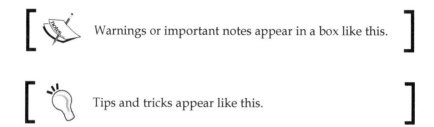

Warnings or important notes appear in a box like this.

Tips and tricks appear like this.

Reader feedback

Feedback from our readers is always welcome. Let us know what you think about this book—what you liked or may have disliked. Reader feedback is important for us to develop titles that you really get the most out of.

To send us general feedback, simply send an e-mail to feedback@packtpub.com, and mention the book title via the subject of your message.

If there is a book that you need and would like to see us publish, please send us a note in the **SUGGEST A TITLE** form on www.packtpub.com or e-mail suggest@packtpub.com.

If there is a topic that you have expertise in and you are interested in either writing or contributing to a book, see our author guide on www.packtpub.com/authors.

Customer support

Now that you are the proud owner of a Packt book, we have a number of things to help you to get the most from your purchase.

Downloading the example code for this book

You can download the example code files for all Packt books you have purchased from your account at http://www.PacktPub.com. If you purchased this book elsewhere, you can visit http://www.PacktPub.com/support and register to have the files e-mailed directly to you.

Errata

Although we have taken every care to ensure the accuracy of our content, mistakes do happen. If you find a mistake in one of our books—maybe a mistake in the text or the code—we would be grateful if you would report this to us. By doing so, you can save other readers from frustration and help us improve subsequent versions of this book. If you find any errata, please report them by visiting http://www.packtpub. com/support, selecting your book, clicking on the **errata submission form** link, and entering the details of your errata. Once your errata are verified, your submission will be accepted and the errata will be uploaded on our website, or added to any list of existing errata, under the Errata section of that title. Any existing errata can be viewed by selecting your title from http://www.packtpub.com/support.

Piracy

Piracy of copyright material on the Internet is an ongoing problem across all media. At Packt, we take the protection of our copyright and licenses very seriously. If you come across any illegal copies of our works, in any form, on the Internet, please provide us with the location address or website name immediately so that we can pursue a remedy.

Please contact us at copyright@packtpub.com with a link to the suspected pirated material.

We appreciate your help in protecting our authors, and our ability to bring you valuable content.

Questions

You can contact us at questions@packtpub.com if you are having a problem with any aspect of the book, and we will do our best to address it.

1
Compiling and Using MySQL Plugins

As you progress through this book you will see several examples of how to use MySQL plugins. This chapter is designed to help you compile and install the UDFs (User Defined Functions) and MySQL plugins that will be created in the following chapters. Do not miss it; you will need this knowledge in every single chapter later on.

UDF libraries

MySQL comes with a small utility called `mysql_config`, which aids the supply of some of the required options to your compiler. In most cases you need:

```
shell$ mysql_config --cflags
```

This will print something such as the following:

```
-I/opt/mysql-5.1/include/mysql -g -Wreturn-type -Wtrigraphs -W -Wformat
-Wsign-compare -Wunused-function -Wunused-value -Wunused-parameter -m64
-DUNIV_LINUX
```

Both MySQL plugins and UDFs need to be compiled as shared libraries. How this is done depends on the platform.

Linux

Under Linux, UDFs should be compiled as follows:

```
gcc -o udf_library.so udf_library.c `mysql_config --cflags` -shared -fPIC
```

The `mysql_config` in backticks will apply the results for the command as switches to `gcc`, so the include directories as well as other required build options are automatically inserted. The `-shared` option tells the compiler that we are creating a shared library and `-fPIC` enables Position Independent Code, which is required for dynamic linking of this shared library.

Mac OS X

Compiling on Mac OS X is very much like compiling on Linux, but the way shared libraries are defined is slightly different:

```
gcc -o udf_library.so udf_library.c `mysql_config --cflags` -bundle
```

A *bundle* is the Mac OS X equivalent of a shared library. If the UDF needs to call functions in the server binary (for example, if it uses the DBUG debugging facility) the command line will need to be:

```
gcc -o udf_library.so udf_library.c `mysql_config --cflags`
-bundle -Wl,-undefined -Wl,dynamic_lookup
```

Windows

Setting up for compiling UDFs in Windows is generally more involved than in other operating systems.

As everywhere, we need to have the required libraries and include files installed. To do this we run the MySQL installer. If you already have MySQL installed, you can use this tool to modify your installation. The following screenshot shows that we have selected **Custom** to do this, but a complete install will also give the required files:

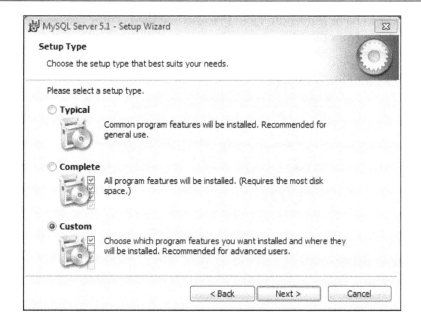

Now we need to select **Developer Components** and then **C Include Files / Lib Files** to have them included in the installation. Once this is done the installer should look similar to this:

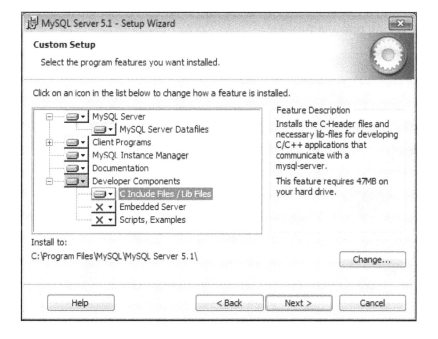

Also, you need to have Microsoft Visual Studio installed. There are free express editions available from the Microsoft website, which we can use.

In Visual Studio we need to create a new empty project to put our source code into and set up the build environment:

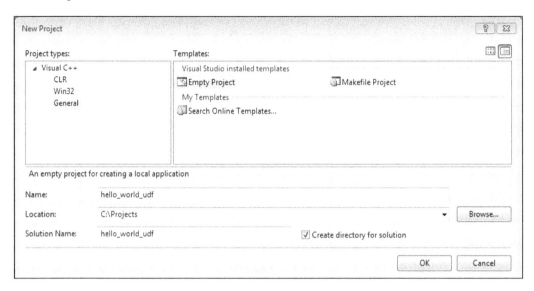

Then we need to add a source file to this project. We can either create a new `.cpp` file or add an existing one to a project:

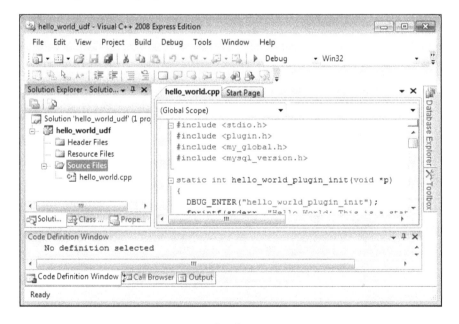

Now we need to modify the project properties to set up everything required to compile the UDF. To start with, inside the **General** configuration section, we need to set the **Configuration Type** to a `.dll` file (a Windows dynamic link library):

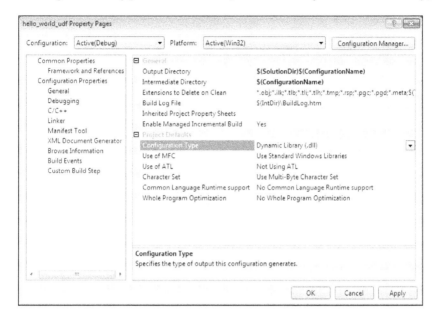

Then in the **C/C++** section we need to add the MySQL include path to **Additional Include Directories**:

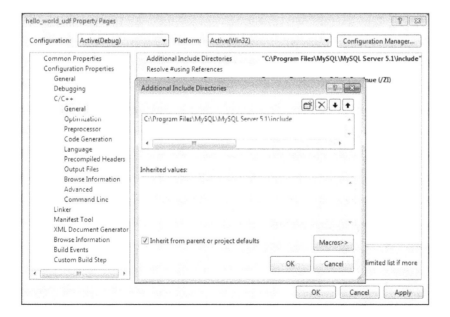

Finally, we need to create a definitions file that lists the functions from this library which we wish to export for MySQL to use. It may look as follows:

```
EXPORTS
  udf_hello_world
  udf_hello_world_init
  udf_hello_world_deinit
```

This is then added to the **Linker** configuration in the **Input** section under **Module Definition File**. This gives a hand-typed dialog, so we need to type in the full path to the definitions file we just created:

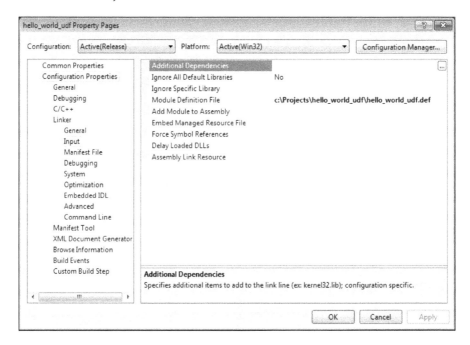

We can then compile our UDF and, if successful, we will have a brand new `.dll` file:

Installing a UDF

Now that we have our UDF, we need to install it in the MySQL server. For security reasons MySQL will only load plugins and UDFs from the location defined in the `plugin_dir` system variable. This variable can only be set during the startup of the MySQL server. By default it is in the `lib/mysql/plugin` subdirectory inside the directory where MySQL is installed. So we need to put our UDF library there.

We can then tell MySQL to load the library using:

```
CREATE FUNCTION my_udf_function RETURNS STRING SONAME 'my_udf_function.so'
```

More details on how to use this syntax and how to solve UDF loading errors are in the UDF chapter of this book.

Plugin libraries

Building and installing plugin libraries is very much like building and installing UDFs. The include and library paths are the same but some further build options are needed. This is slightly complicated by the fact that some plugin types (namely Information Schema and Storage Engine plugins) require the MySQL source to be downloaded for the version of the MySQL server you have installed. This is so that the plugin can have access to data and functions that are only "half-public" and are not declared in the installed C header files.

Linux

When compiling on Linux and using just the normal plugin API we can compile in the same way as with UDFs:

```
gcc -omy_plugin.so my_plugin.c `mysql_config --cflags` -shared -fPIC
-DMYSQL_DYNAMIC_PLUGIN
```

Notice that the main difference here is `-DMYSQL_DYNAMIC_PLUGIN`. This sets up the necessary environment for the plugin at compile time.

For plugins that require access to the MySQL server source, compiling is slightly different (suppose, the MySQL source tree is in `/Sources/mysql-5.1.35`):

```
gcc  omy_plugin.so my_plugin.cc `mysql_config   cflags`
—I/Sources/mysql 5.1.35/include/  I/Sources/mysql 5.1.35/regex
—I/Sources/mysql 5.1.35/sql  shared  fPIC  fno exceptions
—fno rtti  DMYSQL_DYNAMIC_PLUGIN
```

Typically, such a plugin will be in C++, not C. It is compiled exactly the same way the main server is—without exceptions or runtime type identification. Technically, it could use exceptions, but then it may need to use g++ instead of gcc as a C++ compiler. Either way, it needs extra include paths that point to the include/, regex/, and sql/ directories of the MySQL source tree.

Mac OS X

Just as in the UDF case, compiling plugins on Mac OS X is almost the same as on Linux. You can use the same command line and only replace -shared -fPIC with -bundle or –bundle -Wl,-undefined -Wl,dynamic_lookup as explained before.

Windows

In Windows we can compile MySQL plugins that do not require the inclusion of the MySQL source code (everything except Information Schema and Storage Engine plugins) using a process very similar to compiling UDFs.

First, we need to create an empty project file to contain the source and build environment:

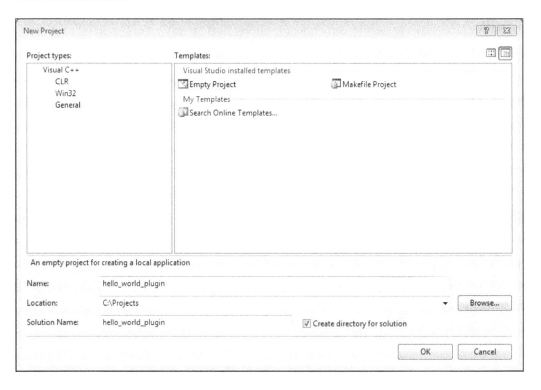

We can then add or create a `.cpp` file containing the source for our plugin:

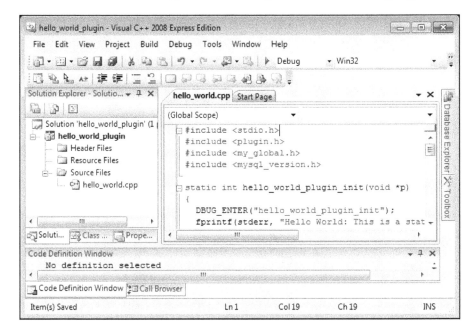

This project needs to be a `.dll`, not an executable one. We can set this in the project's **Property Pages** dialog:

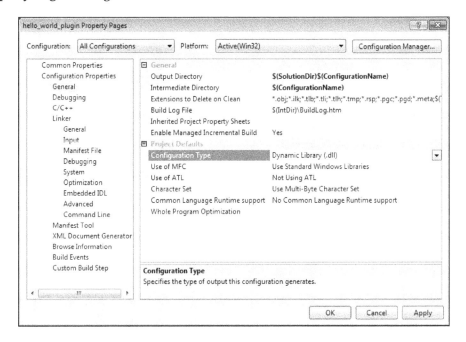

We now need to set up the C/C++ include paths so that the MySQL include path is in them:

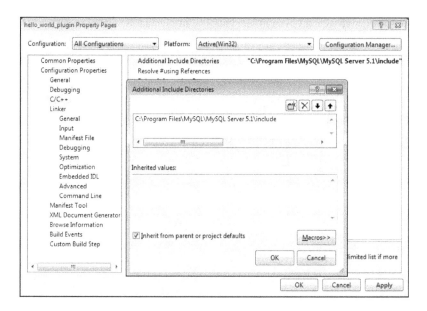

This final step is different to compiling the UDFs. We need to add a C/C++ preprocessor definition so that the include files set up everything we need for a MySQL plugin. To do this we simply add MYSQL_DYNAMIC_PLUGIN to the definitions list:

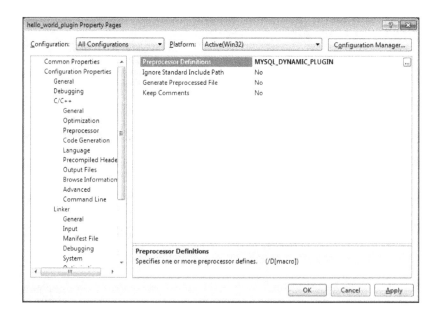

Installing a plugin

Just as with UDFs, our MySQL plugin needs to be in `plugin_dir` before it can be added to MySQL. Once it is located there the syntax is very simple. All of the details about how to use the plugin are in the plugin itself. So we simply need:

```
INSTALL PLUGIN my_plugin SONAME 'my_plugin.so'
```

Automatic builds, packaging

Specifying all compiler options manually, as we did in a previous section, gets more complicated as the number of files grows. When a plugin consists of more than a couple of files, an appropriate `Makefile` becomes almost a requirement. And it is absolutely unavoidable if we want to distribute our great plugin, as we cannot expect our users to copy and paste complex command lines from a `README` file. We want the process of configuring and building a plugin to be as simple as possible. But first we need to decide whether a plugin should be built from inside the MySQL source tree or standalone.

UDFs and standalone plugins

UDFs and certain plugin types (for example, full-text parser plugins, some Daemon plugins, or newer plugin types added after MySQL 5.1) do not require MySQL sources for building; the API for them is complete and self-sufficient. These plugins can be distributed and built independently from MySQL. Writing a `Makefile` or `configure.ac` for such a plugin does not differ from writing them for any other project—we only need to set the installation path correctly. When using `automake` and `libtool`, a simple `Makefile.am` can look like this:

```
plugindir= $(libdir)/mysql/plugin
plugin_LTLIBRARIES=    my_plugin.la
my_plugin_la_SOURCES= my_plugin.c
my_plugin_la_LDFLAGS= -module -rpath $(plugindir)
my_plugin_la_CFLAGS=   -DMYSQL_DYNAMIC_PLUGIN
```

This file sets the installation directory to be `mysql/plugin/` inside the library path, which is usually `/usr/lib`. However, strictly speaking, the user has to use the same library path that his MySQL installation uses. It specifies the build target to be `my_plugin.la` — it is a libtool control file, a text file with information about `my_plugin.so`. The latter will be built automatically. It tells the libtool that we are building a library for dynamic loading with `dlopen()` (the `-module` option does that) and where it will be installed. The last line adds `-DMYSQL_DYNAMIC_PLUGIN` to the compiler command line. There is no need to specify `-fPIC`, `-shared`, or `-bundle`; libtool will use them automatically, depending on the platform we are building on. It knows a large number of operating systems, compilers, linkers, and their corresponding command-line switches for building dynamically loaded modules.

In addition to `Makefile.am`, a complete project will need a `configure.ac` file, `AUTHORS`, `NEWS`, `ChangeLog`, and `README` files. The last four files are required by automake, but they can be empty. The `configure.ac` file is used by autoconf to generate a `configure` script, which, in turn, will generate `Makefile`. A minimal `configure.ac` could be as simple as:

```
AC_INIT(my_plugin, 0.1)
AM_INIT_AUTOMAKE
AC_PROG_LIBTOOL
AC_CONFIG_FILES([Makefile])
AC_OUTPUT
```

It sets the name and version of our software package, initializes automake and libtool, and specifies that the result of the `configure` script should be a `Makefile`.

Plugins that are built from the MySQL source tree

If we need to have access to the MySQL source tree for our plugin, we can at least do it with style. Plugins that are built from the MySQL source tree can be integrated seamlessly into the MySQL build system. Additionally, we will get support for Microsoft Windows builds and the ability to link the plugin *statically* into the server, so that it becomes a part of the `mysqld` binary. Unlike standalone plugins, we will only need three auxiliary files here.

On UNIX-like systems, MySQL 5.1 is built using autotools and make. A `plug.in` file will be the source file for autoconf, and `Makefile.am` for automake. To build MySQL on Windows one needs CMake, and thus our plugin should come with a `CMakeLists.txt` file. All of these three files can use the full power of autotools or CMake, if necessary, but for a minimal working plugin they only need to contain a few simple lines.

plug.in

The plug.in file describes the plugin to the MySQL configure script. A plugin is detected automatically by autoconf as long as its plug.in file can be found in a directory located in the plugin/ or storage/ subdirectory in the MySQL source tree (in other words, it should be either plugin/*/plug.in or storage/*/plug.in). A plug.in file can use all autoconf and m4 macros as usual. Additionally, MySQL defines a few macros specifically for using in the plug.in files. They all are documented in the config/ac-macros/plugin.m4 file in the MySQL source tree. The most important of them are described as follows:

- MYSQL_PLUGIN([name],[long name], [description], [group,group...])

  This is usually the first line in any plug.in file. This macro is mandatory. It declares a new plugin. The name will be used in the configure options such as --with-plugin-foo and --without-plugin-foo. The long name and the description will be printed in the ./configure --help output. "Groups" are preset configuration names that one can specify in the --with-plugin=group option. Any group name can be used, but max, max-no-ndb, and default are commonly used. Most plugins add themselves to the max and max-no-ndb groups.

- MYSQL_PLUGIN_STATIC([name],[libmyplugin.a])

  This macro declares that a plugin name supports static builds, that is, it can be built as a static library and linked statically into the server binary. It specifies the name of this static library, which can be later referred to in Makefile.am as @plugin_myplugin_static_target@. It will be expanded to libmyplugin.a if a static build is selected, otherwise it will be empty.

- MYSQL_PLUGIN_DYNAMIC([name],[myplugin.la])

  Similarly, this macro declares that a plugin can be built as a shared library and loaded into the server dynamically. It introduces a Makefile.am substitution @plugin_myplugin_dynamic_target@, which is myplugin.la if this shared library needs to be built, and empty otherwise.

- MYSQL_PLUGIN_ACTIONS([name],[ACTION-IF-SELECTED])

  The ACTION-IF-SELECTED code will be executed only if this plugin is selected by configure either for static or dynamic builds. Here we can check for system headers, libraries, and functions that are used by the plugin. Normal AC_ macros can be used here freely.

An example of a `plug.in` file can look like

```
MYSQL_PLUGIN(my_plugin,[My Plugin Example],
             [An example of My Plugin], [max,max-no-ndb])
MYSQL_PLUGIN_STATIC(my_plugin,[libmy_plugin.a])
MYSQL_PLUGIN_DYNAMIC(my_plugin,[my_plugin.la])
```

With such a file in place, say in `plugin/my_plugin/plug.in`, all we need to do is to run `autoreconf -f` to recreate the `configure` script. After that, there is no distinction between our plugin and official MySQL plugins:

```
$ ./configure --help
`configure' configures this package to adapt to many kinds of systems.
...
  --with-plugins=PLUGIN[[[,PLUGIN..]]]
                Plugins to include in mysqld. (default is: none)
                Must be a configuration name or a comma separated
                list of plugins.
                Available configurations are: none max max-no-ndb
                all.
                Available plugins are: partition daemon_example
                ftexample archive blackhole csv example federated
                heap ibmdb2i innobase innodb_plugin myisam
                myisammrg my_plugin ndbcluster.
...
  === My Plugin Example ===
  Plugin Name:       my_plugin
  Description:       An example of My Plugin
  Supports build:    static and dynamic
  Configurations:    max, max-no-ndb
```

A new plugin is mentioned in the "available plugins" list and described in detail at the end of the `configure --help` output.

Makefile.am

As in the case of standalone plugins, we need a `Makefile.am` file. It will be converted by automake and the `configure` script to a `Makefile`, and it defines how the plugin, static or shared library, should be built. This file is more complex than for standalone plugins because it needs to cover both static and dynamic builds. Of course, when a plugin supports only one way of linking, only static or only dynamic, `Makefile.am` gets much simpler. Let's analyze it line by line:

```
pkgplugindir =  $(pkglibdir)/plugin

INCLUDES = -I$(top_srcdir)/include -I$(top_builddir)/include \
           -I$(top_srcdir)/sql

pkgplugin_LTLIBRARIES = @plugin_my_plugin_shared_target@
my_plugin_la_LDFLAGS = -module -rpath $(pkgplugindir)
my_plugin_la_CXXFLAGS= -DMYSQL_DYNAMIC_PLUGIN
my_plugin_la_SOURCES = my_plugin.c

noinst_LIBRARIES = @plugin_my_plugin_static_target@
libmy_plugin_a_SOURCES= my_plugin.c

EXTRA_LTLIBRARIES = my_plugin.la
EXTRA_LIBRARIES = libmy_plugin.a


EXTRA_DIST = CMakeLists.txt plug.in
```

The file starts with defining pkgplugindir—a place where a plugin will be installed.

Then we set the search path for the #include directives; it needs to contain at least the include/ directory where most of the headers are, and often the sql/ directory too, especially when we need to access internal server structures.

Now we can specify automake build rules for the targets. A shared target is a libtool library (LTLIBRARIES) that should be installed in pkgplugindir (because we used the pkgplugin_ prefix). And we specify the source files, compiler and linker flags that are needed to build the my_plugin.la library. If a user decides not to build a dynamic version of our plugin, @plugin_my_plugin_shared_target@ will be empty and no libtool library will be built.

Similarly, we specify rules for the static target. It is a library (LIBRARIES), and it should not be installed (noinst_). Indeed, as it will be linked into the server statically, becoming a part of the server binary, there is no need to install it separately. In this case, we do not need any special compiler or linker flags, we only specify the sources.

Because a user may decide to build either a static or a shared library, the name of the build target is not known before the configure script is run. However, automake needs to know all possible targets in advance, and we list them in the EXTRA_ variables.

We end the file by listing all remaining files that are part of the plugin source distribution, but are not mentioned in other rules. The automake needs to know about them, otherwise the make dist command will work incorrectly.

CMakeLists.txt

In MySQL 5.1, of all plugin types, only Storage Engine plugins can be integrated into the MySQL build system on Windows. One does this by providing an appropriate CMakeLists.txt file. All of the CMake power is available there, but a minimal CMakeLists.txt file is as simple as this:

```
INCLUDE("${PROJECT_SOURCE_DIR}/storage/mysql_storage_engine.cmake")
SET(my_plugin_SOURCES my_plugin.c)
MYSQL_STORAGE_ENGINE(my_plugin)
```

We only specify the name of the storage engine, my_plugin, and the source files, and include the file that does all of the heavy job.

Summary

Using the information in this chapter we should be able to compile all of the UDFs and plugins for this book as well as any others. We should be able to prepare all of the auxiliary files for plugins to be built with configure && make, as a standalone project or as a part of MySQL, either dynamically or statically. We can package them for distributing in the source form that allows the user to build and install the plugin easily.

2

User Defined Functions

Way back in 1998, MySQL 3.21 introduced a framework that allowed users to create new SQL functions easily. It made it possible for developers to write their own functions in C/C++ and load them dynamically into the running server. The functions loaded within this framework were called User Defined Functions or UDFs.

Today not much has changed with UDFs, they are more stable and slightly more secure than they used to be, and they can be declared aggregate for use together with GROUP BY queries. However, many UDFs that worked in 1998 with MySQL 3.21.24 would still work at the time of writing in 2010, with MySQL 5.1.47.

MySQL UDFs are not part of the newer MySQL Plugin API, but there are future plans to make this happen. In the meantime, they can serve as an introduction to MySQL plugins. And sometimes UDFs can be used together with plugins to complement their functionality. In this chapter, we will cover creating User Defined Functions and write several of our own UDFs, working up from a basic static output to an aggregate summing function.

Writing UDFs

UDFs can be of two types, normal and aggregate. Normal UDFs take inputs and deliver an output just like an ordinary function in most programming languages. When run on a set of rows, they will return a result for every row. Aggregate UDFs take a group of rows, process each row, and produce a result at the end. In other words, they will return one result per group. Therefore, aggregate functions are useful for tasks such as adding up a group of values or calculating an average.

Whether MySQL considers a given UDF as an aggregate or a normal type depends on how it was installed. However, the API is somewhat different too, and we need to take care to install UDFs that use the aggregate API as aggregate and normal UDFs as normal. Otherwise they will not only fail to work correctly, but may as well crash the whole server.

Why write UDFs

There are several advantages and disadvantages to UDFs that we should be aware of. UDFs are much easier to develop than is hacking raw code into the MySQL server. If our function were hacked into the server, we would need to change the MySQL source every time we upgraded, which is never easy. MySQL code base evolves quite rapidly and to implement the same function we would need different code changes in every new version. UDFs, on the other hand, continue to work when the server is upgraded. They will not even need to be recompiled.

Also, UDFs have many benefits as compared to Stored Functions written in SQL. For example, UDFs are typically much faster and can be declared aggregate, while stored functions cannot. There are few alternatives to UDFs when custom aggregation functionality is needed.

UDFs are designed for development speed, the API is easy to access, and compilation is much quicker than rebuilding the entire server just to add a tiny function. They are also designed for portability between different MySQL versions.

Although UDFs are much faster than SQL stored functions, they are slightly slower in execution when compared to built-in functions. When running the `udf_floatsum()` function from the end of this chapter on a table with 10,000,000 rows, I got:

Query	Execution time
SELECT UDF_FLOATSUM(a) FROM t1;	1.40 seconds
SELECT SUM(a) FROM t1;	1.36 seconds

As we can see, on my system, MySQL 5.1.47 runs this query about 3% slower when using UDFs compared to native functions.

While UDFs are easier to develop, they offer little extra safety over raw MySQL server hacking. If your UDF code crashes, it will take the MySQL server with it. This is due to the UDF code literally getting bolted onto the server code during runtime.

Installing and using UDFs

To install a normal function in MySQL we can use the following command:

```
CREATE FUNCTION my_func RETURNS INTEGER SONAME 'udf_my_func.so';
```

Whereas with an aggregate function we do it like this:

```
CREATE AGGREGATE FUNCTION my_total_func RETURNS INTEGER
  SONAME 'udf_my_total_func.so';
```

Each shared library can contain multiple UDFs inside, which is useful when installing a group of related functions. If we have multiple UDFs in one shared library, we need to perform CREATE FUNCTION for every UDF contained in it. In Windows, dynamic libraries have the .dll extension, so instead this would be:

```
CREATE FUNCTION my_func RETURNS INTEGER SONAME 'udf_my_func.dll';
```

Once installed, the details of a UDF get stored in the mysql.func table, so that MySQL can automatically load the UDFs back in upon server startup. Once a few UDFs are installed, the table may look as follows:

```
mysql> SELECT * FROM mysql.func;
```

```
+---------------------+-----+--------------------+-----------+
| name                | ret | dl                 | type      |
+---------------------+-----+--------------------+-----------+
| udf_staticexample   |   2 | udf_static.so      | function  |
| udf_intexample      |   2 | udf_integer.so     | function  |
| udf_textexample     |   0 | udf_textexample.so | function  |
| udf_textexample2    |   0 | udf_textexample.so | function  |
| udf_floatsum        |   1 | udf_floatsum.so    | aggregate |
+---------------------+-----+--------------------+-----------+
5 rows in set (0.00 sec)
```

If at any point in time you wish to uninstall a UDF, there is a DROP FUNCTION statement in MySQL. This is run as follows:

```
mysql> DROP FUNCTION my_func;
```

When installed, a UDF can be used just like any native MySQL function, for example, in a SELECT statement. A normal UDF will process and return a result for every row:

```
mysql> SELECT my_example(my_ints) FROM my_table;

+----------------------+
| my_example(my_ints)  |
+----------------------+
|                  99  |
|                  27  |
+----------------------+
2 rows in set (0.00 sec)
```

Whereas aggregate functions will return a single result for an entire group of rows:

```
mysql> SELECT my_aggregate_example(my_ints) FROM my_table;

+-------------------------------+
| my_aggregate_example(my_ints) |
+-------------------------------+
|                           126 |
+-------------------------------+
1 row in set (0.00 sec)
```

An attempt to install a UDF may fail, resulting in an error. In most cases, the causes are easy to find and normally not too difficult to resolve. A few of the common ones are as follows:

```
ERROR 1126 (HY000): Can't open shared library 'my_udf.so' (errno: X )
```

This error means that there is a problem opening the UDF shared library or one of its dependencies. There are two things to look out for here. Firstly, the filename in Windows will always be the UDF dynamic library filename, regardless of which library cannot be opened. However, in Linux/Unix based operating systems it will be the name of the library that is causing the problem.

The second thing to look at is the errno part of the error message. In Linux/Unix this will show a number indicating the error that has occurred. MySQL cannot yet interpret Windows error codes with regard to opening UDFs, but there is work in progress to make this happen.

When it comes to error codes, MySQL comes with a very useful utility called `perror`. Now, say we get this error:

```
ERROR 1126 (HY000): Can't open shared library 'my_udf.so' (errno: 2 )
```

If we run `perror` on error code 2 we should see:

```
shell$ perror 2
OS error code   2:  No such file or directory
```

So we can say that the operating system has reported to MySQL that it cannot find `my_udf.so`. MySQL only loads UDFs from the path stored in the `plugin_dir` server configuration variable, that is, the UDF shared library needs to be there and it needs to be readable by the operating system user that MySQL is run under (usually `mysql`).

If the error is for another shared library, then the operating system cannot find that library in the library path. We can check this by running `ldd` on the UDF shared library to see what the UDF depends on and what it cannot find. For example:

```
shell$ ldd my_udf.so
  linux-vdso.so.1 =>   (0x00007ffff22c9000)
  my_dependency.so => not found
  libc.so.6 => /lib64/libc.so.6 (0x00007fb6a91dc000)
  /lib64/ld-linux-x86-64.so.2 (0x00000035d5c00000)
```

Here we can see that `my_dependency.so` is not found. There are three ways we can resolve this:

1. Find `my_dependency.so` and copy it to a known library path (such as `/usr/lib/`)
2. Alter the list of known library paths to include the directory where `my_dependency.so` is located
3. Embed the full path to `my_dependency.so` in `my_udf.so`

For this second option in Linux, we can do this by adding this directory to the `/etc/ld.so.conf` file and then running `ldconfig` to update the library path cache.

For the third option in Linux we can do it by adding `-Wl,-rpath -Wl,/path/to/my_dependency.so` to the `gcc` command line when linking `my_udf.so`.

As stated earlier, Windows handles things a bit differently. For example, we do not know the exact filename that caused the problem or the failure error code. Luckily, Windows has a utility called Process Monitor, which can help us to find this out. With this utility we can see file open calls as they happen and it will show real errors when failures happen. You can download it from `http://technet.microsoft.com/en-us/sysinternals/bb896645.aspx`. In the following example we try to install a UDF called `my_udf` from `my_udf.dll`. As can be seen here, we get an error because the file cannot be opened, but the error code is not very helpful. To resolve the problem we will take a look at the file monitor inside the Process Monitor window to see what has actually happened:

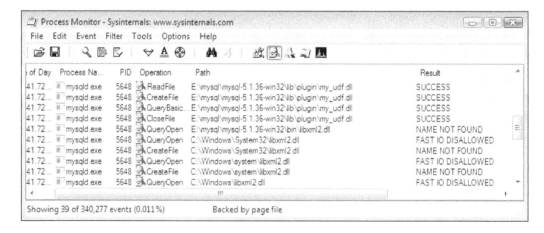

In the following screenshot there is a filter on the `mysqld.exe` process and with this we can see that the file, `my_udf.dll`, was found and was perfectly readable. The actual problem comes from a dependency library, `libxml2.dll`. Windows searches for it in the predefined library paths, but fails. To fix this problem we simply need to put `libxml2.dll` into one of the Windows library paths:

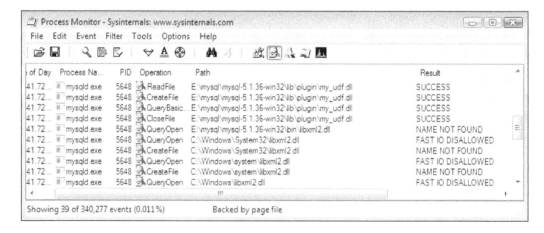

There are other common errors we can get when installing UDFs, but they are normally easier to diagnose:

```
ERROR 1127 (HY000): Can't find symbol 'my_udf' in library
```

This error shows that MySQL has loaded the library, but while searching it for the functions inside, it could not find what it was expecting. This is usually due to the wrong name for the UDF used in the CREATE FUNCTION command.

```
ERROR 1044 (42000): Access denied for user 'username'@'localhost' to
database 'mysql'
```

When installing a UDF, MySQL needs to insert an entry into the func table of the mysql database because MySQL remembers all installed UDFs to be able to load them automatically when restarted. To fix this permission error, we need to install our UDF as a user who has INSERT privileges to the mysql database.

```
ERROR 1123 (HY000): Can't initialize function 'my_udf'; UDFs are
unavailable with the --skip-grant-tables option
```

With the --skip-grant-tables option, MySQL server ignores the privileges table, including the func table required to install UDFs. Without access to this table, UDFs are disabled. Simply restarting MySQL without this option or issuing the FLUSH PRIVILEGES statement will let us install and use UDFs again.

```
ERROR 1146 (42S02): Table 'mysql.func' doesn't exist
```

Somehow the func table has been dropped, and without it we cannot install UDFs. MySQL comes packaged with a utility called mysql_upgrade, which will create the missing table for us.

```
ERROR 145 (HY000): Table './mysql/func' is marked as crashed and should
be repaired
```

The func table is a MyISAM table, and as such is not crash-resilient. We could expect to see this error if the MySQL server crashes when installing or removing a UDF. To fix this, follow the usual MyISAM repair instructions as found in the MySQL manual.

Defining UDFs

All functions in the UDF API start with the name of the UDF itself. For example, if the UDF is called name (that is, installed with CREATE FUNCTION name and used like SELECT name()) the corresponding C functions may be called: name(), name_init(), name_deinit(), and so on. The following table lists all UDF API functions and their purpose:

Function	Normal / Aggregate	Description
name_init()	Both	Initialize the UDF for use. It is called for every statement that uses the UDF name.
name_deinit()	Both	De-initialize the function and clean up memory usage. It is called after the statement that used the UDF name.
name()	Both	The main body of the UDF name, the function that returns a result to the user. It is called for every row (or for every group of rows if the function is declared aggregate).
name_add()	Aggregate	Called for every row of the group.
name_clear()	Aggregate	Called before the first row of every group.
name_reset()	Aggregate. Unused since MySQL 4.1.1	Called for the first row of every group. This function was doing the job of both name_clear and name_add for the first row — starting a new group and processing the first row in this group. It was removed from the API in MySQL 4.1.1 and replaced with name_clear, because it could not handle the case of the empty group. However, you may see it in old UDF examples.

When calling a UDF inside MySQL, firstly name_init() is called with the following prototype:

```
my_bool name_init(UDF_INIT *initid, UDF_ARGS *args,
                  char *message)
```

 Pay attention to the difference between *UDF arguments*, which are arguments passed to the User Defined Function from the SQL (for example, 1, 2, and "foo" in SELECT name(1,2,"foo")), and *arguments of C functions* such as name_init(), name(), and others.

This function should be used to check the metadata of the UDF arguments, such as their types, and prepare the UDF for execution, for example, allocate the memory. Typically, for MySQL, the name_init() function should return 0 for success or 1 for failure. In the latter case, an error message should be written into the buffer pointed to by message, so that the user could see what went wrong. Two other arguments of this function are args, which contains the metadata of the UDF arguments, and initid, which is used to return the metadata of the result (see? argument metadata are already known here, and MySQL wants to know the result metadata. The way MySQL works, it needs to know all metadata before it starts executing the query, that is, before it starts working with the data) and to preserve the internal UDF context between the calls.

A pointer to the UDF_INIT structure, initid, is passed as a first argument to all C functions that implement the UDF, and it can be used to store the context of the execution and share it between the different function calls. Typically, we would allocate some memory for use in the UDF and store a pointer to it inside the UDF_INIT structure. The second purpose of UDF_INIT is to allow us to tell MySQL about the metadata of the UDF result. This structure has the following members:

Member	Type	Description
const_item	my_bool	Set to 1 if the UDF will always return the same result in this query.
decimals	unsigned int	Number of digits after decimal point (this is often called *scale*) in the UDF result. Setting it only makes sense when the UDF is declared as RETURNS REAL.
max_length	unsigned long	The maximum length of the UDF return result (length of its string representation if the result is numeric).
maybe_null	my_bool	Set to 1 if the UDF can return NULL in this query.
ptr	char *	A free-to-use pointer. Not used by the server. Reserved for internal UDF use.

- const_item: It is set by MySQL to 1 if all UDF arguments are constants, and to 0 otherwise, which is a reasonable default for a well-behaving function without side effects. Thus, we only need to set it to 1 if the UDF is a true constant and always returns the same value independent of the arguments. Similarly, we need to set const_item to 0 if the function is truly volatile, and may return different results even if called with exactly the same arguments.

- decimals: It is set by MySQL to the largest scale of the UDF arguments. The supported values are from 0 to 30. Anything larger than that (MySQL internally uses 31 here) means that no scale was specified, and MySQL will not limit the number of digits after a decimal point in the UDF return result.

- max_length: Its default value is set depending on the result type. For the INTEGER return type it is 21, for the REAL return type it is usually 17 plus the value in decimals, and for the STRING return type it is the largest value of max_length of all UDF arguments.

- maybe_null: It is set to 0 by default unless any of the arguments may be NULL, which usually works well for functions such as CONCAT() or FORMAT(). If the UDF can never return NULL (such as the ISNULL() function) this should be set to 0. If the UDF can return NULL even when all arguments are not NULL (such as the NULLIF() function) this should be set to 1.

- ptr: This is a `char*` pointer that MySQL never uses for anything. We can store there any data we want. `initid` is passed to every function in the UDF API, and if we put any value in `initid->ptr` in, say `name_init()`, we will be able to use it in `name()`, `name_add()` or any other function. In other words, this is an easy way to keep the execution context (such as allocated memory buffer) around and preserve it between function calls. Unlike using a global variable, if our UDF is invoked from many SQL statements in many connections in parallel, every such invocation will have its own `initid` and thus its own `initid->ptr`.

The second argument of the `name_init()` function is a pointer to the `UDF_ARGS` structure. It contains the metadata of the arguments that have been passed from MySQL to the UDF. It has pointers to the arguments' values too, but only the values of the constant arguments are filled in at the time when `name_init()` is called. In `SELECT name(5, t1.c1)` the value of 5 is, naturally, known, but the value of column `c1` in the table `t1` is not. Later, when the same `UDF_ARGS` structure is passed to the `name()` or `name_add()` functions all argument values will be filled in, so that the function can compute the UDF return result. The `UDF_ARGS` structure has the following members:

Member	Type	Description
arg_count	unsigned int	The number of arguments passed to the UDF. All arrays below will be of this length.
arg_type	enum Item_result*	An array of types of the arguments.
args	char**	An array of pointers to arguments' values.
lengths	unsigned long*	An array of lengths of each argument value.
maybe_null	char*	An array indicating whether each argument can be NULL in this query.
attributes	char**	An array of names of the arguments.
attribute_lengths	unsigned long*	An array of the lengths of each argument name

- arg_count: It should be used as a count for the number of array elements in the rest of the members of the structure.

- `arg_type`: This array contains the type of every argument passed to the UDF. This can be one of `STRING_RESULT`, `INT_RESULT`, `REAL_RESULT`, and `DECIMAL_RESULT`.

- `args` array: It contains pointers to the actual argument data. It is either a `char*` pointer for the `STRING_RESULT` or `DECIMAL_RESULT` arguments, a `long long*` for `INT_RESULT`, a `double*` for `REAL_RESULT`, or a null pointer if the argument value is NULL or unknown. Note that string values are not zero terminated!

- `lengths`: This array contains the length of each argument value in the `args` member. This is most useful for string arguments. For integer and real types it contains the maximum length of the argument.

- `maybe_null`: This array indicates whether or not each argument could be NULL.

- `attributes`: This array contains names of each argument. This is either an appropriate part of the SQL statement that corresponds to this particular UDF argument, or an alias name, if it was specified. For example, for `SELECT name(1+log(2e3), 15 as bar)` the name of the first argument will be "1+log(2e3)" and the name of the second one will be "bar".

- `attribute_lengths`: It holds the length of each attribute name. Just as with string attribute values, attribute name strings are not zero terminated.

The `name_deinit()` function should be used to clean up after the UDF execution. Often this only entails freeing up any memory pointed to by `initid->ptr`. The de-initialization function is called with the following prototype:

```
void name_deinit(UDF_INIT *initid)
```

 This is the only function inside a UDF that cannot return an error condition.

The function that does all the work for normal UDFs and the result function for aggregate UDFs is the `name()` function.

We can see in the CREATE FUNCTION calls that a return type of the UDF is specified when loading it into the server. This type should match the function prototype chosen when writing the code of the UDF (or bad things could happen). The following table outlines the different return types and the equivalent function prototypes needed in C:

Type	C function
STRING or DECIMAL	`char *name(UDF_INIT *initid, UDF_ARGS *args, char *result, unsigned long *length, char *is_null, char *error)`
INTEGER	`long long name(UDF_INIT *initid, UDF_ARGS *args, char *is_null, char *error)`
REAL	`double name(UDF_INIT *initid, UDF_ARGS *args, char *is_null, char *error);`

 There is **no** check to see if the type in CREATE FUNCTION matches the prototype. A user must ensure the type is correct when installing a UDF or it may not function as desired.

With the STRING type we get a `result` buffer where we can store a UDF return value, but it is only 766 bytes long. If a result longer than that is required we need to use `malloc()` to allocate memory for it. As a UDF can return a binary string with null bytes in it, we should always store the length of the returned string in `*length`, so that MySQL knows how long the result should be.

Irrespective of the return type, all variants of the `name()` function get `is_null` and `error` arguments. The `*is_null` should be set to 1 if we want our UDF to return NULL in this particular invocation, and `*error` should be set to 1 if an error has occurred during execution.

With aggregate functions MySQL repeatedly calls two additional functions, `name_add()` and `name_clear()`. These are designed to perform one calculation per row, while a result is returned only once per group of rows. For every row in a group, MySQL calls `name_add()` and before each group starts, MySQL calls `name_clear()`. These functions are declared as follows:

```
void name_add(UDF_INIT *initid, UDF_ARGS *args,
              char *is_null, char *error)
void name_clear(UDF_INIT *initid, char *is_null, char *error)
```

Execution sequence of a UDF

With a normal function MySQL simply calls three functions in sequence upon every SQL statement that uses the UDF. With aggregate UDFs there are five functions to call and rows and groups of rows to loop over. This creates the following execution flow for each UDF type:

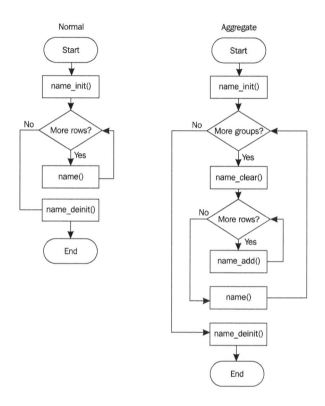

UDF error handling

Ideally most, if not all, possible error conditions should be detected in the `name_init()` function of the UDF. In case of an error, this function needs to write a zero-terminated error message string in the `message` buffer and return 1 to indicate a failure. Error messages must be less than `MYSQL_ERRMSG_SIZE` bytes long (which means less than 512 bytes long in MySQL 5.1) and should preferably be less than 80 characters to fit nicely within a terminal screen.

There is no error message facility in `name()`, `name_add()`, or `name_clear()` functions; all you can do is set the `*error` argument to 1. This will return `NULL` and if the UDF is to be run on subsequent rows, all further invocations will return `NULL` too (in fact, the UDF will not be invoked for these rows).

UDF security

UDFs must be placed in the directory stored in the `plugin_dir` MySQL configuration variable. Usually this is `lib/mysql/plugin/` or `lib/plugin/` relative to the directory where MySQL is installed. We can find out where this is on our particular installation by running:

```
mysql> SHOW VARIABLES LIKE 'plugin_dir';
+---------------+----------------------------+
| Variable_name | Value                      |
+---------------+----------------------------+
| plugin_dir    | /opt/mysql/lib/mysql/plugin |
+---------------+----------------------------+
1 row in set (0.00 sec)
```

When using MySQL 5.1 any attempt to explicitly specify a path in the CREATE FUNCTION statement will result in an error.

Both the `name_init()` and `name_deinit()` functions are optional and can be omitted if empty. However, at least one of the functions besides `name()`, that is `name_init()`, `name_deinit()`, `name_add()`, or `name_clear()`, must be present in the UDF shared library to reduce the chance of loading as a UDF something that was not meant to be (tricks such as CREATE FUNCTION exit SONAME 'libc.so' were possible in the past). It is possible to disable this protection by using the `--allow-suspicious-udfs` command-line option, but this is not recommended.

Gotchas with UDFs

UDFs are a great way to add functionality, with more flexibility than MySQL Stored Procedures. They do, however, have drawbacks that developers should be wary of:

- The `mysql.func` table needs to exist. If it does not, running the `mysql_upgrade` command-line utility will create it for you.

- Running the MySQL server with the `--skip-grant-tables` option disables UDFs.

- Imagine a UDF as a code that is part of the server. As such, if your UDF crashes, for example with a Segmentation Fault, it will take out the MySQL server with it.

- All functions in the UDF must be thread-safe. It is possible that the UDF could be called multiple times simultaneously from different threads. You need to keep this in mind when using global or static variables. Protect them from concurrent modifications with mutexes, or avoid them altogether. Allocate what you need in `name_init()` and free it in `name_deinit()`.

- The `name()` function cannot generate error messages. Hence, you must do all your error checking in `name_init()`.

- You need to have `INSERT` privileges on the MySQL database to be able to install UDFs (and `DELETE` privileges to uninstall them).

- MySQL UDFs can only be installed from the `plugin_dir` path as described in the *UDF security* section of this chapter.

A constant integer output UDF

To show the basic construction of a UDF we will start with a simple constant function that returns an integer. The output of this UDF will be the same no matter what arguments are passed to the UDF. To make the example a little more complex and to demonstrate the `initid->ptr` usage we will allocate a small amount of memory upon initialization to store our integer. This example will be called `udf_staticexample`:

```
#include <stdlib.h>
#include <string.h>
#include <mysql.h>
```

These are the standard includes needed for this example. The header `mysql.h` contains the structures and constants that we will use.

```
my_bool udf_staticexample_init(UDF_INIT *initid,
                               UDF_ARGS *args, char *message)
{
```

We are calling this UDF `udf_staticexample` so all functions need to be prefixed with this. We start with the `udf_staticexample_init()` function, which as we have seen before, prepares the UDF for execution in the context of an SQL statement.

```
long long *staticint = malloc(sizeof(long long));
if (staticint == NULL)
{
  strcpy(message, "staticexample() allocation error");
  return 1;
}
```

Here we declare a pointer to a type `long long` and allocate memory for it. If the allocation fails, we put an error message into the `message` buffer and return 1 to indicate that an error has occurred. This error will then be passed on to the client.

```
*staticint = 318749;
initid->ptr = (char*) staticint;
```

Set out new `long long` to a value of 318749 and put the pointer to this variable into `initid->ptr`. Notice that we have to typecast it as a `char*` so that we do not get compiler warnings.

```
    initid->const_item=1;
    initid->maybe_null=0;
    return 0;
}
```

The result of this UDF is always the same and it cannot be NULL, so we set these `initid` members appropriately and return 0 to indicate a success.

```
    void udf_staticexample_deinit(UDF_INIT *initid)
    {
        free(initid->ptr);}
```

Our `udf_staticexample_deinit()` function needs to clear up the `initid->ptr` so that we do not end up with a memory leak. In this case, only a few bytes would be leaked, but it could be a lot worse in larger UDFs.

```
    long long udf_staticexample(UDF_INIT *initid,
                        UDF_ARGS *args, char *is_null, char *error)
    {
        return *(long long*) initid->ptr;
    }
```

This UDF is of the INTEGER type so we define the main `udf_staticexample()` function to return a `long long`. We return the value by dereferencing a pointer that we set up in the initialization function.

Once this UDF is compiled this is what we will get from the MySQL command line:

```
Welcome to the MySQL monitor.   Commands end with ; or \g.
Your MySQL connection id is 1
Server version: 5.1.47 Source distribution


Type 'help;' or '\h' for help. Type '\c' to clear the current
input statement.


mysql> CREATE FUNCTION udf_staticexample RETURNS INTEGER SONAME 'udf_
staticexample.so';
Query OK, 0 rows affected (0.00 sec)
```

```
mysql> SELECT udf_staticexample();
+---------------------+
| udf_staticexample() |
+---------------------+
|              318749 |
+---------------------+
1 row in set (0.00 sec)
```

An integer echoing UDF

The next example is designed to show how to deal with inputs. It is similar to the previous one, but will demonstrate how to perform argument checking. As you remember, this check should happen in the initialization function, so that we can give a proper error message when there is a problem. We will call this UDF, udf_intexample, and will make it accept only one argument, which has to be an integer for the function to succeed:

```
#include <string.h>
#include <mysql.h>
my_bool udf_intexample_init(UDF_INIT *initid,
                            UDF_ARGS *args, char *message)
{
```

As before, we include everything needed for this example and create an initialization function with the same prefix as the function name.

```
if (args->arg_count != 1)
{
  strcpy(message,
         "udf_intexample() can only accept one argument");
  return 1;
}
```

We want to ensure that only one argument is accepted for this UDF so we check that arg_count is 1. If it is not, we stick an error message into the message buffer and return 1 to indicate that the function failed.

```
if (args->arg_type[0] != INT_RESULT)
{
  strcpy(message,
         "udf_intexample() argument has to be an integer");
  return 1;
}
```

OK, so we have exactly one argument, but for all we know it could be some string or a floating point number. That's pretty useless when we are dealing with integers. So we check `arg_type` for the first argument to make sure it is an integer. If it is not, again, we complain to the user that the input is invalid.

```
    return 0;
}
```

If we get this far, it's a success! We return 0 to indicate this and go on to the `udf_intexample()` function. As for `udf_intexample_deinit()`, because we did not allocate any memory in the initialization function and there is nothing else to de-initialize, we do not need it at all.

```
long long udf_intexample(UDF_INIT *initid, UDF_ARGS *args,
                         char *is_null, char *error)
{
    return *(longlong*) args->args[0];
}
```

Now that we have made sure the argument is an integer we can get its value (by dereferencing a properly casted pointer) and return it back to the user.

Once we have compiled and installed this UDF we can see the following:

```
Welcome to the MySQL monitor.  Commands end with ; or \g.
Your MySQL connection id is 2
Server version: 5.1.47 Source distribution


mysql> CREATE FUNCTION udf_intexample RETURNS INTEGER SONAME 'udf_
intexample.so';
Query OK, 0 rows affected (0.00 sec)


mysql> SELECT udf_intexample('hello');
ERROR 1123 (HY000): Can't initialize function 'udf_intexample'; udf_
intexample() the argument has to be an integer
```

We do not like this; it is a string so it is getting caught by our integer check.

```
mysql> SELECT udf_intexample('2');
ERROR 1123 (HY000): Can't initialize function 'udf_intexample'; udf_
intexample() argument has to be an integer
```

Even though this is an integer, it is enclosed in quotes, so it is treated as a string and fails appropriately.

```
mysql> SELECT udf_intexample(2.2);
ERROR 1123 (HY000): Can't initialize function 'udf_intexample'; udf_
intexample() argument has to be an integer
```

As the argument has a decimal point in it, it is a decimal type, thus failing the integer check again.

```
mysql> SELECT udf_intexample(2543,3452);
ERROR 1123 (HY000): Can't initialize function 'udf_intexample'; udf_
intexample() can only accept one argument
```

We have supplied two integers here. However, our UDF can only take one argument.

```
mysql> SELECT udf_intexample(2543);

+----------------------+
| udf_intexample(2543) |
+----------------------+
|                 2543 |
+----------------------+

1 row in set (0.00 sec)
```

And there we have it! We supplied a single integer and the UDF behaved exactly as expected!

```
mysql> SELECT udf_intexample(10*3-CAST(2.2 AS UNSIGNED));

+--------------------------------------------+
| udf_intexample(10*3-CAST(2.2 AS UNSIGNED)) |
+--------------------------------------------+
|                                         28 |
+--------------------------------------------+

1 row in set (0.00 sec)
```

Naturally, expressions are fine too, as long as the result type is an integer.

A simple static text output UDF

Returning text in a MySQL UDF can be slightly more complex than dealing with numbers. MySQL gives us a memory buffer to use when returning a string but it is only 766 bytes long. This is fine for some tasks, but not big enough to hold a long string or a blob, so what we do is allocate our own buffer for this purpose. Either way, we need to tell MySQL how long the resulting string is.

The next piece of example code has two UDFs inside it, the first showing how to use the memory buffer that MySQL has given us and the second allocating its own memory. Both are simple UDFs which will just return the MySQL version number that UDF was compiled against:

```
#include <stdlib.h>
#include <string.h>
#include <mysql.h>
my_bool udf_textexample_init(UDF_INIT *initid,
                             UDF_ARGS *args, char *message)
{
  initid->const_item = 1;
  return 0;
}
```

As with previous examples we create the initialization function. We set `initid->const_item` to 1 here because the return value is always the same.

We do not need the de-initialization function in this example, so we do not create it.

```
char *udf_textexample(UDF_INIT *initid, UDF_ARGS *args,
                      char *result, unsigned long *res_length,
                      char *null_value, char *error)
{
  strcpy(result, MYSQL_SERVER_VERSION);
  *res_length = strlen(MYSQL_SERVER_VERSION);
  return result;
}
```

The return function declaration is different this time to account for the extra data required for the string result. MYSQL_SERVER_VERSION is declared in `mysql_version.h`, which is included via `mysql.h`. We copy this into `result`, which is 766 bytes long, and set the length of our returned string in `*res_length`. We then return a pointer to the data.

The following is our second UDF in the same file. It does exactly the same thing, but allocates the memory for the text first:

```
my_bool udf_textexample2_init(UDF_INIT *initid,
                              UDF_ARGS *args, char *message)
{
  char* statictext = strdup(MYSQL_SERVER_VERSION);
```

Here we have allocated memory and copied `MYSQL_SERVER_VERSION` into it.

```
if (statictext == NULL)
{
  strcpy(message, "udf_textexample2() allocation error");
  return 1;
}
```

Allocation is unlikely to fail, it is hardly possible that you do not have enough RAM for the few bytes that we wish to allocate. If, however, the worst happens at least we end up with an error rather than crashing the server.

```
initid->max_length = strlen(MYSQL_SERVER_VERSION);
initid->ptr = statictext;
initid->const_item = 1;
```

The `initid->max_length` is set as `strlen()` to make it easier to pass to the main `udf_textexample2()` function. We then set `initid->ptr` to the pointer of `statictext` and, of course, this function always has the same return value, so `initid->const_item` is set.

```
  return 0;
}
void udf_textexample2_deinit(UDF_INIT *initid)
{
  free(initid->ptr);
}

char *udf_textexample2(UDF_INIT *initid, UDF_ARGS *args,
                       char *result, unsigned long *res_length,
                       char *null_value, char *error)
{
  *res_length = initid->max_length;
  return initid->ptr;
}
```

We end this UDF by setting the result length to the same value as `initid->max_length` we set earlier and returning the value inside `initid->ptr`. We completely ignore the `result` buffer that has been provided for us.

When running this through MySQL we get:

```
Welcome to the MySQL monitor.  Commands end with ; or \g.
Your MySQL connection id is 1
Server version: 5.1.47 Source distribution
```

```
Type 'help;' or '\h' for help. Type '\c' to clear the current
input statement.
```

```
mysql> CREATE FUNCTION udf_textexample RETURNS STRING SONAME
'udf_textexample.so';
Query OK, 0 rows affected (0.00 sec)
```

```
mysql> CREATE FUNCTION udf_textexample2 RETURNS STRING SONAME
'udf_textexample.so';
Query OK, 0 rows affected (0.00 sec)
```

This shows that we can have two UDFs inside one shared library. It can be very convenient if you have a library of related functions you wish to use.

```
mysql> SELECT udf_textexample();
```

```
+------------------ +
| udf_textexample() |
+------------------ +
| 5.1.47            |
+------------------ +
1 row in set (0.00 sec)
```

Our first function returns the version string, as expected.

```
mysql> SELECT udf_textexample2();
```

```
+------------------- +
| udf_textexample2() |
+------------------- +
| 5.1.47             |
+------------------- +
1 row in set (0.00 sec)
```

Also, as expected, the text returned from the second function is exactly the same.

A summing aggregate UDF

As discussed earlier in this chapter, aggregate UDFs are great for performing operations on groups of rows. Things work slightly differently here, we have a new keyword to use when installing UDFs and two extra functions to deal with individual rows and to clean up after every group of rows.

Let's write an aggregating UDF that will add up floating point numbers. We will call it udf_floatsum:

```
#include <stdlib.h>
#include <string.h>
#include <mysql.h>

my_bool udf_floatsum_init(UDF_INIT *initid, UDF_ARGS *args,
                          char *message)
{
  double* float_total = malloc(sizeof(double));
  *float_total = 0;
  initid->ptr = (char*) float_total;
```

To aggregate we need an accumulator, a variable of the type double to keep the running totals as we are seeing rows one by one. Different queries invoking our UDF must have different running totals, in other words, initid->ptr is exactly what's needed. We allocate memory for one double and save a pointer to it in initid->ptr.

```
  if (args->arg_count != 1)
  {
    strcpy(message,
           "udf_floatsum() can only accept one argument");
    return 1;
  }
  if (args->arg_type[0] != REAL_RESULT)
  {
    strcpy(message, "udf_floatsum() argument has to be "
                    "a floating point number");
    return 1;
  }
```

Just as we have in previous UDFs, we are setting the restriction of one argument and the value of this argument has to be a floating point number.

 It is always enough to run these sorts of checks only in the name_init() function. There is no need to repeat them in, say, name_add() or name(), because metadata (number of arguments and their types) never change throughout the statement execution.

```
  initid->decimals = 3;
  return 0;
}
```

Just for the sake of an example, we have set our UDF to return 3 decimal places.

```
void udf_floatsum_deinit(UDF_INIT *initid)
{
  free(initid->ptr);
}

void udf_floatsum_add(UDF_INIT *initid, UDF_ARGS *args,
                      char *is_null, char *error)
{
  double* float_total;
  float_total = (double*)initid->ptr;
  if (args->args[0])
    *float_total += *(double *)args->args[0];
}
```

This is called for every row, and for the purposes of aggregation we are retrieving the `float_total` pointer from `initid->ptr` and adding the new value to it. We also take special care of NULL values; in such a case a pointer to the argument value will be null and we skip this row.

```
void udf_floatsum_clear(UDF_INIT *initid, char *is_null,
                        char *error)
{
  double* float_total;
  float_total = (double*)initid->ptr;
  *float_total = 0;
}
```

The `udf_floatsum_clear()` function is called to prepare the UDF before starting to work on rows from a new group. In this case we need to clear our running total by setting it to zero.

```
double udf_floatsum(UDF_INIT *initid, UDF_ARGS *args,
                    char *is_null, char *error)
{
  double* float_total;
  float_total = (double*)initid->ptr;
  return *float_total;
}
```

This function is called at the end of every group to retrieve the running total before it gets cleared again and returns it as the UDF result.

When installing and running inside MySQL we will see the following:

```
mysql> CREATE AGGREGATE FUNCTION udf_floatsum RETURNS REAL SONAME
'udf_floatsum.so';
Query OK, 0 rows affected (0.00 sec)
```

As we can see here, the installation is slightly different. The keyword AGGREGATE is used to signify that this is an aggregate function.

```
mysql> CREATE TABLE t1 (a INT, b FLOAT);
Query OK, 0 rows affected (0.01 sec)


mysql> INSERT INTO t1 VALUES (1,1.1),(2,5.34),(1,8.231),
    -> (1,9.8523),(2,9.37567);
Query OK, 5 rows affected (0.01 sec)
Records: 5  Duplicates: 0  Warnings: 0
mysql> SELECT * FROM t1;
+------+---------+
| a    | b       |
+------+---------+
|    1 |     1.1 |
|    2 |    5.34 |
|    1 |   8.231 |
|    1 |  9.8523 |
|    2 | 9.37567 |
+------+---------+
5 rows in set (0.00 sec)
```

We insert five rows of data into this table. The first column has two distinct values, which we will use for grouping.

```
mysql> SELECT a, udf_floatsum(b),sum(b) FROM t1 GROUP BY a;
+------+-----------------+------------------+
| a    | udf_floatsum(b) | sum(b)           |
+------+-----------------+------------------+
|    1 |          19.183 | 19.1832996606827 |
|    2 |          14.716 | 14.7156705856323 |
+------+-----------------+------------------+
2 rows in set (0.00 sec)
```

When running the UDF in this query we can see that it has added up all of the floats in both groups separately. Comparing the result with the built-in SUM() we see that our result is rounded off to the third digit after the decimal point, exactly as specified in initid->decimals.

Further reading

There is a UDF repository run by Roland Bouman that contains various useful functions in both source and binary forms. This can be found at `http://www.mysqludf.org/`.

To make the UDF API even easier to use, Hartmut Holzgraefe, a MySQL Support Manager at Sun Microsystems, has created a UDF generator. This generates the source code for you based on an XML description of what the UDF should do. More information on this can be found at its PECL site at: `http://pear.php.net/package/CodeGen_MySQL_UDF/`

Summary

We can now see that writing a UDF is not too complex. MySQL has a lot of built-in functionality to help with the task. UDFs make a good compromise between easy and limited Stored Procedures and the ultimate power and complexity of modifying the source code of the MySQL server.

3
Daemon Plugins

We begin with Daemon plugins as an introduction to the new MySQL Plugin API due to their simplicity. Plugin API is designed to facilitate the adding of extra code to MySQL without having to recompile the entire server. A typical use of a Daemon plugin would be to create threads to execute some background code. This gives us a basic structure to start with which can be followed later with other plugin types.

In this chapter we will cover the basic information needed to write a Daemon plugin and use some examples to illustrate how this could be applied in practical usage. Background knowledge of POSIX threads is useful for this chapter, but we will go through things simply and explain what is going on at every step.

A look inside a Daemon plugin

Unlike UDFs, MySQL plugins store all of the metadata in the plugins shared library. So when installing a plugin you only need to specify the name of the plugin and its shared library filename. This eliminates much of the user error while installing. With UDFs it is very easy to choose the wrong return type or forget the AGGREGATE keyword, but with plugins this is not possible.

Why write a Daemon plugin

Just like UDFs and other MySQL plugin types the Daemon plugin can be used to add extra functionality to MySQL with the same advantages and disadvantages.

Daemon plugins are ideal for writing code that needs to reside in the server but does not need to communicate with it—such as a heartbeat plugin or monitoring plugins—because the simple Daemon plugin API does not provide any means for a server and a plugin to communicate with each other.

Installing and using Daemon plugins

Installing plugins is relatively easy because all of the information about a plugin is stored inside it. To install a plugin we can use the INSTALL PLUGIN statement as follows:

```
mysql> INSTALL PLUGIN my_plugin SONAME 'my_plugin.so';
```

Likewise, to remove a plugin we use:

```
mysql> UNINSTALL PLUGIN my_plugin;
```

When a plugin is installed it is initialized instantly and this means that the code we write will start automatically when our plugin is installed.

Upon installing a plugin it is added to the mysql.plugin table so MySQL knows it is installed and can load it again on startup. In other words, similar to UDFs, all installed plugins are loaded automatically when a server is started.

A plugin is de-initialized when either it is uninstalled or the MySQL server is being shut down. It is worth noting at this time that if the MySQL server crashes for any reason the de-initialization of the plugin will not happen.

If a plugin is installed, we can prevent it from being loaded and executed at startup with the --disable-plugin-my-plugin or --plugin-my-plugin=OFF commands. If we do not do that MySQL will try to load it because the default behavior is --plugin-my-plugin=ON. If the plugin fails to load, MySQL will note that fact in the error log and will continue without this plugin. If we want to be sure that a plugin is absolutely loaded in the server, and that the server will not simply ignore a plugin failure, we can use --plugin-my-plugin=FORCE. In this mode the server will exit if our plugin fails to load.

As we can see below, the mysql.plugin table simply contains the plugin name and the filename for the shared library containing the plugin:

```
mysql> SELECT * FROM mysql.plugin;
+-----------+--------------+
| name      | dl           |
+-----------+--------------+
| my_plugin | my_plugin.so |
+-----------+--------------+
1 row in set (0.01 sec)
```

MySQL has a SHOW command to give us information about installed plugins. This is very useful to see if a plugin is actually running. If there was a problem during initialization then the status for the plugin will be marked as DISABLED. A sample output for SHOW PLUGINS can be seen below:

```
mysql> SHOW PLUGINS\G

...

*************************** 11. row ***************************
   Name: my_plugin
 Status: ACTIVE
   Type: DAEMON
Library: my_plugin.so
License: GPL
11 rows in set (0.00 sec)
```

Information Schema also includes a table for use with plugins, and it contains more detail than SHOW PLUGINS. It shows version information supplied by the plugin as well as the plugin description:

```
mysql> SELECT * FROM information_schema.plugins WHERE PLUGIN_NAME='my_
plugin'\G

*************************** 1. row ***************************
           PLUGIN_NAME: my_plugin
        PLUGIN_VERSION: 1.0
         PLUGIN_STATUS: ACTIVE
           PLUGIN_TYPE: DAEMON
   PLUGIN_TYPE_VERSION: 50147.0
        PLUGIN_LIBRARY: my_plugin.so
PLUGIN_LIBRARY_VERSION: 1.0
         PLUGIN_AUTHOR: Andrew Hutchings
    PLUGIN_DESCRIPTION: Daemon example, shows a declaration
        PLUGIN_LICENSE: GPL
1 row in set (0.00 sec)
```

Technically, loading of plugins is very similar to loading of UDFs. Problems that can arise, ways of solving them, and error messages are similar to those of UDFs. They were described in a previous chapter.

The role of a version

As we have seen, there are three two-component version numbers in the INFORMATION_SCHEMA.PLUGINS table. One of them, PLUGIN_VERSION, is purely informational. It is a number that a plugin author can specify arbitrarily, and MySQL itself does not do anything with it. The other two are very important though. They are used to protect the API, to make sure that if a plugin is loaded it uses the same API version that the server provides. This is one of the main differences to UDFs. UDF API is not versioned. Hence, it was not developed and still has only those features that it did in 3.21.24. Extending UDF API is risky; any change and old UDFs may start crashing the server.

Plugin API, on the other hand, is safe. It is protected by a version, and this version is part of every plugin library, the API version that the plugin was compiled against. When a plugin is loaded the server verifies that the version is supported by the server and refuses to load a plugin otherwise. That is, the server can *guarantee* that all loaded plugins are fully compatible with the server, and no crash can happen because of API mismatch.

The API is protected with two version numbers, as it contains two parts — one is common to all plugin types. It is version 1.0, as can be seen in the PLUGIN_LIBRARY_ VERSION column above. The other one is specific to each plugin type. For Daemon plugins this version is 50147.0, as seen in the PLUGIN_TYPE_VERSION column, and it is derived from the MySQL server version (which was 5.1.47 in my examples).

Defining Daemon plugins

The most basic of Daemon plugins needs no code at all; only a declaration is required. A plugin declaration is an instance of a st_mysql_plugin structure:

```
struct st_mysql_plugin
{
  int type;
  void *info;
  const char *name;
  const char *author;
  const char *descr;
  int license;
  int (*init)(void *);
  int (*deinit)(void *);
  unsigned int version;
  struct st_mysql_show_var *status_vars;
  struct st_mysql_sys_var **system_vars;
  void *__reserved1
};
```

The `type` defines what type of plugin this will be, which in turn defines what it can do. In MySQL 5.1, `type` can be set to one of the following enumerated values:

Type	Description
MYSQL_UDF_PLUGIN	UDF plugin (not yet implemented)
MYSQL_STORAGE_ENGINE_PLUGIN	Storage engine plugin
MYSQL_FTPARSER_PLUGIN	Full text index parser plugin
MYSQL_DAEMON_PLUGIN	Daemon plugin
MYSQL_INFORMATION_SCHEMA_PLUGIN	Information Schema plugin

In this chapter we are talking about Daemon plugins so this should be set to `MYSQL_DAEMON_PLUGIN`.

The `info` member is a pointer to the descriptor of the plugin and its members. It contains the information specific to this particular plugin type (while the `st_mysql_plugin` structure itself contains the information applicable to any plugin, independently of its type). It always starts with an API version number and for Daemon plugins this is all it contains. For other plugin types it may also contain plugin methods that the server will call, but Daemon plugins are not designed to communicate with the server, and their descriptor structure contains nothing besides the version:

```
struct st_mysql_daemon my_daemon_plugin =
{ MYSQL_DAEMON_INTERFACE_VERSION };
```

Next we have the `name` member, which specifies the name of the plugin as it will be used by MySQL. This is the name that needs to be used in the INSTALL PLUGIN statement, the name that will be seen in SHOW PLUGINS and SHOW ENGINES, the name that all plugin configuration variables and command-line options will start from. That is, the name of the plugin should be a valid SQL identifier and should be good for the command line too. A safe choice would be a name that consists of only Latin letters, digits, and an underscore. Plugin names are not case-sensitive.

The `author` member is a string containing details about the author; it can contain anything we wish. It must be in UTF-8 and can be arbitrarily long, but MySQL will only show the first 64 characters of it.

The final string member is `descr`, which should contain a description of the plugin. Again we are free to put whatever we like here, but we would normally put a short line stating what the plugin does. Again, it is supposed to be UTF-8, but it can be as long as you want.

In the next member, each plugin specifies its license. This does not strictly do anything as such, but should help with accidental distribution of a plugin under the wrong license. There are currently three possible values for the `license` member:

License	Description
PLUGIN_LICENSE_PROPRIETARY	Any proprietary license
PLUGIN_LICENSE_GPL	GPL license
PLUGIN_LICENSE_BSD	BSD license

Then we come to the `init` and `deinit` members, which are pointers to the plugin initialization and de-initialization functions. The initialization function is called when the plugin is loaded during INSTALL PLUGIN or server startup. The de-initialization function is called when a plugin is unloaded, which, again, can happen for two reasons, UNINSTALL PLUGIN or server shutdown. In a Daemon plugin the initialization function is often used to fork a thread to run the main function of the plugin. Both the initialization and the de-initialization functions should return 0 on success or 1 on failure.

The `version` member should be used for the current version of our plugin. A two-component version is encoded as a hexadecimal number, where the lower 8 bits store the second component (minor version) and all others bits store the first component (major version). For example, if the version is set to 0x205, MySQL will show it as "2.5", and if the version is set to 0x123FF, MySQL will show it as "291.255". Unfortunately, there is no way to store in this member a more complex version such as "1.10.14b-RC2".

MySQL has many *status variables* that can be seen with the SHOW STATUS statement, and there are different third-party tools that analyze this data, how the status variables change over time, draw graphs, and so on. A plugin can benefit from that and make its status and various statistics and performance values visible as MySQL status variables. A pointer to the list of the plugin status variables is stored in the `status_vars` member.

Similarly, there is a SHOW VARIABLES statement. It lists all MySQL *system variables*, variables that are used to alter the behavior of the server. They can have server-wide or session-only effect, some of them can be set on the command line or in the configuration file. They can be modifiable run-time or read-only. This is all available to plugins too. A plugin can add new system variables to the server, global or session, with or without command-line option support, modifiable or read-only. As we would expect, a pointer to the array of these variables goes into the `system_vars` member.

Finally there is one `__reserved1` member, which is unused in MySQL 5.1 and should be set to NULL.

MySQL provides two macros that help to declare plugins. A plugin declaration starts from the `mysql_declare_plugin()` macro. It takes one argument, a unique identifier for this plugin library, it will be used automatically as needed to avoid name clashes when plugins are linked statically into the server. This identifier must be the same one that was used as a plugin name in the `plug.in` file (see Chapter 1). We can put many plugins in one library, but they all need to be declared in one place, after the `mysql_declare_plugin()` macro, separated by commas. We end the list of plugin declarations with a `mysql_declare_plugin_end` macro.

A complete example of the plugin declarations can be seen as follows:

```
mysql_declare_plugin(my_plugin)
{
  MYSQL_DAEMON_PLUGIN,
  &my_plugin_info,
  "my_plugin",
  "Andrew Hutchings (Andrew.Hutchings@Sun.COM)",
  "Daemon example, shows a declaration",
  PLUGIN_LICENSE_GPL,
  my_plugin_init,
  my_plugin_deinit,
  0x0100,
  NULL,
  NULL,
  NULL
},
{
  MYSQL_DAEMON_PLUGIN,
  &my_plugin2_info,
  "my_plugin2",
  "Sergei Golubchik (serg@mariadb.org)",
  "Another Daemon example, shows a declaration",
  PLUGIN_LICENSE_GPL,
  my_plugin2_init,
  NULL,
  0xC0FFEE,
  status,
  vars,
  NULL
}
mysql_declare_plugin_end;
```

This declares two plugins. We can see that the first one:

- is a Daemon plugin
- has an `info` structure called `my_plugin_info`
- is called `my_plugin` and was written by me (Andrew Hutchings)
- is described as an example plugin
- is GPL licensed
- has initialization and de-initialization functions
- is of version 1.0
- has no system or status variables

The second plugin can be interpreted similarly. It is also a Daemon plugin of version 49407.238 with initialization function, without de-initialization function, with both status and system variables.

Status variables

Status variables can be used to give feedback to the user and any application that reads status variables. To create them we need to define a zero-terminated array of structures of the type `st_mysql_show_var`. This structure is defined in `plugin.h` as:

```
struct st_mysql_show_var {
  const char *name;
  char *value;
  enum enum_mysql_show_type type;
};
```

In this structure `name` is the name of the status variable that will be seen when executing `SHOW STATUS`. The `value` member is a pointer to the memory that will contain the data for this status variable. It will be casted to the appropriate pointer type and dereferenced as needed. What it will be casted to depends on the `type` member, according to the following table:

Type	C type
SHOW_BOOL	bool *
SHOW_INT	unsigned int *
SHOW_LONG	long *
SHOW_LONGLONG	long long *
SHOW_DOUBLE	double *
SHOW_CHAR	char *
SHOW_CHAR_PTR	char **

Type	C type
SHOW_ARRAY	st_mysql_show_var *
SHOW_FUNC	int (*)(MYSQL_THD, struct st_mysql_show_var*, char *)

The last two types are special. Elements of these types do not define rows in SHOW STATUS, they define other elements of the st_mysql_show_var structure.

SHOW_ARRAY specifies that value is not really a value, but a pointer to another zero-terminated array of status variables. The corresponding name of the SHOW_ARRAY element will be used as a *prefix* added to all the names of status variables in the referenced array. The variables beginning with Com_ in the normal SHOW STATUS output is an example of this in action.

The SHOW_FUNC function is more interesting. The value is interpreted as a pointer to a function that generates the st_mysql_show_var structure. This function should have the following prototype:

```
int my_status_var(MYSQL_THD thd,
                  struct st_mysql_show_var *var, char *buff)
```

The first argument is a pointer to the thread object of the current connection, var points to a st_mysql_show_var structure that we need to fill in, and buff is a preallocated 1024-byte buffer. The function needs to set var->type and var->value (the var->name member will be ignored by MySQL) to form a valid status variable structure. And if needed, var->type can be set to SHOW_ARRAY or even to SHOW_FUNC again, and MySQL will handle this situation correctly. A buffer buff is provided as convenience storage; the function may store the value there and point var->value to it. The return value of this function is ignored.

So, putting this together we can have something similar to the following to make our plugin add new status variables to a server:

```
struct st_mysql_show_var my_status_vars[]=
{
  {"data_size",     (char *)&data_size,       SHOW_LONG},
  {"avg_text_size", (char *)&avg_text_size,   SHOW_LONGLONG},
  {0,0,0}
};
```

We would then use my_status_vars in the plugin declaration.

System variables

If status variables can be seen as output variables, then system variables can be seen as input variables. MySQL plugins can have variables that are visible in SHOW VARIABLES so that users can modify the settings of a plugin. They can also be set at the command line when starting mysqld if the options are set to do this. To create system variables we use an array of macros as follows:

```
struct st_mysql_sys_var* my_sysvars[]= {
  MYSQL_SYSVAR(my_var),
  MYSQL_SYSVAR(my_other_var),
  NULL
};
```

It does not create any system variables by itself, it only creates a list of variables to put into a plugin declaration. The MYSQL_SYSVAR() macro is expanded into a pointer to a system variable structure. Such a structure needs to be created first. In other words, our system variables my_var and my_other_var need to be declared before we can put them in an array. We do this by using other macros depending on the type of variable we require. Macros to create global variables are summarized in the following table:

Macro to Create a Global Variable	Corresponding C Type
MYSQL_SYSVAR_BOOL(name, varname, opt, comment, check, update, def)	char
MYSQL_SYSVAR_STR(name, varname, opt, comment, check, update, def)	char*
MYSQL_SYSVAR_INT(name, varname, opt, comment, check, update, def, min, max, blk)	int
MYSQL_SYSVAR_UINT(name, varname, opt, comment, check, update, def, min, max, blk)	unsigned int
MYSQL_SYSVAR_LONG(name, varname, opt, comment, check, update, def, min, max, blk)	long
MYSQL_SYSVAR_ULONG(name, varname, opt, comment, check, update, def, min, max, blk)	unsigned long
MYSQL_SYSVAR_LONGLONG(name, varname, opt, comment, check, update, def, min, max, blk)	long long
MYSQL_SYSVAR_ULONGLONG(name, varname, opt, comment, check, update, def, min, max, blk)	unsigned long long
MYSQL_SYSVAR_ENUM(name, varname, opt, comment, check, update, def, typelib)	unsigned long
MYSQL_SYSVAR_SET(name, varname, opt, comment, check, update, def, typelib)	unsigned long long

To create session, or thread-local, variables we need to use a different set of macros. They start with MYSQL_THDVAR instead of MYSQL_SYSVAR, and they do not take the varname parameter:

Macro to Create a Session Variable	Corresponding C Type
MYSQL_THDVAR_BOOL (name, opt, comment, check, update, def)	char
MYSQL_THDVAR_STR (name, opt, comment, check, update, def)	char*
MYSQL_THDVAR_INT (name, opt, comment, check, update, def, min, max, blk)	int
MYSQL_THDVAR_UINT (name, opt, comment, check, update, def, min, max, blk)	unsigned int
MYSQL_THDVAR_LONG (name, opt, comment, check, update, def, min, max, blk)	long
MYSQL_THDVAR_ULONG (name, opt, comment, check, update, def, min, max, blk)	unsigned long
MYSQL_THDVAR_LONGLONG (name, opt, comment, check, update, def, min, max, blk)	long long
MYSQL_THDVAR_ULONGLONG (name, opt, comment, check, update, def, min, max, blk)	unsigned long long
MYSQL_THDVAR_ENUM (name, opt, comment, check, update, def, typelib)	unsigned long
MYSQL_THDVAR_SET (name, opt, comment, check, update, def, typelib)	unsigned long long

The parameters of all these macros are as follows:

Name	Description
name	The name of the system variable, excluding the plugin name. It will be shown in SHOW VARIABLES; it can be used in SELECT and SET, or on the command line. The name of the plugin will be prepended to the name automatically.
varname	The associated C or C++ variable. A global system variable (MYSQL_SYSVAR) will store its value in this C or C++ variable. Session variables (MYSQL_THDVAR) have no varname parameter; the storage for the value will be created automatically in every thread as necessary.
opt	System variable options, see the following table.
comment	The comment describing the system variable. If a variable can be set on the command line, this comment will be visible in the mysqld --help --verbose output.
check	A pointer to a function that checks if the value is valid. It can be NULL.
update	A pointer to a function used to store the new value. It can be NULL too.

Name	Description
def	The default value for the variable.
min	The minimum value for the variable. It can only be specified for numeric system variables.
max	The maximum value for the variable. It can only be specified for numeric system variables.
blk	Block size, a value will be a multiple of this number. It can only be specified for numeric system variables.
typelib	A structure defining the list of values of entities for an ENUM or SET system variable

The opt parameter helps you define extra options for the variable. Multiple options can be used by using an or ('|') to join them together. A description of these options can be seen as follows:

Option	Description
PLUGIN_VAR_READONLY	System variable cannot be modified at runtime.
PLUGIN_VAR_NOSYSVAR	It is not a system variable (only a command-line option).
PLUGIN_VAR_NOCMDOPT	It is not a command-line option (only a system variable).
PLUGIN_VAR_NOCMDARG	Command-line option does not take an argument.
PLUGIN_VAR_RQCMDARG	Command-line option must be used with an argument.
PLUGIN_VAR_OPCMDARG	Command-line option can optionally take an argument.
PLUGIN_VAR_MEMALLOC	If set, the memory will be allocated for the value of this string variable. If unset, the variable can only be set on the command line, not at runtime, and it will point directly into the *argv[] array.

For ENUM and SET variables we need to create a TYPELIB structure that provides a list of allowed values. A TYPELIB structure is defined in include/typelib.h as follows:

```
typedef struct st_typelib {
  unsigned int count;
  const char *name;
  const char **type_names;
  unsigned int *type_lengths;
} TYPELIB;
```

However, we only need to set count correctly and put the list of values into type_names as an array of strings. Other TYPELIB members are used in different places in MySQL, but not for system variables.

Now, let's look at the examples:

```
static char turbo;
static MYSQL_SYSVAR_BOOL(turbo_mode, turbo,
        PLUGIN_VAR_READONLY | PLUGIN_VAR_NOCMDARG,
        "Enabled <<turbo>> mode", NULL, NULL, 0);
```

Suppose, our plugin (called "ourplugin") supports a turbo mode, and when enabled everything works much faster. Unfortunately, it cannot activate this turbo mode at runtime, and once a plugin is started, the mode cannot be changed. The variable declaration above does just that. First, it declares a static C variable `turbo`. If we need to check if the turbo mode is active, we simply write `if (turbo)`. Then we create a global MySQL system variable that is bound to our `turbo` variable. The variable is called `turbo_mode`, and being a variable of `ourplugin`, its full name will be `ourplugin_turbo_mode`. For example, to see its value with a `SELECT` statement, a user will need to type:

```
mysql> SELECT @@global.ourplugin_turbo_mode;
```

We have declared this variable with the `PLUGIN_VAR_READONLY` flag to prevent runtime modifications of it with the `SET` statement. Our plugin simply cannot enable turbo mode at runtime. But it can be activated at startup with a command-line option:

```
shell$ mysqld_safe --enable-ourplugin-turbo-mode
```

It can also be activated from a configuration file. This variable has no custom check or update functions, and by default (see the last parameter in the declaration), the turbo mode is disabled.

```
static unsigned long long log_size;
static MYSQL_SYSVAR_ULONGLONG(log_size, log_size,
        PLUGIN_VAR_RQCMDARG, "Upper limit for a log file size",
        NULL, NULL, 102400, 1024, 1099511627776, 1024);
```

The second example for our hypothetical plugin introduces a variable that limits the size of log files. It is a global updatable system variable, one can modify its value with

```
mysql> SET GLOBAL ourplugin_log_size=20480;
```

or on the command line

```
shell$ mysqld_safe --ourplugin-log-size=20480
```

Because we have specified PLUGIN_VAR_RQCMDARG, the corresponding command-line option must be used with an argument. It will be an error to write --ourplugin-log-size and not provide a number. In the declaration, we have specified that a value of our variable must between 1024 and 1099511627776 (in other words, 1KB-1TB), and must be always divisible by 1024. If a user tries to set it to an incorrect value, MySQL will adjust it automatically.

```
static const char *mode_names[] = {
  "NORMAL", "TURBO", "SUPER", "HYPER", "MEGA"
};
static TYPELIB modes = { 5, NULL, mode_names, NULL };
static MYSQL_THDVAR_ENUM(mode, PLUGIN_VAR_NOCMDOPT,
      "one of NORMAL, TURBO, SUPER, HYPER, MEGA",
      NULL, NULL, 0, &modes);
```

This is a very advanced turbo mode from the first example. It can be in one of the five modes, can be changed at runtime, and even per thread. Different clients may enable different modes; the mode of one connection does not affect others.

The above means that we need to have a *session* variable for the mode, not a global one. And because it takes one value out of a fixed list of values, MYSQL_THDVAR_ENUM is a good match here. As explained above, we need to create a TYPELIB with the list of allowed values, and use it when declaring our system variable. Just for the sake of this example we make it PLUGIN_VAR_NOCMDOPT and MySQL will not create a --ourplugin-mode command-line option for this variable. As a result, this variable can only be changed in SQL, with the SET statement. However, usually it is better and certainly more user friendly to provide a corresponding command-line option for every system variable, and a system variable for every command-line option. Now, this is a session variable. How can we access its value from our plugin? Unlike a global system variable, it cannot store its value in a normal C or C++ variable, because such a variable cannot have different values in different threads. This is why MySQL provides a special macro to access a value of a session system variable. We cannot write simply if (mode == 0) as before, but we use if (THDVAR(thd,mode) == 0) instead. It can be assigned too; THDVAR(thd,mode)=3 will work as expected. The type of the THDVAR(thd,mode) will be unsigned long, as listed in the table previously.

There are two parameters of the `MYSQL_SYSVAR_*` and `MYSQL_THDVAR_*` macros that we have not touched yet. The `check()` and `update()` function callbacks are called when the system variable is altered. The `check()` function is used to add custom checks to a variable to make sure the setting is acceptable. The `update()` function can be used to perform additional actions when a variable is updated, for example, when a variable `memory_buffer_size` is updated one may want to resize the corresponding memory buffer. There are two functions instead of one, `check_and_update()`, because a `SET` statement can modify many variables at once. In this case, MySQL first calls the `check()` function for all these variables, and then their `update()` functions. In other words, MySQL tries to maintain an "all or nothing" behavior. An `update()` function, if provided, should try not to fail as all the preconditions for it to succeed should have been verified in a `check()` function. And a `check()` function, in turn, should avoid having any side effects, because they will persist even if the update is canceled. These functions have the following prototypes:

```
int check(MYSQL_THD thd, struct st_mysql_sys_var *var,
          void *save, struct st_mysql_value *value);
```

Here `thd` is the thread object for the connection that is changing the variable, `var` is the structure of the system variable, `save` is a pointer to where the data should be saved, and `value` is the value passed to the function. A minimal check function should get the result of the expression behind the `value` in the appropriate type and store it in a `*save`. If a check function is not provided at all, MySQL will do it automatically.

```
void update(MYSQL_THD thd, struct st_mysql_sys_var *var,
            void *var_ptr, const void *save);
```

Here we, again, have `thd` and `var` pointers. A `save` pointer gives a new value of the updated variable, and `var_ptr` is a pointer to the variable to be updated. A minimal update function needs to update the `*val_ptr` with the value of `*save`. Again, if no update function is provided, MySQL will do it automatically.

A Hello World! Daemon plugin

Now, let's look at our first complete plugin example. This plugin is probably the most basic plugin we can have. It simply prints a message into the MySQL error log when loaded:

```
#include <stdio.h>
#include <mysql/plugin.h>
#include <mysql_version.h>
```

These are the basic includes required for most Daemon plugins. The most important being `mysql/plugin.h`, which contains macros and data structures necessary for a MySQL plugin.

```
static int hello_world_plugin_init(void *p)
{
  fprintf(stderr, "Hello World: "
          "This is a static text daemon example plugin!\n");
  return 0;
}
```

In the plugin initialization function we simply write a message to `stderr`. MySQL redirects `stderr` to the error log (if there is one) so our message will end up there. We then return 0 to indicate that the initialization was successful.

```
struct st_mysql_daemon hello_world_info =
{ MYSQL_DAEMON_INTERFACE_VERSION };
```

This structure is used for the `info` part of the plugin declaration. In Daemon plugins it simply contains the API version that this plugin was compiled against. The Daemon plugin API version matches the MySQL server version, which means MySQL Daemon plugins can only be used with a MySQL server version they have been compiled against. Indeed, for a Daemon plugin to do something non-trivial it will invariably need access to the server's internal functions and data structures that change with every MySQL version. Other plugins that are implemented according to a certain functionality API are separated from the server internals and are binary compatible with a wide range of server releases.

Having defined all of the functions and auxiliary structures, we can declare a plugin:

```
mysql_declare_plugin(hello_world)
{
```

This is a Daemon plugin so we need to specify it as such with this defined constant:

```
MYSQL_DAEMON_PLUGIN,
```

`info` points to the structure declared earlier. With other plugin types this may contain additional information valuable to the plugin functionality:

```
&hello_world_info,
```

We are calling this plugin "hello_world". This is its name for the INSTALL PLUGIN command and any plugin status:

```
"hello_world",
```

The author string, is useful for providing contact information about the author of the plugin:

```
"Andrew Hutchings (Andrew.Hutchings@Sun.COM)",
```

A Simple line of text that gives a basic description of what our plugin does:

```
"Daemon hello world example, outputs some static text",
```

This plugin is licensed under GPL so we set the license type to this:

```
PLUGIN_LICENSE_GPL,
```

This is our initialization function that has been defined earlier in the code:

```
hello_world_plugin_init,
```

As our simple plugin does not need a de-initialization function, we put NULL here:

```
NULL,
```

This plugin is given version 1.0 because it is our first GA release of the plugin. In future versions we can increment this:

```
0x0100,
```

There are no status or system variables in this example. Hence, everything below the version is set to NULL:

```
NULL,
NULL,
NULL
}
mysql_declare_plugin_end;
```

We can now install this plugin using the INSTALL PLUGIN syntax as described earlier in this chapter:

```
Welcome to the MySQL monitor. Commands end with ; or \g.
Your MySQL connection id is 2
Server version: 5.1.47 Source distribution


Type 'help;' or '\h' for help. Type '\c' to clear the current
input statement.


mysql> INSTALL PLUGIN hello_world SONAME 'hello_world.so';
Query OK, 0 rows affected (0.00 sec)
```

Going to the error log we see:

```
090801 22:18:00 [Note] /home/linuxjedi/Programming/Builds/mysql-5.1.47/
libexec/mysqld: ready for connections.
Version: '5.1.47'  socket: '/tmp/mysql.sock'  port: 3306  Source
distribution
Hello World: This is a static text daemon example plugin!
```

A system and status variables demo plugin

Let's see a more complex example. This plugin shows how to create system and status variables. It has one global system variable and one status variable, both defined as `long long`. When you set the global system variable, its value is copied into the status variable.

```c
#include <stdio.h>
#include <mysql/plugin.h>
#include <mysql_version.h>

long long system_var = 0;
long long status_var = 0;

struct st_mysql_show_var vars_status_var[] =
{
  {"vars_status_var", (char *) &status_var, SHOW_LONGLONG},
  {0, 0, 0}
};
```

We have one status variable in this plugin called `vars_status_var` which is bound to the `status_var` variable defined near the top of this source code. We are defining this variable as `long long` so we use the `SHOW_LONGLONG` type.

```c
int sysvar_check(MYSQL_THD thd,
                 struct st_mysql_sys_var *var,
                 void *save, struct st_mysql_value *value)
{
```

This function is to be called before our system variable is updated. A plugin is not required to provide it but it can be used to check if the data entered is valid and, as an example, we will only allow values that are not too close to `status_var`.

```c
long long buf;
value->val_int(value, &buf);
```

First we retrieve the new value-to-be and store it in `buf`.

```
*(longlong*) save = buf;
```

We then set `save` to the contents of `buf`, so that the update function could access it and store the value in our `system_var` variable. If we do not implement our own `sysvar_check()` function for our system variable, MySQL will provide a default one that performs all of the above (but nothing of the following).

```
    if (buf * 2 < status_var || buf > status_var * 3)
      return 0;
    else
      return 1;
}
```

This is our special condition. In this example we allow an update only if the new value is either less than a half of or three times bigger than the value of `status_var`. We return 0 when the new value is valid, and an update should be allowed, and 1 when an update should be canceled. In our update function we copy the value of the `system_var` to a `status_var`, to see how its value changes in SHOW STATUS and to get a different range on valid values for the `system_var` on every update. Note that the update function cannot return a value. It is not supposed to fail!

```
void sysvar_update(MYSQL_THD thd,
                   struct st_mysql_sys_var *var,
                   void *var_ptr, const void *save)
{
  system_var = *(long long *)save;
  status_var = system_var;
}
```

We update our `system_var` variable without any mutex protection, even though many threads may try to execute the SET statement at the same time. Nevertheless, it is safe. MySQL internally guards all accesses to global system variables with a mutex, which means we do not have to.

```
MYSQL_SYSVAR_LONGLONG(vars_system, system_var, 0,
  "A demo system var", sysvar_check, sysvar_update,
  0, 0, 123456789, 0);
```

This is the declaration for our system variable. It is a `long long` and is called `vars_system`. In fact as this is a variable for the `vars` plugin, the full name will be `vars_vars_system` in SHOW VARIABLES. It is associated with the `system_var` variable in the code, has the check function `sysvar_check()` and an update function `sysvar_update()` as defined above, and it can only take values between 0 and 123456789.

```
struct st_mysql_sys_var* vars_system_var[] = {
  MYSQL_SYSVAR(vars_system),
  NULL
};
```

This is the structure which stores all system variables to be passed to the declaration for this plugin. As we only have one variable we shall only include that.

```
struct st_mysql_daemon vars_plugin_info=
{ MYSQL_DAEMON_INTERFACE_VERSION };

mysql_declare_plugin(vars)
{
  MYSQL_DAEMON_PLUGIN,
  &vars_plugin_info,
  "vars",
  "Andrew Hutchings",
  "A system and status variables example",
  PLUGIN_LICENSE_GPL,
  NULL,
  NULL,
  0x0100,
  vars_status_var,
  vars_system_var,
  NULL
}
mysql_declare_plugin_end;
```

This is very similar to the declaration of our first plugin, but this one has structures for the status variables and system variable listed.

When putting our new plugin into action we should see the following:

```
mysql> INSTALL PLUGIN vars SONAME 'vars.so';
Query OK, 0 rows affected (0.00 sec)


mysql> SHOW STATUS LIKE 'vars_%';

+------------------+-------+
| Variable_name    | Value |
+------------------+-------+
| vars_status_var  | 0     |
+------------------+-------+
1 row in set (0.00 sec)


mysql> SHOW VARIABLES LIKE 'vars_%';

+------------------+-------+
| Variable_name    | Value |
+------------------+-------+
| vars_vars_system | 0     |
+------------------+-------+
1 row in set (0.00 sec)
```

Our status and system variables are both set to 0 by default.

```
mysql> SET GLOBAL vars_vars_system=2384;
Query OK, 0 rows affected (0.00 sec)


mysql> SHOW STATUS LIKE 'vars_%';

+------------------+-------+
| Variable_name    | Value |
+------------------+-------+
| vars_status_var  | 2384  |
+------------------+-------+
1 row in set (0.00 sec)


mysql> SHOW VARIABLES LIKE 'vars_%';

+------------------+-------+
| Variable_name    | Value |
+------------------+-------+
| vars_vars_system | 2384  |
+------------------+-------+
1 row in set (0.00 sec)
```

Setting our system variable to 2384 has altered both the system variable and the status variable, so we have success!

```
mysql> SET GLOBAL vars_vars_system=2383;
ERROR 1210 (HY000): Incorrect arguments to SET
```

Our special check function works too. The variable cannot be updated to a value that is too close to its old value!

A simple monitoring plugin

Our previous examples have demonstrated how to create a plugin and how to use status and system variables, but they did not do anything practically useful. The next plugin will record the connection statistics every five seconds into a log file so that load spikes can be recorded or monitored using an external application.

This plugin will remove any previous copy of the log file, create a new one, and then start a thread to retrieve the data and record it every five seconds. Upon removal of the plugin or shutdown, the plugin will record the shutdown time and close the file gracefully:

```
#include <string.h>
#include <mysql/plugin.h>
#include <mysql_version.h>
#include <my_global.h>
#include <my_sys.h>

#define MONITORING_BUFFER 1024

extern ulong thread_id;
extern uint thread_count;
extern ulong max_connections;
```

There are three internal MySQL variables we wish to monitor in our example. They are declared in `sql/mysqld.cc` so we need to declare them here as `extern` to be able to access them. The `thread_id` variable is used for the `Connections` status variable, `thread_count` for the `Threads_connected`, and `max_connections` is the `max_connections` system variable.

In theory, our plugin could read as well as alter them, and this can be a very powerful tool. But remember, with great power comes great responsibility.

```
static pthread_t monitoring_thread;
static int monitoring_file;
```

We will need these variables in our plugin. Because there can be only one monitoring file and only one monitoring thread, we can declare these variables on the global scope.

```
pthread_handler_t monitoring(void *p)
{
```

This function will be run in our monitoring thread, which is created during initialization. It has an endless loop retrieving data. This loop will sleep for five seconds, retrieve the current time and date, and then write the statistics to the file.

```
char buffer[MONITORING_BUFFER];
char time_str[20];
while(1)
{
  sleep(5);
  get_date(time_str, GETDATE_DATE_TIME, 0);
  sprintf(buffer, "%s: %u of %lu clients connected, "
                  "%lu connections made\n",
                  time_str, thread_count,
                  max_connections, thread_id);
  write(monitoring_file, buffer, strlen(buffer));
}
}
```

`get_date()` is a function that can be found in MySQL sources in `mysys/mf_getdate.c`. It is designed to return the current date and time in a MySQL format. Using MySQL functionality in this way is convenient, but it makes our plugin dependent on MySQL internals, which are not part of the plugin API and can change virtually anytime. Luckily, Daemon plugins already depend on the MySQL server version, they cannot be made more dependent than that. However, if a plugin is separated from the server by an API, adding such a dependency on the server internals may be undesirable. An ultimate solution for this problem, Server Services, is described in the Appendix for this book.

```
static int monitoring_plugin_init(void *p)
{
```

Our initialization function has more work to do this time. We need to open the file we are recording to and create the thread that will handle the monitoring.

```
pthread_attr_t attr;
char monitoring_filename[FN_REFLEN];
char buffer[MONITORING_BUFFER];
char time_str[20];

fn_format(monitoring_filename, "monitor", "", ".log",
          MY_REPLACE_EXT | MY_UNPACK_FILENAME);
```

The `fn_format()` function is designed to build a filename and path compatible with the current operating system given a set of parameters. More details on its functionality can be found in `mysys/mf_format.c`.

In this example our output file will be called `monitor.log` and should be found in the data directory of your MySQL installation.

```
unlink(monitoring_filename);
monitoring_file = open(monitoring_filename,
                       O_CREAT | O_RDWR, 0644);
if (monitoring_file < 0)
{
  fprintf(stderr, "Plugin 'monitoring': "
                  "Could not create file '%s'\n",
                  monitoring_filename);
  return 1;
}
```

We wish to unlink (delete) any old file with the same filename and create a new one to write to. We could instead append and/or rotate the file, but we are aiming for simplicity in this example. If the file cannot be created then the plugin will fail with an error.

```
get_date(time_str, GETDATE_DATE_TIME, 0);
sprintf(buffer, "Monitoring started at %s\n", time_str);
write(monitoring_file, buffer, strlen(buffer));
```

A line of text is written to our new file to signify when the monitoring was started.

```
pthread_attr_init(&attr);
pthread_attr_setdetachstate(&attr,
                            PTHREAD_CREATE_JOINABLE);
```

Pthreads (POSIX threads) is a GNU library to control the creation and handling of threads. This initializes the new thread and sets its state as a *joinable* thread. This means that this thread can pass its exit status back to the main thread upon termination. We could alternatively create a *detached* thread here.

```
    if (pthread_create(&monitoring_thread, &attr,
                       monitoring, NULL) != 0)
    {
      fprintf(stderr, "Plugin 'monitoring': "
                      "Could not create monitoring thread!\n");
      return 1;
    }
```

This creates a new thread for monitoring. If the thread creation fails, an error message is written to the error log and the initialization function returns a failure.

```
      return 0;
    }
```

If we have managed to get this far we should have the file successfully opened and a thread started and running.

```
    static int monitoring_plugin_deinit(void *p)
    {
      char buffer[MONITORING_BUFFER];
      char time_str[20];

      pthread_cancel(monitoring_thread);
      pthread_join(monitoring_thread, NULL);
```

Now that we are shutting down this plugin we need to clean things up. We start from the monitoring thread. The first function tells the thread to terminate, the second waits until it actually does.

```
      get_date(time_str, GETDATE_DATE_TIME, 0);
      sprintf(buffer, "Monitoring stopped at %s\n", time_str);
      write(monitoring_file, buffer, strlen(buffer));
      close(monitoring_file);
```

To complete the log file we write a message signifying the termination of the plugin. The file is then closed.

```
      return 0;
    }

    struct st_mysql_daemon monitoring_plugin =
    { MYSQL_DAEMON_INTERFACE_VERSION };

    mysql_declare_plugin(monitoring)
```

```
{
    MYSQL_DAEMON_PLUGIN,
    &monitoring_plugin,
    "monitoring",
    "Andrew Hutchings",
    "Daemon monitoring example, monitors MySQL",
    PLUGIN_LICENSE_GPL,
    monitoring_plugin_init,
    monitoring_plugin_deinit,
    0x0100,
    NULL,
    NULL,
    NULL
}
mysql_declare_plugin_end;
```

The plugin called `monitoring` is declared exactly as before, nothing new here.

When we install this plugin, run a few connections, and then uninstall the plugin, we should see in the file `monitor.log` something similar to the following:

```
Monitoring started at 2009-08-01 22:22:57
2009-08-01 22:23:02: 2 of 151 clients connected, 7 connections made
2009-08-01 22:23:07: 2 of 151 clients connected, 8 connections made
2009-08-01 22:23:12: 3 of 151 clients connected, 9 connections made
2009-08-01 22:23:17: 3 of 151 clients connected, 9 connections made
2009-08-01 22:23:22: 4 of 151 clients connected, 10 connections made
2009-08-01 22:23:27: 3 of 151 clients connected, 10 connections made
2009-08-01 22:23:32: 2 of 151 clients connected, 10 connections made
2009-08-01 22:23:37: 2 of 151 clients connected, 10 connections made
Monitoring stopped at 2009-08-01 22:23:41
```

System Status Variables plugin

At the end of the chapter, let's try to create a different Daemon plugin. This plugin, called `sys_status`, does not start any threads and does not do anything in the background. It uses the status variables to provide access to the `getrusage()` statistics. The `getrusage()` system call returns information about the process resource usage such as number of page faults, number of signals received, and number of context switches. How could we let MySQL users see this information?

As we remember, status variables are defined in terms of pointers to data. That is, SHOW STATUS takes the st_mysql_show_var structure and shows the data pointed to by its value member. It works well when a value to show is stored in a variable; for example, in our vars plugin, where we have stored the value in a status_vars C variable. But in this case we want to show the result of a function call. In other words, we need to use SHOW_FUNC type of a "status variable". And because we have many variables to show and all of their data are obtained from one function call, we put all of these variables in an array and use SHOW_ARRAY to display it. Let's put it all together.

We start by including all headers that we will need:

```
#include <mysql/plugin.h>
#include <mysql_version.h>
#include <sys/time.h>
#include <sys/resource.h>
#include <stdlib.h>
```

In addition to MySQL headers we will need a few system headers to be able to use getrusage(). Now we declare our status variables. We declare only one "variable" of the SHOW_FUNC type; MySQL will invoke the specified function to obtain the real status variable and we will be able to collect getrusage() data and convert it into status variables:

```
static struct st_mysql_show_var sys_status_var[] =
{
  {"Sys", (char *) &make_var_array, SHOW_FUNC},
  {0, 0, 0}
};
```

Let's write this function now. According to the table above, it should be declared as taking a thread context, a status variable structure to fill in, and a convenience buffer as arguments:

```
static int make_var_array(MYSQL_THD thd,
                          struct st_mysql_show_var* var,
                          char *buff)
{
```

In this function we will need to call getrusage() and create an array of status variables. We may as well declare needed local variables now:

```
struct st_mysql_show_var *status;
struct rusage *rusage;
```

We start by allocating the memory we need. MySQL has provided us with a buffer, and unless we need more than 1024 bytes we can simply use that buffer. However, we will need both an array of status variables and a `rusage` structure, which may not fit into the buffer. Also, we cannot simply `malloc()` the memory, because we will not be able to free it as the plugin API has no call for freeing a memory allocated in the `SHOW_FUNC` function. Luckily, there is a better solution. The `thd_alloc()` function allocates the memory in the connection's local memory pool. This memory is freed automatically at the end of the statement. We do not need to worry about memory leaks. Additionally, `thd_alloc()` can be much faster than `malloc()`, as explained in the Appendix. So, as `rusage` structure has 14 `long` members, we use `thd_alloc()` to allocate an array of 15 status variables—14 for values and one to terminate the array. We also need a memory for the `rusage` structure itself, but that we can safely put in the `buff` buffer:

```
status = thd_alloc(thd, sizeof(*status)*15);
rusage = (struct rusage*) buff;
```

Having done that, we configure our `var` status variable, which is of `SHOW_ARRAY` type, and its value points to the array to show:

```
var->type = SHOW_ARRAY;
var->value = (char*)status;
```

There is no need to set a name of the `var` variable—it will be ignored. MySQL will use the name that we have specified in the `sys_status_var[]` array for the `SHOW_FUNC` type. The name was "Sys" and the new type is `SHOW_ARRAY`. As we remember from before, it means that all variables in the array will automatically get the "Sys_" prefix.

Now, that we have prepared the array, all that is left is to fill it. Now is a good time to invoke `getrusage()` to grab the data. We check the return value, as the function may fail:

```
if (getrusage(RUSAGE_SELF, rusage) == 0)
{
```

And now we create status variables for every `long` member of the `rusage` structure. Basically, we will need to do something like the following and repeat it for all 14 members of the structure:

```
status->name = "maxrss";
status->value = (char*) & (rusage->ru_maxrss);
status->type = SHOW_LONG;
status++;
```

To save on typing and reduce the amount of copy-pasted code we can define a convenience macro for it:

```
#define show_rusage(X)                                  \
    status->name = #X;                                  \
    status->value = (char*) & (rusage->ru_ ## X);       \
    status->type = SHOW_LONG;                            \
    status++;
```

This makes filling the array as easy as the following:

```
        show_rusage(maxrss);
        show_rusage(ixrss);
        show_rusage(idrss);
        show_rusage(minflt);
        show_rusage(majflt);
        show_rusage(nswap);
        show_rusage(inblock);
        show_rusage(oublock);
        show_rusage(msgsnd);
        show_rusage(msgrcv);
        show_rusage(nsignals);
        show_rusage(nvcsw);
        show_rusage(nivcsw);
    }
```

The members of the rusage structure have quite cryptic names. You can find the complete description of all information returned by getrusage() by typing man getrusage either at the shell prompt or in the Google search form.

The array is done. We just need to terminate it with a zero element—an element with no name:

```
    status->name = 0;
    return 0;
}
```

This is it. We declare the plugin as usual, and we are done:

```
static struct st_mysql_daemon sys_status =
{ MYSQL_DAEMON_INTERFACE_VERSION };

mysql_declare_plugin(sys_status)
{
  MYSQL_DAEMON_PLUGIN,
  &sys_status,
  "sys_status",
  "Sergei Golubchik",
  "Export getrusage() via SHOW STATUS",
  PLUGIN_LICENSE_GPL,
  NULL,
  NULL,
  0x0100,
  sys_status_var,
  NULL,
  NULL
}
mysql_declare_plugin_end;
```

Now we can build, install it, and try it out:

```
mysql> show status like 'sys%';

+----------------+-------+
| Variable_name  | Value |
+----------------+-------+
| Sys_maxrss     | 0     |
| Sys_ixrss      | 0     |
| Sys_idrss      | 0     |
| Sys_minflt     | 3584  |
| Sys_majflt     | 0     |
| Sys_nswap      | 0     |
| Sys_inblock    | 0     |
| Sys_oublock    | 0     |
| Sys_msgsnd     | 0     |
| Sys_msgrcv     | 0     |
| Sys_nsignals   | 0     |
| Sys_nvcsw      | 10    |
| Sys_nivcsw     | 19    |
+----------------+-------+
13 rows in set (0.00 sec)
```

Works!

Summary

Daemon plugins, even if very limited in functionality, can serve as a good introduction into MySQL plugin programming. In this chapter we have learned the basics of the plugin API which are features common to all plugin types. We know how to declare a plugin, why API versions are needed, how to create new status and system variables, and new command-line options. To understand better the concepts in this chapter we have developed four Daemon plugins and tried them out. We will use this knowledge in all of the following chapters where we will study other more complex, plugin types. And we start in the next chapter with the Information Schema plugins.

4
Information Schema Plugins

The Information Schema was introduced in MySQL 5.0 as a standard way of providing database metadata accessible using normal SELECT queries. To make this work the metadata is made available via read-only tables in a database called INFORMATION_SCHEMA. In the MySQL mailing lists these tables are often informally referred to as *I_S tables*. The name of the schema, names of tables, and their structure is defined in the SQL standard (ISO/IEC 9075-11:2003 part 11). However, MySQL extends the standard by providing more tables than the standard dictates. This is where plugins come into the game. There is an Information Schema plugin type in MySQL 5.1. Plugins of this type can add new tables to the INFORMATION_SCHEMA database. These plugins are great for exposing information (possibly a lot of it) to the user in tabular form. Often these plugins are not distributed as standalone, but accompany other plugins, for example, complex storage engines, and expose their statistics or other internal information to the user.

In this first chapter on Information Schema plugins we will go over the basics of this plugin type and illustrate them with two simple example plugins.

Why write Information Schema plugins

The MySQL plugin API provides plugin developers with two ways of reporting status or statistical information to the user. Status variables were discussed in the previous chapter. They are best suited for reporting a small number of values that can be sorted into a fixed number of categories.

For example, we can use status variables to report the total number of disk syncs that our storage engine plugin has done, or the total number of different words that our full-text parser plugin has seen in the text. But we cannot use status variables to report, for example, a frequency distribution of words or word lengths—how many words of each length our full-text parser plugin has seen or (for a storage engine plugin) how many blocks each index takes and the block fill factor per index because the number of words or indexes may be very large, and because it is not known in advance, we cannot create a static array of all needed status variables.

Information Schema plugins, on the other hand, are perfect for that. They allow us to present large amounts of information in tabular form. The user can easily filter or group the information as necessary and generate reports using all of the power of SQL. Sometimes, Information Schema plugins are used as standalone if they expose information about the system or MySQL internals, like all of the working plugin examples in this book do. However, often they supplement other plugins; for example, full-text parsers or storage engines, like in the usage examples above.

Installing and using Information Schema plugins

As with all MySQL plugins the Information Schema plugins are installed and removed using INSTALL PLUGIN and UNINSTALL PLUGIN as follows:

```
mysql> INSTALL PLUGIN is_my_plugin SONAME 'is_my_plugin.so';
mysql> UNINSTALL PLUGIN is_my_plugin;
```

Upon initialization our table is created in the INFORMATION_SCHEMA. It is visible, in SHOW TABLES. However, it is not populated until queried, and every time it is queried its content is generated anew; it works as a kind of virtual table that is materialized whenever it is queried.

When running SHOW PLUGINS we should see:

```
mysql> SHOW PLUGINS\G

...

*************************** 10. row ***************************
    Name: IS_MY_PLUGIN
  Status: ACTIVE
    Type: INFORMATION SCHEMA
 Library: is_my_plugin.so
 License: GPL
...
```

Alternatively, we can get this from one of the predefined tables
in `INFORMATION_SCHEMA`:

```
mysql> SELECT * FROM INFORMATION_SCHEMA.PLUGINS WHERE PLUGIN_NAME='IS_MY_
PLUGIN'\G
*************************** 1. row ***************************
          PLUGIN_NAME: IS_MY_PLUGIN
       PLUGIN_VERSION: 0.16
        PLUGIN_STATUS: ACTIVE
          PLUGIN_TYPE: INFORMATION SCHEMA
  PLUGIN_TYPE_VERSION: 50137.0
       PLUGIN_LIBRARY: is_my_plugin.so
PLUGIN_LIBRARY_VERSION: 1.0
        PLUGIN_AUTHOR: Andrew Hutchings
   PLUGIN_DESCRIPTION: An information schema plugin
       PLUGIN_LICENSE: GPL
1 row in set (0.00 sec)
```

Tables in `INFORMATION_SCHEMA` are read-only, as dictated by the SQL Standard.
According to the Standard, write access to them should be denied to everyone. If we
try to run an update query on such a table we will see:

```
mysql> UPDATE MY_IS_TABLE SET VERSION=1;
ERROR 1044 (42000): Access denied for user 'root'@'localhost' to database
'information_schema'
```

Yes, even the almighty `root` user that has `ALL PRIVILEGES ON *.*` cannot modify
these tables!

The creation of Information Schema plugins

The basic structure of the Information Schema plugins in similar to that of Daemon
plugins. They need to be declared with `mysql_declare_plugin`, and can have status
and system variables. The initialization function, though, is a requirement for them,
not an option, as this is the function where we define a new Information Schema
table and tell MySQL what should happen when it is queried.

Defining Information Schema plugins

Just like with any other plugin type we use a macro to declare a plugin. This time
we set the plugin type to MYSQL_INFORMATION_SCHEMA_PLUGIN. An example of the
definition may look like this:

```
mysql_declare_plugin(mysql_is_my_plugin)
{
  MYSQL_INFORMATION_SCHEMA_PLUGIN,
  &mysql_is_my_plugin,
  "IS_MY_PLUGIN",
  "Andrew Hutchings (Andrew.Hutchings@Sun.COM)",
  "An information schema plugin",
  PLUGIN_LICENSE_GPL,
  is_my_plugin_init,
  is_my_plugin_deinit,
  0x0010,
  NULL,
  NULL,
  NULL
}
```

The differences start when we get to the initialization function. It still has the
same prototype:

```
int static_table_init(void *p);
```

However, this time p is a pointer to an ST_SCHEMA_TABLE structure that we need to
fill in. It is a structure that defines the layout of the Information Schema table and the
function calls for it. This structure is defined in sql/table.h as follows:

```
typedef struct st_schema_table
{
  const char* table_name;
  ST_FIELD_INFO *fields_info;
  TABLE *(*create_table)(THD *thd, TABLE_LIST *table_list);
  int (*fill_table)(THD *thd, TABLE_LIST *tables, COND *cond);
  int (*old_format)(THD *thd,
                    struct st_schema_table *schema_table);
  int (*process_table)(THD *thd, TABLE_LIST *tables,
                       TABLE *table, bool res,
                       LEX_STRING *db_name,
                       LEX_STRING *table_name);
  int idx_field1, idx_field2;
  bool hidden;
  uint i_s_requested_object;
} ST_SCHEMA_TABLE;
```

The fact that we need to include anything from `sql/` and may work with types such as `TABLE_LIST` or `COND` automatically means that plugins of this type strongly depend on internal MySQL data structures. These plugins will typically only work with the MySQL version they were compiled for.

The following table outlines the usage of elements for the structure:

Name	Description
table_name	The name for the Information Schema table. After calling the plugin initialization function MySQL sets this member to match the plugin name; that is, we do not need to do anything with it.
fields_info	An array of `ST_FIELD_INFO` structures describing the fields of the table.
create_table	A function that creates a `TABLE` structure for our table. It is always the same for any Information Schema table, and MySQL sets it automatically to the necessary function.
fill_table	The main function of our plugin. It generates the data that will be shown in our Information Schema table.
old_format	This is only used for built-in MySQL Information Schema tables that have `SHOW` statement counterparts (For example, the `INFORMATION_SCHEMA.PLUGINS` table has a `SHOW PLUGINS` counterpart). As plugins cannot add or replace `SHOW` statements, this member is never used for them.
process_table	This function is only used by built-in MySQL Information Schema tables that have their `fill_table` member set to `get_all_tables()` defined in `sql_show.cc`. It is never used in plugins.
idx_field1 and idx_field2	These members, again, are normally only used by built-in MySQL Information Schema tables; the functions and data structures to use them are not available to plugins.
hidden	Set to `true` if the data should only be available via the corresponding `SHOW` command, not as a table in the `INFORMATION_SCHEMA`. Plugins should never set it, as they cannot provide a new `SHOW` command.
i_s_request ed_object	The table opening method, not used here. This member, too, is only used by `get_all_tables` and is completely ignored for plugins

In other words, the only members of `ST_SCHEMA_TABLE` that we would ever need to set are `fields_info` and `fill_table`.

The `fields_info` member is an array of structures that defines the fields of our Information Schema table. The structure itself is defined in `sql/table.h` as the following:

```
typedef struct st_field_info
{
  const char* field_name;
  uint field_length;
  enum enum_field_types field_type;
  int value;
  uint field_flags;
  const char* old_name;
  uint open_method;
} ST_FIELD_INFO;
```

A `fields_info` array needs to have as many elements (these very structures) as there are fields in our Information Schema table, plus one more with `field_name` being NULL to denote the end of the array. The following table details the elements of this structure:

Name	Description
field_name	The name of this field, usually defined in uppercase.
field_length	This is complicated. It means the maximum number of characters if the field is of a VARCHAR or TEXT type, the number of bytes for BLOB, the display width for integers, the number of digits for FLOAT or DOUBLE, and both the precision and scale (encoded as *precision*100+scale*) for DECIMAL.
field_type	An enum denoting the field type. See below.
value	Unused.
field_flags	Field attributes. MY_I_S_UNSIGNED if the field is unsigned, MY_I_S_MAYBE_NULL if the field may have NULL values (that is, if the field is not NOT NULL), or both as MY_I_S_UNSIGNED | MY_I_S_MAYBE_NULL.
old_name	The field name for the corresponding SHOW statement. It is only used for Information Schema tables that have a SHOW statement counterpart.
open_method	This is only used by get_all_tables and is of no importance for plugins

A `field_type` denotes the type of the field. It uses the same `enum_field_types` that should be familiar to anybody who has used the MySQL C client library. However, only a subset of types is supported for fields of the Information Schema tables. The supported types and the corresponding `enum_field_types` constants are listed as follows:

Constant	MySQL Type
MYSQL_TYPE_TINY	TINYINT
MYSQL_TYPE_SHORT	SMALLINT
MYSQL_TYPE_INT24	MEDIUMINT
MYSQL_TYPE_LONG	INT
MYSQL_TYPE_LONGLONG	BIGINT
MYSQL_TYPE_TIME	TIME
MYSQL_TYPE_DATE	DATE
MYSQL_TYPE_DATETIME	DATETIME
MYSQL_TYPE_TIMESTAMP	TIMESTAMP
MYSQL_TYPE_FLOAT	FLOAT
MYSQL_TYPE_DOUBLE	DOUBLE
MYSQL_TYPE_DECIMAL	DECIMAL
MYSQL_TYPE_NEWDECIMAL	DECIMAL
MYSQL_TYPE_TINY_BLOB	TINYBLOB
MYSQL_TYPE_MEDIUM_BLOB	MEDIUMBLOB
MYSQL_TYPE_BLOB	BLOB
MYSQL_TYPE_LONG_BLOB	LONGBLOB
MYSQL_TYPE_STRING	VARCHAR or TEXT (depending on the length)

Out of these only MYSQL_TYPE_STRING, MYSQL_TYPE_LONGLONG, MYSQL_TYPE_LONG, MYSQL_TYPE_DECIMAL, and MYSQL_TYPE_DATETIME are really used by built-in MySQL Information Schema tables. It would be a safe bet to limit ourselves to these five types, whenever possible.

So, for example, we can define the `fields_info` array as follows:

```
ST_FIELD_INFO my_is_fields[] =
{
  {"A_VARCHAR", 30, MYSQL_TYPE_STRING, 0, 0, 0, 0},
  {"AN_INT", 10, MYSQL_TYPE_LONG, 0, 0, 0, 0},
  {0, 0, MYSQL_TYPE_NULL, 0, 0, 0, 0}
};
```

The `fill_table()` function is used to fill our table with data when it is about to be queried. As we have seen above, it should have the following prototype:

```
int fill_table(THD *thd, TABLE_LIST *tables, COND *cond);
```

The arguments of this function are as follows:

Argument	Description
`thd`	The thread context object for the connection that executes the query
`tables`	A pointer into the list of tables of the current query to the element that corresponds to our Information Schema table. More precisely, it corresponds to the automatically created temporary table that will substitute our table in the query. This is the table that we need to fill with data in the `fill_table()` function.
`cond`	The WHERE clause for the query. It can be used for the so called *condition pushdown*. This means evaluating the condition (or a part of it) directly in the `fill_table()` and putting only those rows into the temporary table that can satisfy the WHERE clause, as opposed to putting all rows into it and relying on MySQL to filter the garbage out. In certain cases this trick can speed up the queries significantly. We will discuss *condition pushdown* in the next chapter.

To fill the destination temporary table with data we have `store()` methods of the MySQL `Field` class and the `schema_table_store_record()` utility function. First, we go over all fields of the table using their `store()` methods to store data in the row. When all fields have got the values, that is when we have completely filled one row with data, we call `schema_table_store_record()` to write this row to the temporary table. We repeat this procedure until we have written all of the rows we wanted.

There are five store methods in the `Field` class. Any one of them can be used depending on the type of the data we want to store:

- `Field::store(const char *to, uint length, CHARSET_INFO *cs)`
- `Field::store(longlong nr, bool unsigned_val)`
- `Field::store(double nr)`
- `Field::store_decimal(const my_decimal *d)`
- `Field::store_time(MYSQL_TIME *ltime, timestamp_type t_type)`

For example, to store a UTF-8 string in the first field of the table we use:

```
tables->table->field[0]->store(my_str, strlen(my_str),
                               system_charset_info);
```

This example shows that all fields (objects of the `Field` class) are accessed via the `tables->table->field[]` array. And that to store a string MySQL needs to know its character set. If the string is in UTF-8 or pure 7-bit ASCII we can use `system_charset_info` (which is always UTF-8). If we are lucky and the string is in binary or in the Latin1 character set we can use `my_charset_bin` or `my_charset_latin1` respectively. Otherwise, we will need to use one of the `get_charset()`, `get_charset_by_name()`, or `get_charset_by_csname()` functions, but details on working with the MySQL character sets are beyond the scope of this book. Further information is available in the `include/m_ctype.h` and `mysys/charset.c` files in the MySQL source distribution.

There is an important detail to keep in mind. If the field is declared with the `MY_I_S_MAYBE_NULL` flag, in other words if the field value can be NULL, we need to set its "nullness" for every row, as the store methods will not do it for us. For example, if the field in question could be NULL the previous example should be modified to:

```
tables->table->field[0]->set_notnull();
tables->table->field[0]->store(my_str, strlen(my_str),
                               system_charset_info);
```

On the other hand, to set it to NULL we simply write:

```
tables->table->field[0]->set_null();
```

Now, to write a row with data to the temporary table we will need a MySQL utility function whose prototype, unfortunately, is not exported to plugins. That is, we have to declare it in our plugin. This is done as follows:

```
bool schema_table_store_record(THD *thd, TABLE *table);
```

And we use it simply as:

```
result = schema_table_store_record(thd, tables->table);
```

As almost always in MySQL this function returns 0 on success and 1 on failure.

A Static Table example

To familiarize ourselves with the extra structures and functions required for an Information Schema plugin, we will start with a simple example. This plugin will create an Information Schema table called VERSIONS that will return a few rows of data with the version numbers for various MySQL internals:

```
#include <mysql_priv.h>
```

To see MySQL internal data structures such as TABLE_LIST, TABLE, and Field we need to include the mysql_priv.h file. This is a mega-header that includes almost everything else and a kitchen sink too. At least this is the case in MySQL 5.1 and earlier versions, but it will change in one of the future MySQL releases. Still in 5.1 it is the only header we include, everything else we may need is included by it.

```
bool schema_table_store_record(THD *thd, TABLE *table);
```

As discussed above we need to declare a schema_table_store_record() function.

```
static ST_FIELD_INFO versions_fields[] =
{
  {"NAME", 30, MYSQL_TYPE_STRING, 0, 0, 0, 0},
  {"VERSION", 10, MYSQL_TYPE_LONG, 0, 0, 0, 0},
  {0, 0, MYSQL_TYPE_NULL, 0, 0, 0, 0}
};
```

Now we define the structure of our table. It has two columns — one of type VARCHAR(30) called NAME, and the other of type INT(10) called VERSION. The array is terminated with an empty element.

```
static int fill_versions(THD *thd, TABLE_LIST *tables,
                         COND *cond)
{
```

We start implementing our fill_table function — the one that fills the temporary table with data. As we will need the table and character set pointers quite often, we copy them into local variables for convenience:

```
CHARSET_INFO *cs = system_charset_info;
TABLE *table = tables->table;
```

These are the values we put into the first column:

```
const char *version_str = "MySQL Version ID";
const char *protocol_str = "MySQL Protocol Version";
const char *frm_str = "MySQL FRM Version";
```

Let's put them into the table, one by one. As shown previously, we store the string in the first field:

```
table->field[0]->store(version_str,
                       strlen(version_str), cs);
```

And the corresponding number (MYSQL_VERSION_ID is MySQL version as a number, for example, 50147 for 5.1.47) in the second field:

```
table->field[1]->store(MYSQL_VERSION_ID);
```

Having done that, we insert the row into the temporary table:

```
if (schema_table_store_record(thd, table))
  return 1;
```

Similarly we insert two more rows:

```
table->field[0]->store(protocol_str,
                       strlen(protocol_str), cs);
table->field[1]->store(PROTOCOL_VERSION);
if (schema_table_store_record(thd, table))
  return 1;

table->field[0]->store(frm_str, strlen(frm_str), cs);
table->field[1]->store(FRM_VER);
if (schema_table_store_record(thd, table))
  return 1;
```

We are done, and if we have not failed so far, we report a success:

```
  return 0;
}
```

In the initialization function we set up the ST_SCHEMA_TABLE structure, as described previously:

```
static int versions_init(void *p)
{
  ST_SCHEMA_TABLE *schema = (ST_SCHEMA_TABLE*) p;
  schema->fields_info = versions_fields;
  schema->fill_table = fill_versions;
  return 0;
}
```

Our simple plugin has neither a de-initialization function nor system or status variables. What is left is to declare the plugin, and we are done:

```
static struct st_mysql_information_schema versions =
{ MYSQL_INFORMATION_SCHEMA_INTERFACE_VERSION };

mysql_declare_plugin(versions)
{
  MYSQL_INFORMATION_SCHEMA_PLUGIN,
  &versions,
  "VERSIONS",
  "Andrew Hutchings (Andrew.Hutchings@Sun.COM)",
  "A simple static information schema table",
```

```
        PLUGIN_LICENSE_GPL,
        versions_init,
        NULL,
        0x0100,
        NULL,
        NULL,
        NULL
    }
    mysql_declare_plugin_end;
```

When we build and install this plugin we should see something like:

```
mysql> SHOW TABLES FROM INFORMATION_SCHEMA LIKE 'VERSIONS';
+-------------------------------------------+
| Tables_in_INFORMATION_SCHEMA (VERSIONS)   |
+-------------------------------------------+
| VERSIONS                                  |
+-------------------------------------------+
1 row in set (0.00 sec)


mysql> SHOW CREATE TABLE INFORMATION_SCHEMA.VERSIONS\G
*************************** 1. row ***************************
       Table: VERSIONS
Create Table: CREATE TEMPORARY TABLE 'VERSIONS' (
  `NAME` varchar(30) NOT NULL DEFAULT '',
  `VERSION` int(10) NOT NULL DEFAULT '0'
) ENGINE=MEMORY DEFAULT CHARSET=utf8
1 row in set (0.00 sec)
```

See? It says TEMPORARY and ENGINE=MEMORY, because for the duration of the query our Information Schema table is materialized using a temporary table.

```
mysql> SELECT * FROM INFORMATION_SCHEMA.VERSIONS;
+-----------------------+---------+
| NAME                  | VERSION |
+-----------------------+---------+
| MySQL Version ID      |   50147 |
| MySQL Protocol Version |     10 |
| MySQL FRM Version     |       6 |
+-----------------------+---------+
3 rows in set (0.00 sec)
```

Here we can see that the new Information Schema table has been created successfully and we can query it to get the data.

```
mysql> SELECT * FROM INFORMATION_SCHEMA.VERSIONS
    --> WHERE NAME LIKE '%FRM%';

+--------------------+---------+
| NAME               | VERSION |
+--------------------+---------+
| MySQL FRM Version  |       6 |
+--------------------+---------+
1 row in set (0.00 sec)
```

We do not need to do anything special to support WHERE or ORDER BY or any other SQL features; everything just works automatically.

A System Information plugin

In the previous chapter we created a Daemon plugin that exported getrusage() data via status variables. For the sake of the example we will now do the same with the Information Schema table. However, to not repeat ourselves we will go beyond getrusage() and will also use other Linux system information functions. Yes, unfortunately this plugin is unlikely to work on anything except Linux. One can create a portable system information plugin by using, for example, the SIGAR library (http://sigar.hyperic.com) but for simplicity we will keep the example free from external dependencies.

```
#include <mysql_priv.h>
#include <sys/sysinfo.h>
bool schema_table_store_record(THD *thd, TABLE *table);
```

We start the plugin as usual, with the exception of sys/sysinfo.h that we need for system information functions. Then we declare fields; for simplicity we will use a name/value pair, the value being a long long integer:

```
static ST_FIELD_INFO sys_usage_fields[] =
{
  {"RESOURCE", 255, MYSQL_TYPE_STRING, 0, 0, 0, 0},
  {"VALUE", 20, MYSQL_TYPE_LONGLONG, 0, 0, 0, 0},
  {0, 0, MYSQL_TYPE_NULL, 0, 0, 0, 0}
};
```

Now we can perform our `fill_table` function starting by declaring local variables, as usual:

```
int fill_sys_usage(THD *thd, TABLE_LIST *tables, COND *cond)
{
  CHARSET_INFO *cs= system_charset_info;
  TABLE *table= tables->table;
  rusage rusage;
  rlimit limit;
```

Now we need to write rows into the table, one by one. As we have seen in the previous example, the procedure is always the same—set the value of the first column, set the value of the second column, and store the row. Let's create a macro to avoid copy-pasting the same lines over and over:

```
#define INSERT(NAME,VALUE)                             \
  table->field[0]->store(NAME, sizeof(NAME)-1, cs);   \
  table->field[1]->store(VALUE);                       \
  if (schema_table_store_record(thd, table))           \
    return 1;
```

Now we can start inserting rows:

```
INSERT("Total physical memory",
       get_phys_pages() * getpagesize());
```

We get the total number of physical memory pages and then multiply this by the page size to obtain the total memory size in bytes.

```
INSERT("Available physical memory",
       get_avphys_pages() * getpagesize());
```

Then do the same with the amount of free physical memory. This value may turn out to be lower than expected because it does not include caches and buffers, which often take up most of the available system memory.

```
INSERT("Number of CPUs", get_nprocs());
```

This simply gives the total number of CPUs available to the operating system. This also includes the multiple cores of a CPU and will show double the amount for Hyper Threaded CPUs.

```
if (getrusage(RUSAGE_SELF, &rusage))
    return 1;
```

This function gets details about the current CPU and block I/O usage for the current process. In fact, it is supported in other operating systems and may give more information in those operating systems.

```
INSERT("CPU user time (seconds)",  rusage.ru_utime.tv_sec);
```

The operating system records the amount of user CPU time the current process uses, and we can display this information.

```
INSERT("CPU system time (seconds)", rusage.ru_stime.tv_sec);
```

Likewise the system time used by the current process is recorded, and this can be displayed as well.

```
INSERT("Block input operations", rusage.ru_inblock);
INSERT("Block output operations", rusage.ru_oublock);
```

Block I/O is also reported by the `getrusage()` function. We display this as two separate rows.

```
if (getrlimit(RLIMIT_AS, &rlimit))
  return 1;
```

In POSIX operating systems we can define limits to things such as the number of open files on a per-user basis. It is often interesting to know this from a MySQL perspective, because if the limits are too low unusual error messages can be displayed in MySQL.

```
INSERT("Maximum virtual memory", rlimit.rlim_cur);
if (getrlimit(RLIMIT_DATA, &rlimit))
  return 1;
INSERT("Maximum data memory", rlimit.rlim_cur);
```

Using the user limits data we obtained we can give the maximum amount of virtual and data memory available to the process.

```
if (getrlimit(RLIMIT_FSIZE, &rlimit))
  return 1;
INSERT("Maximum file size", rlimit.rlim_cur);
```

The maximum file size can limit the size of the tables in MySQL, so it is important that this is set high. This variable will show us what this is currently set to.

```
if (getrlimit(RLIMIT_NOFILE, &rlimit))
  return 1;
INSERT("Maximum number of files", rlimit.rlim_cur);
```

Finally we get the number of files limit. If set too low, it can cause problems for installations with many tables. Knowing it will help to diagnose and prevent these problems.

```
    return 0;
}
```

There are many more values that `getrusage()` reports and many more limits that `getrlimit()` knows about. New rows can be added easily, but the mentioned examples are enough to illustrate the concept.

We finish the plugin with the initialization function and a declaration, just as in the first example:

```
int sys_usage_init(void *p)
{
  ST_SCHEMA_TABLE *schema= (ST_SCHEMA_TABLE*) p;
  schema->fields_info= sys_usage_fields;
  schema->fill_table= fill_sys_usage;
  return 0;
}

struct st_mysql_information_schema is_sys_usage =
{ MYSQL_INFORMATION_SCHEMA_INTERFACE_VERSION };

mysql_declare_plugin(is_sys_usage)
{
  MYSQL_INFORMATION_SCHEMA_PLUGIN,
  &is_sys_usage,
  "SYS_USAGE",
  "Andrew Hutchings (Andrew.Hutchings@Sun.COM)",
  "Information about system resource usage",
  PLUGIN_LICENSE_GPL,
  sys_usage_init,
  NULL,
  0x0010,
  NULL,
  NULL,
  NULL
}
mysql_declare_plugin_end;
```

So we should now have a table in Information Schema called `SYS_USAGE` and when queried it will give us live data about the system. Running on a Linux system gives us:

```
mysql> select * from information_schema.sys_usage;
+----------------------------+---------------------+
| RESOURCE                   | VALUE               |
+----------------------------+---------------------+
| Total physical memory      |          4050092032 |
| Available physical memory  |          1227526144 |
| Number of CPUs             |                   2 |
| CPU user time (seconds)    |                   0 |
| CPU system time (seconds)  |                   0 |
| Block input operations     |               17832 |
| Block output operations    |                  48 |
| Maximum virtual memory     | 9223372036854775807 |
| Maximum data memory        | 9223372036854775807 |
| Maximum file size          | 9223372036854775807 |
| Maximum number of files    |                1024 |
+----------------------------+---------------------+
11 rows in set (0.01 sec)


mysql> select benchmark(100000000, 2*2);
+---------------------------+
| benchmark(100000000, 2*2) |
+---------------------------+
|                         0 |
+---------------------------+
1 row in set (4.36 sec)


mysql> select * from information_schema.sys_usage;
+----------------------------+---------------------+
| RESOURCE                   | VALUE               |
+----------------------------+---------------------+
| Total physical memory      |          4050092032 |
| Available physical memory  |          1226723328 |
| Number of CPUs             |                   2 |
| CPU user time (seconds)    |                   4 |
| CPU system time (seconds)  |                   0 |
| Block input operations     |               17832 |
| Block output operations    |                  48 |
| Maximum virtual memory     | 9223372036854775807 |
| Maximum data memory        | 9223372036854775807 |
| Maximum file size          | 9223372036854775807 |
| Maximum number of files    |                1024 |
+----------------------------+---------------------+
11 rows in set (0.00 sec)
```

In this example we have shown one set of results, run a query that takes just over 4 seconds of user CPU time to execute, and got another set of results that shows the increase in user CPU time. We now have a diagnostics tool inside MySQL!

Summary

In this chapter we have learned the basic structure of an Information Schema plugin. We have discussed how it works, how it defines the table structure, and how it fills it with the data. At the end of the chapter we have used this knowledge to develop two fully functional Information Schema plugins.

In the next chapter we will look into more complex aspects of Information Schema plugins such as condition pushdown and exposing internal MySQL data structures.

5
Advanced Information Schema Plugins

We have seen in the previous chapter how to create a basic Information Schema plugin and then further adapt this knowledge to expose the information about the server operating system. In this chapter we will talk about advanced features of the Information Schema plugins. We will discuss how to access MySQL internal data structures and display them in Information Schema tables, and we will look at condition pushdown optimization.

Accessing MySQL internals

One of the important use cases for the Information Schema plugin is to provide more server diagnostics to the user, that is, to expose the data about the MySQL internals. To do it we need to be able to find and use the internal data structures. Of course MySQL is an open source project and we can see where the data is that we need to capture. Typically, the data we need will be declared in the `sql/` directory of the source code, but sometimes they can be in `mysys/` or elsewhere.

In order to access the internals we need to define a `MYSQL_SERVER` macro that the server uses internally to see all of the declarations. Without it we only get a highly filtered view, appropriate for plugins. In particular, we need this macro to access the `THD` object. There are other tricks that may be needed to get the data we want. For instance, we may want to make our plugin access a private class member, in which case we need to extend the class so there are public accessors for the private data. An example of this can be seen in the Information Schema cached queries plugin created by Roland Bouman at: `http://rpbouman.blogspot.com/2008/07/inspect-query-cahce-using-mysql.html` (yes, the word "cache" is spelled incorrectly in the URL, it's not a typo in the book).

Condition pushdown

Condition pushdown is not a new kind of wrestling move but a special optimization in the MySQL server. It allows the Storage Engine and Information Schema plugins to use the WHERE condition to filter the rows returned to MySQL, as opposed to letting MySQL process the WHERE condition internally after the rows have been received. So it is effectively pushing down the WHERE condition into the plugin. This optimization is not always meaningful to use. However, if the total number of rows is large, while the number of rows that satisfy the WHERE clause is small, and generating rows is relatively expensive—in such a case this optimization can bring huge performance benefits. For example, the INFORMATION_SCHEMA.COLUMNS table uses it, because it needs to open a table to get the information about its columns, and it is far better to open only one table that the user is interested in, than to open every table in every database, potentially thousands of them.

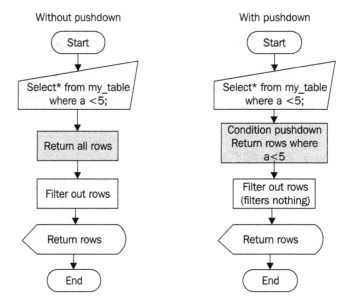

In these flowcharts, we can see the roles of the MySQL server in light gray and the Information Schema plugin in dark gray. In the first flowchart, without condition pushdown, all rows for the table are generated and returned. MySQL then filters them to satisfy the WHERE condition for the user. A similar thing happens when you query a normal table that does not use indexing. In the second example, the Information Schema plugin takes the WHERE condition and uses it so that unneeded rows are not even generated. The results are also filtered by MySQL but it will be applying the filter on a lot less rows, and in many cases it will not filter anything out (it depends on the implementation of the condition pushdown).

Depending on the plugin this optimization may or may not be beneficial. For example, condition pushdown is used quite a lot by the MySQL NDB Cluster storage engine that converts the WHERE clause to NDBAPI calls to filter rows in the cluster storage nodes rather than the MySQL server. In many situations this will give a good performance gain, because different cluster nodes can perform the filtering in parallel and, most importantly, rows that fail the WHERE condition will not be sent over the network to the MySQL server. Similarly, condition pushdown is very important for other engines that store the data remotely, such as the Federated storage engine. As for Information Schema tables, condition pushdown makes sense when generating a row is an expensive operation. All tables that provide information about tables fall into this category. To know table metadata MySQL has to open this table, and opening a table is not cheap. As big MySQL installations can potentially have many thousands of tables, opening them all when only one table will match the WHERE clause is simply not acceptable. This is why tables such as INFORMATION_SCHEMA.TABLES, INFORMATION_SCHEMA.COLUMNS, INFORMATION_SCHEMA.TRIGGERS, and a few others have to utilize condition pushdown to be usable.

Using condition pushdown

Condition pushdown is quite complex to implement and there will not be many cases where it will be advantageous to use it in an Information Schema. That said, we will cover the basics here.

The conditions are stored in a tree of Item objects. The hierarchy of Item classes is huge (hundreds of classes) and even the base class is very complex. It is one of the most fundamental classes in MySQL. It is used for expressions, and anything that may have a value. There is an Item class (more precisely, a class derived from the base Item class) for a field in a table, for a user variable, for a parameter in a prepared statement, for an SQL function, for a subquery, for each comparison, mathematical or logical operator, and so on. There are also very special Item classes, for example, for using in GROUP BY or HAVING clauses with an expression that refers to another expression in the SELECT clause. Luckily, for condition pushdown we will only need a few percent of all that functionality and complexity. Don't let item.h header scare you!

We will not go into deep detail here, because although pushed conditions can bring dramatic performance improvements they are not exactly easy to use and could well span a few chapters on their own. In fact, Item classes were never designed to be used by plugins and working with them is not much easier than hacking MySQL server source code directly.

For the purpose of optimizing Information Schema tables, we are only interested in the conditions of the form `field=constant`, where `field` is a field in our Information Schema table. Alternatively, other comparison operators such as `<=,>,` or `BETWEEN` can be used. Possibly many of these conditions can be used together in a `WHERE` clause, combined with `OR` or `AND` operators. The corresponding part of the `Item` hierarchy is shown in the following simplified graph (it is simplified, because it omits seven intermediate classes — between `Item` and `Item_field`, between `Item` and `Item_func`, and so on):

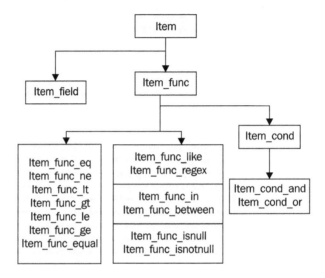

An expression in MySQL is represented as a tree of `Item` objects. Every class derived from `Item_func` has the `arguments()` method that returns an array of arguments of this function or operator. To parse the expression tree and extract constants for early checking, which is the whole point of condition pushdown, one needs to do something like the following:

1. Check if `COND` is, in fact, an `Item_cond_or` or `Item_cond_and` instance.

2. If yes, repeat the procedure recursively for each of the `COND` arguments. Otherwise, check if it is one of the operators we support, for example, if it is `Item_func_eq` or `Item_func_equal`.

3. If yes, check if one of its arguments is `Item_field` that corresponds to the field of our table that we can optimize on. Also, check if the other argument is a constant. If everything is good, remember that the user only wants rows where a given field must be equal to the given constant.

We will not go into details about how to check the `Item` type, how to find if the `Item` is a constant, or how to map `Item_field` to a table. This is because, not surprisingly, MySQL already has a function that implements all of the above. Unfortunately, this function, just like `schema_table_store_record()`, was not designed to be used by plugins. We need to declare its prototype in our plugin. Furthermore, it uses a structure that is declared in `sql/sql_show.cc`; we need to declare it in our plugin too. We do this as follows:

```
typedef struct st_lookup_field_values
{
  LEX_STRING value1, value2;
  bool value1_is_wildcard, value2_is_wildcard;
} LOOKUP_FIELD_VALUES;

bool calc_lookup_values_from_cond(THD *thd, COND *cond,
          TABLE_LIST *table, LOOKUP_FIELD_VALUES *lookups);
```

This function will traverse the `cond` recursively, as explained before, and look for conditions like `field1=constant` and `field2=constant`. Here, `field1` and `field2` are fields of our table indicated by the `idx_field1` and `idx_field2` members of our `ST_SCHEMA_TABLE` structure, the one that we set up in the plugin initialization function. If such a condition is found, the string representation of the value of the `constant` will be stored in `value1` or `value2` as appropriate. Two other members of the `LOOKUP_FIELD_VALUES` structure are not used by this function; they are set only for `SHOW ... LIKE` statements.

Using `calc_lookup_values_from_cond()` allows us to implement condition pushdown quickly and easily, but it has its limitations. This function was written to support condition pushdown for `INFORMATION_SCHEMA.TABLES`, `INFORMATION_SCHEMA.COLUMNS`, and other similar MySQL built-in Information Schema tables, in other words, to be able to avoid directory scan by extracting the table and directory name from the query. That is, it assumes that constants are *strings*, it supports at most *two* lookup fields and assumes that they cannot have `NULL` values, and it only supports comparison for equality — that is, `=` and `<=>`. If we would like to support, say, `>=` or `LIKE`, or filter on three fields, we would need to implement our own `cond` traversal function, using `calc_lookup_values_from_cond()` as a good start.

A condition pushdown example

In this example, however, we will not do anything like that — `calc_lookup_values_from_cond()` is good enough for that.

We will create an Information Schema table that contains a list of words. With the WHERE condition we can limit what words are returned, as usual. But in our table all the generated rows are numbered. Depending on whether condition pushdown worked or not, a different number of rows will be generated and we will see it, because row numbers will change.

We start by including `mysql_priv.h` and declaring functions and types that are missing in it:

```
#include <mysql_priv.h>

typedef struct st_lookup_field_values
{
  LEX_STRING value1, value2;
  bool value1_is_wildcard, value2_is_wildcard;
} LOOKUP_FIELD_VALUES;

bool calc_lookup_values_from_cond(THD *thd, COND *cond,
         TABLE_LIST *table, LOOKUP_FIELD_VALUES *lookups);
bool schema_table_store_record(THD *thd, TABLE *table);
```

And we declare the fields of our table, one for the word and one for the number:

```
ST_FIELD_INFO cond_push_fields[] =
{
  {"NUMBER", 10, MYSQL_TYPE_LONG, 0, 0, 0, 0},
  {"TEXT", 100, MYSQL_TYPE_STRING, 0, 0, 0, 0},
  {0, 0, MYSQL_TYPE_NULL, 0, 0, 0, 0}
}
```

Now, let's do it. Fill the table, taking the WHERE clause into account. First, we declare our local variables—for the character set and the table, as usual, the array or words that we will put in the table, a sequence number for counting generated rows, and a condition pushdown lookup structure.

```
int fill_cond_push(THD *thd, TABLE_LIST *tables, COND *cond)
{
  CHARSET_INFO *cs = system_charset_info;
  TABLE *table = tables->table;
  const char **ptr, *output[] = {"hello", "world", "this",
                                 "is", "a", "test", 0};
  int num;
  LOOKUP_FIELD_VALUES lookups;
```

Then we initialize the `lookups` structure and call the magic function that will analyze the WHERE clause and store the constants in this structure:

```
bzero((char*) &lookups, sizeof(lookups));
if (calc_lookup_values_from_cond(thd, cond,
                                 tables, &lookups))
    return 0;
```

The `calc_lookup_values_from_cond()` returns 1 when a field value is compared to NULL. As our field cannot be NULL, we can return right away—nothing that we can put in the table will satisfy the WHERE condition.

Otherwise we try to fill the table:

```
for (num = 0, ptr = output; *ptr; ptr++)
{
  if (lookups.value1.str &&
      my_strnncoll(cs, (const uchar*)*ptr, strlen(*ptr),
                   (const uchar*)lookups.value1.str,
                   lookups.value1.length))
    continue;
```

If the WHERE clause has given us a value that we can filter on—that is, if the `str` pointer of the `lookups.value1` is not 0—we compare it with the word that we want to put into the row. For comparison we use the `my_strnncoll()` function that compares two strings using the collation, passed as the first argument (`system_charset_info` is `utf8_general_ci`), and takes both strings and their lengths too (indeed, the string is not necessarily zero terminated; after all, one can write WHERE `field='a\0b'`).

If the value matches the word or if there is no value in the `lookups.value1` at all, we store a new row in the table:

```
    table->field[0]->store(++num);
    table->field[1]->store(*ptr, strlen(*ptr), cs);
    if (schema_table_store_record(thd, table))
      return 1;
  }
  return 0;
}
```

That's all. It was not too difficult. Now we only need to set the `idx_field1` in the initialization function and declare the plugin:

```
int cond_push_init(void *p)
{
  ST_SCHEMA_TABLE *schema = (ST_SCHEMA_TABLE*) p;
  schema->fields_info = cond_push_fields;
  schema->fill_table = fill_cond_push;
  schema->idx_field1 = 1;
  return 0;
}

struct st_mysql_information_schema cond_push=
{ MYSQL_INFORMATION_SCHEMA_INTERFACE_VERSION };

mysql_declare_plugin(cond_push)
{
  MYSQL_INFORMATION_SCHEMA_PLUGIN,
  &cond_push,
  "COND_PUSH",
  "Andrew Hutchings (Andrew.Hutchings@Sun.COM)",
  "A simple condition pushdown demo table",
  PLUGIN_LICENSE_GPL,
  cond_push_init,
  NULL,
  0x0010,
  NULL,
  NULL,
  NULL
}
mysql_declare_plugin_end;
```

If we compile and install this plugin, we should see:

```
mysql> select * from information_schema.cond_push;
+-----------+-------+
| INCREMENT | TEXT  |
+-----------+-------+
|         1 | hello |
|         2 | world |
|         3 | this  |
|         4 | is    |
|         5 | a     |
|         6 | test  |
+-----------+-------+
6 rows in set (0.01 sec)
```

There's nothing surprising here. There are six rows in the table.

```
mysql> select * from information_schema.cond_push where text='test';

+--------+------+
| NUMBER | TEXT |
+--------+------+
|      1 | test |
+--------+------+
1 row in set (0.00 sec)
```

Yes! Note that condition pushdown worked—we have put only one single row in the table! Compare this to the result without condition pushdown:

```
mysql> select * from information_schema.cond_push where
concat(text)='test';

+--------+------+
| NUMBER | TEXT |
+--------+------+
|      6 | test |
+--------+------+
1 row in set (0.00 sec)
```

In this case the plugin has put all six rows in the table and MySQL has filtered out the first five. We can use more complex conditions too:

```
mysql> select * from information_schema.cond_push where text='test' and
rand()<2;

+--------+------+
| NUMBER | TEXT |
+--------+------+
|      1 | test |
+--------+------+
1 row in set (0.00 sec)
```

As expected, adding more conditions with AND does not stop condition pushdown.

```
mysql> select * from information_schema.cond_push where
text=concat('te','st');

+--------+------+
| NUMBER | TEXT |
+--------+------+
|      1 | test |
+--------+------+
1 row in set (0.00 sec)
```

It is only important that the field is compared with the constant value. However, the value does not have to be a literal—it can be a result of the expression.

But not everything is perfect:

```
mysql> select * from information_schema.cond_push where text='test' or
text='this';

+--------+------+
| NUMBER | TEXT |
+--------+------+
|      3 | this |
|      6 | test |
+--------+------+
2 rows in set (0.00 sec)
```

We would have naturally preferred this query to use condition pushdown, but it did not. Simply because the `calc_lookup_values_from_cond()` function cannot extract *two* constants corresponding to *one* field. To be able to optimize such a condition, we would need our own implementation of COND tree parsing. Similarly, LIKE is not optimized either:

```
mysql> select * from information_schema.cond_push where text LIKE 'test';

+--------+------+
| NUMBER | TEXT |
+--------+------+
|      6 | test |
+--------+------+
1 row in set (0.01 sec)
```

A User Variables Information Schema plugin

In this plugin we will show how to access MySQL's internal data structures—the list of user variables created in a connection. User variables are used to store data that will persist just for one connection inside the MySQL server. Unfortunately, one of their limitations is that there is no way to see what variables have been created. In this example we will develop an Information Schema table that shows them.

User variables are stored in the `user_vars` member of the THD structure. It is a hash that maps variable names to corresponding `user_var_entry` objects. We simply need to traverse the hash, and for every `user_var_entry` element print its name and its value converted to a string.

To be able to see the user_var_entry and THD definitions we have to define the following macro:

```
#define MYSQL_SERVER
```

Now we can include the obligatory mysql_priv.h and we will get many more declarations than we were getting before. Basically, we can see and do everything that the MySQL server core can see and do. But it comes with a price. Our plugin becomes even more dependent on the server. It not only needs to be compiled for exactly the same server version that it will later work with (this limitation is nothing new for Information Schema plugins) but it also needs to be built exactly as the server was. For example, if the server was built with the *safemalloc* memory debugging facility or with the *safemutex* mutex debugging facility (that is, if the server was built with -DSAFEMALLOC or with -DSAFE_MUTEX) our plugin will have to do exactly the same. Otherwise, a plugin may not load, but more likely it will load, and crash the MySQL. Whether the server was built with any of these facilities can be seen in the server Makefile. Unfortunately, mysql_config does not tell us that.

```
#include <mysql_priv.h>

bool schema_table_store_record(THD *thd, TABLE *table);
ST_FIELD_INFO user_variables_fields[]=
{
  {"NAME", 255, MYSQL_TYPE_STRING, 0, 0, 0, 0},
  {"VALUE", 65535, MYSQL_TYPE_STRING, 0,
                     MY_I_S_MAYBE_NULL, 0, 0},
  {0, 0, MYSQL_TYPE_NULL, 0, 0, 0, 0}
};
```

We declare the table fields as usual, but this time we use the MY_I_S_MAYBE_NULL flag, as the variable values may be NULL.

Now we create the main function that will fill the table:

```
int fill_user_variables(THD *thd, TABLE_LIST *tables,
                        COND *cond)
{
  CHARSET_INFO *cs= system_charset_info;
  TABLE *table= tables->table;
  HASH *user_vars = &thd->user_vars;
  char buf[1024];
  String tmp(buf, sizeof(buf), cs);
```

First, we have defined all the required local variables. Everything is straightforward here. However, the String class deserves a clarification. We need a String object to be able to get the value of a user variable — the user_var_entry::val_str() method takes a pointer to a String as an argument. An instance of this class represents, as we could easily guess a string. A string, as a sequence of characters, its length in bytes, and the associated character set. The String class has quite a lot of utility methods, such as set(), append(), and many others. The string can grow automatically using malloc(), if needed, the memory will be freed in the destructor. What is important for us here is the String can be constructed from a memory buffer. In this case it will not allocate memory but will store the data in the buffer as long as the buffer size is sufficient. If the string grows too large the String will transparently allocate memory and copy the data into it. Practically, it means that if we use a reasonably large buffer (but not too large — it is allocated on the stack) we can avoid almost all malloc() calls in the String class. This is extremely convenient, and indeed, we can see this pattern almost everywhere in MySQL server code.

```
for (ulong idx= 0; idx < user_vars->records; idx++)
{
```

HASH objects store a counter which contains the number of records in the hash. We use it to figure out how many records we need to go through.

```
my_bool is_null;
user_var_entry *current_var =
        (user_var_entry*) hash_element(user_vars, idx);
```

Records in the HASH can be retrieved not only by a key (the user variable name, in this case), but also by the number (because a HASH is built on top of an array). We use it to iterate over all records in the hash.

```
String *str = current_var->val_str(&is_null, &tmp,
                              NOT_FIXED_DEC);
```

We need the string representation of the value of the user variable regardless of what type the value actually is at the moment. Luckily, the user_var_entry object has a var_str() method that does just that. We use it to get the value of the variable.

The method `val_str()` — and in MySQL many objects, including `Item` and `Field`, have method `val_str()` — always returns the value of the object as a string, performing the conversion if necessary. It takes a `String` buffer as an argument and returns a pointer to a `String` with the result. Strictly speaking, the returned pointer does not have to be the same as the argument; it can be a completely different `String`. In `user_var_entry` this method takes two more arguments — a pointer to a variable where it returns whether the value is `NULL`, and a number of decimals, that will be used in a float-to-string conversion if the value of a variable happens to be a float. A value of `NOT_FIXED_DEC` means that the floating point value should be printed as is, and not rounded to a particular number of decimals after the decimal point.

```
table->field[0]->store(current_var->name.str,
                       current_var->name.length, cs);
```

We store the name of the user variable in the first column of this row.

```
if (is_null)
  table->field[1]->set_null();
else
{
  table->field[1]->set_notnull();
  table->field[1]->store(str->ptr(),
                         str->length(), str->charset());
}
```

Then we store the user variable value in the second column of this row. As the second column is nullable, we need to use `set_null()` and `set_notnull()` methods as appropriate.

```
    if (schema_table_store_record(thd, table))
      return 1;
  }
  return 0;
}
```

The rest of the plugin is the same as in other Information Schema plugins:

```
int user_variables_init(void *p)
{
  ST_SCHEMA_TABLE *schema = (ST_SCHEMA_TABLE*) p;
  schema->fields_info = user_variables_fields;
  schema->fill_table = fill_user_variables;
  return 0;
}
```

```
struct st_mysql_information_schema user_variables =
{ MYSQL_INFORMATION_SCHEMA_INTERFACE_VERSION };

mysql_declare_plugin(user_variables)
{
  MYSQL_INFORMATION_SCHEMA_PLUGIN,
  &user_variables,
  "USER_VARIABLES",
  "Andrew Hutchings (Andrew.Hutchings@Sun.COM)",
  "Lists the user variables for a current session",
  PLUGIN_LICENSE_GPL,
  user_variables_init,
  NULL,
  0x0010,
  NULL,
  NULL,
  NULL
}
mysql_declare_plugin_end;
```

We should now have a plugin that gives a table in Information Schema listing all user variables in a current connection. When using it we should see something like the following:

```
mysql> set @my_var="Hello world";
Query OK, 0 rows affected (0.00 sec)

mysql> set @int_var=123456, @real_var=123e+45, @null_var=NULL;
Query OK, 0 rows affected (0.00 sec)

mysql> select * from information_schema.user_variables;
+----------+-------------+
| NAME     | VALUE       |
+----------+-------------+
| null_var | NULL        |
| my_var   | Hello world |
| int_var  | 123456      |
| real_var | 1.23e+47    |
+----------+-------------+
4 rows in set (0.00 sec)
```

A Binary Logs Information Schema plugin

MySQL has quite a few SHOW commands, many of which have Information Schema equivalents. There are, however, exceptions to this. One of them is the SHOW BINARY LOGS command. For this plugin we will take the function from the MySQL server that implements SHOW BINARY LOGS and convert it to an Information Schema plugin. This will also demonstrate another aspect important to Information Schema plugins that deal with MySQL internals—the fact that they need to handle locking. With the user variables it was not an issue, because only the current connection can access its variable. But multiple threads can access binary logs simultaneously so we need to take appropriate precautions to make sure that it does not happen.

```
#define MYSQL_SERVER
#include <mysql_priv.h>
bool schema_table_store_record(THD *thd, TABLE *table);

ST_FIELD_INFO binary_logs_fields[] =
{
  {"LOG_NAME", 255, MYSQL_TYPE_STRING, 0, 0, 0, 0},
  {"FILE_SIZE", 20, MYSQL_TYPE_LONGLONG, 0, 0, 0, 0},
  {0, 0, MYSQL_TYPE_NULL, 0, 0, 0, 0}
};
```

This table has two fields—a filename, which can be a maximum 255 bytes long, and a current file size, which is defined as a long long int.

```
int fill_binary_logs(THD *thd, TABLE_LIST *tables, COND *cond)
{
  TABLE *table = tables->table;
  IO_CACHE *index_file;
  LOG_INFO cur;
  File file;
  char fname[FN_REFLEN];

  uint length;
  int cur_dir_len;
```

The code below was copied with minor adjustments from the sql/sql_repl.cc function show_binlogs()—the very function that implements SHOW BINARY LOGS:

```
if (!mysql_bin_log.is_open())
  return 0;
```

If the binary logging is currently disabled we return an empty result set.

```
pthread_mutex_lock(mysql_bin_log.get_log_lock());
mysql_bin_log.lock_index();
```

Lock the binary log mutex and the binary log index mutex to protect shared data structures that we will be accessing below.

```
index_file = mysql_bin_log.get_index_file();
mysql_bin_log.raw_get_current_log(&cur);
```

We get the index file handle—to read old binary log filenames from it—and the `LOG_INFO` structure that describes the current binary log.

```
pthread_mutex_unlock(mysql_bin_log.get_log_lock());
```

We are done with the current log for now, so we can unlock its mutex. But we keep the other mutex locked, because we will work with the index file below.

```
cur_dir_len = dirname_length(cur.log_file_name);
reinit_io_cache(index_file, READ_CACHE, (my_off_t) 0, 0, 0);
```

The `index_file`, as returned by the `get_index_file()` method, is not a simple OS file handle, but a pointer to the `IO_CACHE` structure (`IO_CACHE` is a MySQL utility functionality that optimizes I/O by using a memory buffer to cache file accesses). It means we need to use corresponding functions to work with it. We want to read the whole file—that is, we need to prepare the `IO_CACHE` for reading and reposition it to the beginning of file.

```
while ((length = my_b_gets(index_file, fname,
                       sizeof(fname))) > 1)
{
```

Loop through every line of the index file.

```
int dir_len;
ulonglong file_length = 0;
fname[--length] = '\0';
dir_len = dirname_length(fname);
length -= dir_len;
table->field[0]->store(fname + dir_len, length,
                   &my_charset_bin);
```

Retrieve and store the filename of the binary log file.

```
if (!(strncmp(fname+dir_len, cur.log_file_name +
                   cur_dir_len, length)))
  file_length = cur.pos;
```

If it corresponds to the current active log file then we use the current log position from the LOG_INFO structure retrieved safely under a mutex.

```
    else
    {
      if ((file = my_open(fname, O_RDONLY|O_SHARE|O_BINARY,
                      MYF(0))) >= 0)
      {
        file_length = (ulonglong)
                  my_seek(file, 0L, MY_SEEK_END, MYF(0));
        my_close(file, MYF(0));
      }
    }
```

Otherwise this is an older log file; so open it, seek to the end, and use this as the file length.

```
    table->field[1]->store(file_length);
```

Then we store this information in the table as well.

```
    if (schema_table_store_record(thd, table))
    {
      mysql_bin_log.unlock_index();
      return 1;
    }
  }
  mysql_bin_log.unlock_index();
  return 0;
```

Unlock the index file now that we are finished with it.

```
}

int binary_logs_init(void *p)
{
  ST_SCHEMA_TABLE *schema = (ST_SCHEMA_TABLE*) p;
  schema->fields_info = binary_logs_fields;
  schema->fill_table = fill_binary_logs;
  return 0;
}

struct st_mysql_information_schema binary_logs=
{ MYSQL_INFORMATION_SCHEMA_INTERFACE_VERSION };

mysql_declare_plugin(binary_logs)
```

```
  {
    MYSQL_INFORMATION_SCHEMA_PLUGIN,
    &binary_logs,
    "BINARY_LOGS",
    "Andrew Hutchings (Andrew.Hutchings@Sun.COM)",
    "Lists the binary logs in use",
    PLUGIN_LICENSE_GPL,
    binary_logs_init,
    NULL,
    0x0010,
    NULL,
    NULL,
    NULL
  }
  mysql_declare_plugin_end;
```

We expect the result to appear as follows:

```
mysql> show binary logs;

+-----------------------------+-----------+
| Log_name                    | File_size |
+-----------------------------+-----------+
| linuxjedi-laptop-bin.000001 |       106 |
| linuxjedi-laptop-bin.000002 |       191 |
| linuxjedi-laptop-bin.000003 |       106 |
| linuxjedi-laptop-bin.000004 |       373 |
+-----------------------------+-----------+

4 rows in set (0.00 sec)
```

These are the results of the standard SHOW BINARY LOGS command. If the plugin works correctly we should see the same in our Information Schema table:

```
mysql> select * from information_schema.binary_logs;

+-----------------------------+-----------+
| LOG_NAME                    | FILE_SIZE |
+-----------------------------+-----------+
| linuxjedi-laptop-bin.000001 |       106 |
| linuxjedi-laptop-bin.000002 |       191 |
| linuxjedi-laptop-bin.000003 |       106 |
| linuxjedi-laptop-bin.000004 |       373 |
+-----------------------------+-----------+

4 rows in set (0.00 sec)
```

Success! The Information Schema table contains exactly the same data.

Summary

We have learned what condition pushdown is and how it can be used to optimize Information Schema plugins that need a lot of processing time per row. We have also looked into some real world examples of Information Schema plugins that access internal MySQL data structures and expose them to the user.

This chapter concludes the subject of Information Schema plugins. In the next chapter we will start looking at full-text parsers.

6
Full-text Parser Plugins

Traditionally, SQL only supported searches *for* values (stored in columns and rows of tables), but not searches *within* values, unless we count LIKE, that lacks expressive power. Still, often users need an ability to search within values (within text documents, that is), so called full-text search.

In 2000, with the version 3.23.23, MySQL introduced a full-text search capability and a new index type called FULLTEXT to support it. Full-text indexes contain individual words from the TEXT, CHAR, or VARCHAR columns, and they can be used by the MATCH ... AGAINST() syntax.

Full-text parser is a component of the full-text search that breaks the value of the TEXT, CHAR, or VARCHAR column into words that will go into the full-text index. It is also used by MATCH ... AGAINST() to split a query string into words and, optionally, recognize Boolean full-text search operators.

Full-text plugins can replace this component or modify its behavior. For example, they can extract the text from the column value (if the column value is a PDF or, say, a URL), they can use a different algorithm for splitting text into words (for example, more suitable for Asian languages), or they can modify the words before they are stored in the index (for example, apply stemming). They can do all of that, or they can replace only part of the built-in full-text parser functionality, and let the rest have the default behavior.

In this chapter we will look at the structure of a full-text parser plugin and create an example parser that uses special rules for splitting text into words.

The full-text parser plugin architecture

Full-text parsers were the first plugin type implemented in the Plugin API. In fact, both the Plugin API and the full-text parsers were developed at the same time within the same project. Unlike Information Schema tables or storage engines, MySQL did not support multiple full-text parsers originally. The support for them was added together with the full-text parser plugins. No wonder the full-text parser API was carefully designed specifically for plugins, and it managed to achieve almost a complete separation of a plugin from the server internals. As a result, the full-text parser API is simple and very stable; it has hardly changed since its inception in 2005, and full-text parser plugin binaries that worked back then can still be loaded in MySQL now and they will work as designed.

Three roles of a full-text parser plugin

When MySQL needs to parse a piece of text, be it for insertion into a full-text index, deletion from a full-text index, or during a full-text search to parse a search query, it does the following:

1. Take the column values if it is an INSERT, UPDATE, or DELETE. Take a query string if it is MATCH ... AGAINST()

2. Split the text into words, and discard the rest

3. For every word: do the required work (insert into the index, delete from the index, search in the index, whatever is needed)

A full-text parser plugin can add itself to the above in three different places. First, it can crawl between step one and step two, and modify the text before it gets parsed. It would be an "extractor" plugin, its job is to convert the data as stored in a table to a text that can be parsed and indexed. If we store PDF or DOC files in MySQL, such a plugin can allow MATCH ... AGAINST() to search in them. If we store only filenames in the table, an "extractor" plugin can open the file, read it, and let MySQL search within file contents even if the table column has only filenames. Or it can allow indexing of remote content and only store URLs in the table.

Second, a full-text parser plugin can replace step two and split the text into words itself. It would be a "tokenizer" plugin. Granted, MySQL's built-in algorithm for word-splitting in the full-text search is not very sophisticated. It does not work with languages where words typically are not separated by spaces. It may make mistakes when parsing words with apostrophes. It is not very flexible; for example, it can ignore all words shorter than the `ft_min_word_len` configuration option, but often one wants to ignore almost all short words, and still keep a few important acronyms. A "tokenizer" plugin can remove these limitations.

And, third, a full-text parser plugin can put itself between step two and step three. That is, MySQL will split the words using a built-in parser (which is quite often still good enough), but a plugin will see and possibly modify every word before MySQL does anything with it (like, stores in the index). It would be a "post-processor" plugin. Such a plugin can, for example, do stemming to improve the quality of the search, or for every word add all related terms to the list (so that, say, searching for "Linux" would find an article about "Ubuntu" or "Gentoo").

We have seen that there are three roles a full-text parser plugin can take—an "extractor", a "tokenizer", or a "post-processor". Of course, it can also take two or all of the three roles, it all depends on how we write it.

Installing and using a full-text parser plugin

Not surprisingly, the full-text parser plugins are installed just like any other plugins. Their use is, however, quite unique. When creating a table or adding an index we need to specify which full-text parser plugin we will use for an index. For example:

```
mysql> CREATE TABLE t1 (a TEXT, FULLTEXT INDEX(a) WITH PARSER my_parser_
plugin);
```

or

```
mysql> ALTER TABLE t1 ADD FULLTEXT INDEX(a) WITH PARSER my_parser_plugin;
```

After that everything works automatically; the server transparently invokes a plugin when some parsing is due. When executing, for example, an INSERT statement on a table that uses one of these plugins the following execution flow will apply:

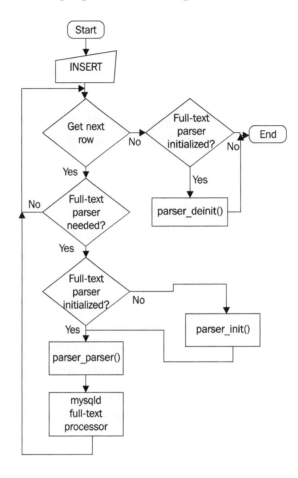

Structure of a full-text parser plugin

The full-text parser plugin is declared similar to any other plugin we have seen so far. The difference is in the info structure, which always depends on the particular plugin type.

For the full-text plugins it is defined as:

```
struct st_mysql_ftparser
{
  int interface_version;
  int (*parse)(MYSQL_FTPARSER_PARAM *param);
```

```
    int (*init)(MYSQL_FTPARSER_PARAM *param);
    int (*deinit)(MYSQL_FTPARSER_PARAM *param);
};
```

Besides the obligatory API version number it contains the callback functions that MySQL will use to perform the parsing job. The parser `init()` function is called once per statement before any parsing is done. The `deinit()` function is called at the end of the statement if the `init()` function was called. The `parse()` function is called somewhere between `init()` and `deinit()` calls, as many times as necessary, and does the actual parsing.

 Do not confuse parser `init()` and `deinit()` functions from the `st_mysql_ftparser` structure with the plugin `init()` and `deinit()` functions from the `st_mysql_plugin` structure. These, as we remember, can be specified for a plugin of any type, and they are called when a plugin is loaded and unloaded.

All of these parser functions take a structure called MYSQL_FTPARSER_PARAM as an argument. This structure contains a pointer to the text that needs to be parsed and pointers to server functions that parse the text and consume parsed words. The complete definition of this structure is as follows:

```
typedef struct st_mysql_ftparser_param
{
  int (*mysql_parse)(struct st_mysql_ftparser_param *,
                     char *doc, int doc_len);
  int (*mysql_add_word)(struct st_mysql_ftparser_param *,
                        char *word, int word_len,
                        MYSQL_FTPARSER_BOOLEAN_INFO *);
  void *ftparser_state;
  void *mysql_ftparam;
  struct charset_info_st *cs;
  char *doc;
  int length;
  int flags;
  enum enum_ftparser_mode mode;
} MYSQL_FTPARSER_PARAM;
```

The following table describes each of the elements inside this structure:

Element	Description
`mysql_parse()`	MySQL's built-in full-text parser. The server would have used it to split a text into words if there were no plugin specified.

Element	Description
mysql_add_word()	A function to process individual words. A full-text parser must call it for every word extracted from the text.
ftparser_state	Not used by MySQL. A plugin can use it for any purpose, to store anything it wants.
mysql_ftparam	Used internally by MySQL to pass information down to mysql_parse() and mysql_add_word(). A plugin should never touch it.
doc	The text to parse.
length	The length of the text to parse
cs	The character set of the text to parse
flags	Either MYSQL_FTFLAGS_NEED_COPY or 0. No other flags exist.
mode	The parsing mode in which the parser should operate. See below

The mysql_parse() function invokes the original MySQL full-text parser. It can be used by "extractor" plugins to let MySQL parse the text that a plugin has extracted. Or by "post-processor" plugins that are not interested in the original text, but only in individual words, and want to kick in after MySQL has parsed the text. In both cases, a plugin invokes the original MySQL parser via the mysql_parse member of the MYSQL_FTPARSER_PARAM structure.

mysql_add_word(), on the other hand, is not an optional function that a plugin *may* invoke—it *must* be invoked for every parsed word. It is this function that consumes parsed words, the words are extracted from the text for the sole reason of being passed into mysql_add_word(). What it will do with them is not always the same, but typically it will accumulate them (add to a list or a tree) and after parsing all words will be inserted in the index, deleted from the index, or searched in the index, as appropriate. A plugin may redefine this function, by changing mysql_add_word pointer to its own function, and then this plugin's own function will be called for every word. This is what "post-processor" plugins do. Of course any such function needs to invoke the original mysql_add_word() at the end, otherwise no parsed word will ever reach MySQL.

The ftparser_state member could be used to share the parsing context between the init(), deinit(), and parse() functions. For example, a "post-processor" plugin may store the original value of the mysql_add_word member there to be able to call it later.

Then, there are, of course, `doc`, `length`, and `cs` members that give us the text to parse, its length in bytes, and its character set. The length is essential, because the text is not necessarily zero terminated. The character set is important, but unfortunately not all MySQL functions that work with it are part of the Plugin API. By using them we would inevitably break the versioning protection and risk a crash any time MySQL developers make a change in the character set code. A complete solution to this problem will come after MySQL 5.1, in the framework of Server Services, which are described in the Appendix. Meanwhile, we will ignore the character set in our plugins below.

Although the `flags` element is there to set flags, currently there is only one flag available called `MYSQL_FTFLAGS_NEED_COPY`. To understand it, we will need an example. Let's say we have an "extractor" plugin that allows us to index files having only their names in the database. That is, we will treat `doc` as a filename, open the file and use `mysql_parse()` to parse it. Such a plugin can be implemented like this:

```
char buf[1024];
FILE *f = fopen(param->doc, "r");
while (fgets(buf, sizeof(buf), f))
  param->mysql_parse(param, buf, strlen(buf));
fclose(f);
```

This is, of course, a very simplified example. It has no error checking, and `param->doc` may be not zero terminated, but it shows the problem. The parsing function `mysql_parse()` will find words in our `buf` and will call `mysql_add_word()` with pointers to words—pointers into our `buf`. However, when we read the next line from the file, `buf` will be overwritten with new content and old words, defined as pointers into it, will change to garbage. Furthermore, when we return from our `parse()` function, `buf` will cease to exist, because it is declared as a local variable on the stack. For our example to work we want `mysql_add_word()` to make a copy of every word that it needs, or to use and discard words right away and not expect them to persist. And we should tell `mysql_add_word()` that it needs to copy words by setting this flag—`MYSQL_FTFLAGS_NEED_COPY`. Sometimes this flag may be set by MySQL too, before invoking our `parse()` function, if MySQL needs `mysql_add_word()` to copy words even if the plugin does not require it. Note that copying all words (and allocating memory for them) adds significant overhead to the full-text processing, so try to use this flag sparingly. For example, MySQL's built-in `mysql_parse()` function does not need to set it; it defines words as pointers into `doc` text, and all words will stay valid as long as the `doc` text itself will, which is long enough for MySQL and does not require copying of words.

Finally there are different modes in which our parser may operate, and the `mode` member tells us which one to use:

Parse mode	Description
MYSQL_FTPARSER_SIMPLE_MODE	This is used, for example, for indexing. The parser should return only words that need to be in the index—that is, stop words, or very short and very long words should be filtered out and not passed to `mysql_add_word()`.
MYSQL_FTPARSER_WITH_STOPWORDS	This mode is used in Boolean searches for phrase matching. When matching a phrase MySQL needs to consider all words, and in this mode the parser must return all words—including stop words, very short and long words, and so on. No word can be filtered out by a parser.
MYSQL_FTPARSER_FULL_BOOLEAN_INFO	This mode is used to parse a query string for Boolean searches. A query string may contain Boolean operators, and a parser must properly recognize them all and set the MYSQL_FTPARSER_BOOLEAN_INFO structure accordingly. This is the only mode where this structure is used. In this mode no stop word should be ignored either.

Now, if we go back to the definition of the `mysql_add_word()` function we will see the last argument, which is of the type `MYSQL_FTPARSER_BOOLEAN_INFO`. This structure is only used in `MYSQL_FTPARSER_FULL_BOOLEAN_INFO` parsing mode; we need to use it to pass the information about Boolean operators to MySQL. It is defined as follows:

```
typedef struct st_mysql_ftparser_boolean_info
{
  enum enum_ft_token_type type;
  int yesno;
  int weight_adjust;
  char wasign;
  char trunc;
  char prev;
  char *quot;
} MYSQL_FTPARSER_BOOLEAN_INFO;
```

Let's look at the individual members of this structure:

Element	Description
type	The type of token passed to mysql_add_word() in the word argument.
yesno	It is greater than 0 if this word should absolutely be present in text for a match to occur. It is less than 0 if the word must not be present in any matching text. It is 0 if the word may be present in matching text (which will increase its relevance), but it is not a requirement. In the default MySQL settings this member corresponds to + (plus) and – (minus) full-text search operators.
weight_adjust	A relative importance of the word in this query. A value greater than 0 increases a word's importance, a value less than zero decreases it. In the default MySQL settings this corresponds to > (greater than) and < (less than) full-text search operators.
wasign	The sign of the word's weight. If it is non-zero the word is considered a noise word; its presence in the text decreases the relevance. In the default MySQL settings this corresponds to the ~ (tilde) full-text search operator.
trunc	If non-zero, the word argument is treated as a prefix. Any word in the text that starts from this prefix will make a match. In the default MySQL settings this corresponds to the * (asterisk) full-text search operator.
prev	It is used by the mysql_parse() function. A plugin can ignore it completely.
quot	It should be initialized to null, and changed to not null on every token that starts a phrase search. In the default MySQL settings this corresponds to " (double quotes) full-text search operator. MySQL automatically changes it back to null at the end of the phrase.

The type, type of token, can be any of the following:

Type	Description
FT_TOKEN_EOF	It is ignored by MySQL. A plugin does not need to use it either. It is enough to return from the parse() function at the end of the text; there is no need to pass the FT_TOKEN_EOF token down to the mysql_add_word() function.
FT_TOKEN_WORD	A word. Just any normal word in the Boolean full-text search query.
FT_TOKEN_STOPWORD	A stop word. A word that is ignored during indexing, it is never present in a full-text index.

Type	Description
FT_TOKEN_LEFT_PAREN	Start of a subexpression. In the default MySQL settings this corresponds to ((left parenthesis) full-text search operators. This token type is also used to mark the beginning of a phrase (because a phrase is also a subexpression, in a sense). MySQL distinguishes between these two cases by looking at the `quot` member.
FT_TOKEN_RIGHT_PAREN	Right parenthesis, end of a subexpression or a phrase search.

For the last two tokens `mysql_add_word()` ignores the `word` argument.

So, in a simple case we can use `MYSQL_FTPARSER_BOOLEAN_INFO` as follows:

```
MYSQL_FTPARSER_BOOLEAN_INFO boolean_info =
  { FT_TOKEN_WORD, 0, 0, 0, 0, 0, 0 };
param->mysql_add_word(param, word, len, &boolean_info);
```

The official documentation for all of these structures, constants, and functions can be found in the plugin header file `plugin.h`. It is well worth looking through when writing plugins of this type.

A PHP full-text parser

To show the layout of a full-text parser plugin we will create a simple parser to parse PHP scripts. PHP syntax has a few peculiarities that are not taken into account by the MySQL built-in full-text parser. In particular, all variable names in PHP start with a dollar sign, which is, in fact, a part of the name; a variable `$while` is not the same as a loop statement `while`. But a dollar sign is not just another character that can be used in variable names—the string `"$foo$bar"` contains two PHP variables, not one. Also, variables can have different scopes; a variable `foo::$bar` is not the same as a variable `$bar`. Let's try to solve this in our full-text parser plugin. According to the above, it will be a "tokenizer" plugin—a plugin that splits the text into words.

As usual, we start by including the required header files:

```
#include <mysql/plugin.h>
#include <stdio.h>
#include <ctype.h>
```

A valid PHP variable name can contain letters, underscores, digits, or bytes with values from 127 to 255. As we will need this check quite often, it makes sense to create a function for it:

```
static int isphpvar(unsigned char x)
{
  return isalnum(x) || x == '_' || (x >= 127 && x <=255);
}
```

Now we can start our main function of a plugin — the parsing function:

```
static int parse_php(MYSQL_FTPARSER_PARAM *param)
{
  char *end = param->doc + param->length;
  char *s = param->doc;
```

In our first full-text parser example we will not bother supporting Boolean mode operators, all tokens will be of the FT_TOKEN_WORD type:

```
MYSQL_FTPARSER_BOOLEAN_INFO bool_info =
  { FT_TOKEN_WORD, 0, 0, 0, 0, 0, 0 };
```

Now we start going through the text, looking for words (according to our definition of a "word"). The dollar sign sometimes means the end of a previous word and a beginning of a new identifier, like in "foobar", but not always. Sometimes it can be in the middle of a word, like in MyClass::$myvar. We will maintain a dollar_ok variable to know if a dollar sign can happen at that place without breaking the current word:

```
for (;;)
{
  char *word_start;
  int dollar_ok;
```

First we skip characters that cannot be part of a word:

```
while (s < end && !isphpvar(*s) && *s != '$')
  s++;
```

And we finish when we have parsed all of the text:

```
if (s >= end)
  break;
```

Otherwise we are at the first character of a new word. We remember the position, and, of course, a dollar sign can happen here—it can be at the beginning of a word:

```
word_start = s;
dollar_ok = 1;
```

Then we go through valid characters (letters, digits, underscore, but excluding a dollar sign). Note that as soon as we have seen one of these characters, we do not expect to see a dollar sign anymore:

```
while (s < end && isphpvar(*s))
{
  dollar_ok = 0;
  while (s < end && isphpvar(*s))
    s++;
```

Here, we have stopped at the first character, which is not a letter, digit, or underscore. We need to check if it is a scope resolution operator—two colons (::). If yes, we skip it and read the next part of the identifier. After two colons we can see a dollar sign again:

```
if (s >= end-1 || s[0] != ':' || s[1] != ':')
  break;
s+=2;
dollar_ok = 1;
}
```

We come here after reading as many letters, digits, underscores, and double colons as possible. If the next character is a dollar sign, and it does not end the word at its current place, we read it too, and a part of the identifier after it:

```
if (s < end && *s == '$' && dollar_ok)
{
  s++;
  while (s < end && isphpvar(*s))
    s++;
}
```

Having read as much as we could without breaking the word, we pass that part of the text to MySQL using the `mysql_add_word()` function, as explained previously:

```
    param->mysql_add_word(param, word_start, s - word_start,
                          &bool_info);
  }
  return 0;
}
```

We end the plugin with declarations, as usual:

```
static struct st_mysql_ftparser ft_php=
{
  MYSQL_FTPARSER_INTERFACE_VERSION,
  parse_php,
  NULL,
  NULL
};

mysql_declare_plugin(fulltext_demo)
{
  MYSQL_FTPARSER_PLUGIN,
  &ft_php,
  "php_code",
  "Sergei Golubchik",
  "Simple Full-Text Parser for PHP scripts",
  PLUGIN_LICENSE_GPL,
  NULL,
  NULL,
  0x0100,
  NULL,
  NULL,
  NULL
}
mysql_declare_plugin_end;
```

When we go ahead, compile, and install our plugin, we can use it as follows:

```
mysql> CREATE TABLE ft_demo (php TEXT, FULLTEXT(php) WITH PARSER php_
code) ENGINE=MyISAM;
Query OK, 0 rows affected (0.01 sec)
```

We create a table with a full-text index, and tell MySQL that this index should use our own parser—php_code.

```
mysql> INSERT ft_demo VALUES ('$a=15; echo $this->var;'), ('echo
$classname::CONST_VALUE;'), ('echo "$foo$bar";'), ('echo
AnotherClass::$varvar;'), ('echo MyClass::CONST_VALUE;');
Query OK, 5 rows affected (0.00 sec)
Records: 5  Duplicates: 0  Warnings: 0


mysql> SELECT * FROM ft_demo;

+------------------------------+
| php                          |
+------------------------------+
| $a=15; echo $this->var;      |
| echo $classname::CONST_VALUE; |
| echo "$foo$bar";             |
| echo AnotherClass::$varvar;  |
| echo MyClass::CONST_VALUE;   |
+------------------------------+
5 rows in set (0.01 sec)
```

We have inserted a few rows with pieces of PHP code into our table. Now, let's try a couple of queries:

```
mysql> select * from ft_demo where MATCH php AGAINST('this');
Empty set (0.00 sec)


mysql> select * from ft_demo where MATCH php AGAINST('$this');

+-------------------------+
| php                     |
+-------------------------+
| $a=15; echo $this->var; |
+-------------------------+
1 row in set (0.01 sec)
```

See, how $this was found, while this was not—because the variable name includes the dollar sign, exactly as we wanted. A few more queries:

```
mysql> select * from ft_demo where MATCH php AGAINST('$varvar');
Empty set (0.00 sec)


mysql> select * from ft_demo where MATCH php AGAINST
('AnotherClass::$varvar');

+-----------------------------+
| php                         |
+-----------------------------+
| echo AnotherClass::$varvar; |
+-----------------------------+

1 row in set (0.00 sec)
```

Again, a complete variable name includes the class name. Simple $varvar is just not in the index.

But not only variable names were indexed:

```
mysql> select * from ft_demo where MATCH php AGAINST('15');

+-------------------------+
| php                     |
+-------------------------+
| $a=15; echo $this->var; |
+-------------------------+

1 row in set (0.01 sec)


mysql> select * from ft_demo where MATCH php AGAINST('echo' in
boolean mode);

+-------------------------------+
| php                           |
+-------------------------------+
| $a=15; echo $this->var;       |
| echo $classname::CONST_VALUE; |
| echo "$foo$bar";              |
| echo AnotherClass::$varvar;   |
| echo MyClass::CONST_VALUE;    |
+-------------------------------+

5 rows in set (0.00 sec)
```

At last, we can see the complete content of the index with the `myisam_ftdump` utility. Note that it internally puts all words into lower case before printing them, independent of how they are stored in the index:

```
shell$ myisam_ftdump -c ft_demo 0
        1             1.3862944 $a
        1             1.3862944 $bar
        1             1.3862944 $classname
        1             1.3862944 $foo
        1             1.3862944 $this
        1             1.3862944 15
        1             1.3862944 anotherclass::$varvar
        1             1.3862944 const_value
        5             0.0000000 echo
        1             1.3862944 myclass::const_value
        1             1.3862944 var
```

The columns are: number of rows that contain the word, word's global weigh (it is zero for `echo`, because this word is present in every row; that is, it cannot be used for distinguishing rows), and the word itself. It is the ultimate proof that our parser worked as we wanted it, and dollar signs and double colons were taken as part of the word.

Summary

In this chapter we have learned the full-text parser API, and created a "tokenizer" plugin which, despite being simple, solves a specific problem that cannot be solved by MySQL's built-in full-text parser. In the next chapter we will look more into the full-text parsers, creating "extractor" and "post-processor" plugins, and a plugin that supports Boolean search operators.

7
Practical Full-text Parsers

In the previous chapter we covered the basics of what a full-text parser plugin can do, how it works, and what is required to create one. In this chapter we will expand on this by going deeper into Boolean mode queries and creating full-text parsers that can be used in real-world applications.

Boolean parsers

The default, natural language, full-text search mode works well for inexperienced users who can simply describe what they want to find using plain English (or any other language) and let the system figure out, with complex statistical and probabilistic analysis, what rows are relevant to them. Other users want more control over what will be found. This is where Boolean search mode is used. It allows users to specify exactly which words must be present in all found rows and which words must not be present. It can search for "phrases" – sequences of words—for prefixes of words, and fine tune the importance of individual words for the result of a query. For Boolean search mode to work, the full-text parser needs to support it; it needs to be able to extract the Boolean search operators from a query and to convey this information to MySQL.

In our example from the previous chapter we ignored Boolean search mode and only sent the search words—not Boolean operators—from the query to the server. In this chapter we will implement a working full-text parser plugin that supports Boolean search operators.

A full-text parser plugin sends the information about Boolean operators to MySQL using the same `mysql_add_word()` function. A parser, of course, can implement any syntax for Boolean operators. In the following table we show the Boolean search syntax as implemented by the MySQL built-in full-text parser:

Operator	Semantics	In the parser
+	The following word must be present in any matched row.	`boolinfo.yesno = 1;` or any positive number
-	The following word must not be present in any matched row.	`boolinfo.yesno = -1;` or any negative number
(no operator)	A row can match with or without the word. But if the word is present in the row, it increases the row relevance.	`boolinfo.yesno = 0;` `boolinfo.wasign = 0;`
~	A row can match with or without the word. But if a word is present in the row, it decreases the row relevance. The word is a noise word.	`boolinfo.wasign = 1;` or anything besides zero. In a sense, this member defines the sign of the word's weight adjusting.
>	Increase a word's weight. This word, if present in a row, increases its relevance more (or decreases more, depending on the `wasign`) than other words.	`boolinfo.weight_adjust++;` where each increment increases the weight by 50%.
<	Decrease a word's weight. This word, if present, increases the row relevance less (or decreases less, depending on the `wasign`).	`boolinfo.weight_adjust--;` where each decrement decreases the weight by 33%.
(	Start of a subexpression	`boolinfo.type = FT_TOKEN_LEFT_PAREN;`
)	End of a subexpression	`boolinfo.type = FT_TOKEN_RIGHT_PAREN;`
*	Wildcard prefix search	`boolinfo.trunc = 1;`

"..."	Literal phrase search	`boolinfo.type = FT_TOKEN_LEFT_PAREN;`
		`boolinfo.quot = "";`
		
		for a phrase start, or
		
		`boolinfo.type = FT_TOKEN_RIGHT_PAREN;`
		
		for a phrase end. The `quot` member can be anything as long as it is not zero. As all words in a phrase must be present for a phrase to match, they all should have `boolinfo.yesno > 0`.

Now let's put this knowledge into practice and create a plugin that supports
Boolean operators.

A Boolean full-text parser

We know the Boolean syntax of the MySQL built-in full-text parser. MySQL already
supports it; there is no fun in reimplementing the same thing. To do something
new we could make a parser that supports AND, OR, and NOT keywords, which is
supposedly a more user-friendly syntax and our users may like it more than
MySQL *plus* and *minus* prefixes.

How could our parser support such a syntax? It could, for example, by doing
look-ahead, reading the next word before sending the current one to MySQL. If the
next word is AND, the current one must have yesno=1. The idea is simple, but the
devil, as always, is in the detail:

- Both words before and after AND must have yesno=1.

- To support foo AND NOT bar we may need to look two words ahead.

- Typically, both words around OR must have yesno=0. But not if an AND is
  involved. In foo OR bar AND bla the second word must have yesno=1.

- In a query string such as foo AND bar OR some AND thing we cannot
  simply have yesno=1 in all four words. It would mean that all four are
  necessary, as if it were foo AND bar AND some AND thing. For our query
  the equivalent MySQL syntax would be (+foo +bar) (+some +thing).
  This is how we need to parse this and similar queries. In other words, we
  will use subexpressions to separate AND and OR words.

- If no operator is used, as in foo bar, we will parse it as foo OR bar.

Can we pull it off? We start, as always, by including the necessary headers:

```
#include <mysql/plugin.h>
#include <stdio.h>
#include <ctype.h>
```

And to finish with the simple stuff we can declare the plugin at once:

```
static struct st_mysql_ftparser ft_andor =
{
  MYSQL_FTPARSER_INTERFACE_VERSION,
  andor_parse,
  NULL,
  NULL
};

mysql_declare_plugin(andor)
```

```
{
  MYSQL_FTPARSER_PLUGIN,
  &ft_andor,
  "andor",
  "Sergei Golubchik",
  "A Full-Text AND/OR boolean parser",
  PLUGIN_LICENSE_GPL,
  NULL,
  NULL,
  0x0100,
  NULL,
  NULL,
  NULL
}
mysql_declare_plugin_end;
```

A "word" extracted from the text is described by a pointer and a length. For convenience we put it in a structure:

```
typedef struct {
  char *start;
  int  len;
  int  yesno;
} WORD;
```

Having a `yesno` property in the same structure will allow us to manipulate it easily when we see an AND or NOT. We can also introduce a handy utility function to read the next word from a piece of text:

```
static char *get_word(WORD *word, char *s, char *end)
{
  word->yesno = 0;
  while (s < end && !isalnum(*s))
    s++;
  word->start = s;
  while (s < end && isalnum(*s))
    s++;
  word->len = s - word->start;
  return s;
}
```

It gets one word from text located between s and end, and returns the new value of the s pointer. It sets the word argument to the found word. If the end of text is reached and no word was extracted, it makes word->start >= end. This function has a very useful property — it can be called many times, even after the end of the text (s >= end) is reached.

Being armed with the `get_word()` function we can now write the main parsing function:

```
static int andor_parse(MYSQL_FTPARSER_PARAM *param)
{
  char *end = param->doc + param->length;
  char *s = param->doc;
  WORD word, next;
  MYSQL_FTPARSER_BOOLEAN_INFO bool_info =
    { FT_TOKEN_WORD, 0, 0, 0, 0, 0, 0 };
```

First, we read the "next" word. Then we start the loop:

```
s = get_word(&next, s, end);
for (;;)
{
```

We never need to read the current word as it is already read, in advance, as `next`. We simply copy the next word into the current one, and read the new next word. Remember, we can safely call `get_word()` as many times as we want, even if the `s` pointer has already reached the end of the text:

```
word = next;
s = get_word(&next, s, end);
```

If there is no current word, it means that we have parsed everything and can return:

```
if (word.start >= end)
  return 0;
```

Otherwise, we go into the details of extracting and interpreting our Boolean operators, of course, if the parsing mode requires it:

```
if (param->mode == MYSQL_FTPARSER_FULL_BOOLEAN_INFO)
{
```

First we check if the next word is AND. If it is, and the current (before the next) word has `yesno==0`, which means there was no AND before the current word, we tell MySQL to start a subexpression. Then we read the next word:

```
if (next.start < end &&
    strncasecmp(next.start, "and", next.len) == 0)
{
  if (word.yesno == 0)
  {
    bool_info.yesno = 0;
    bool_info.type = FT_TOKEN_LEFT_PAREN;
    param->mysql_add_word(param, 0, 0, &bool_info);
    word.yesno = 1;
  }
  s = get_word(&next, s, end);
```

If the next word after AND is NOT, we read the word after it and mark it with
yesno=-1, otherwise we mark the next word with yesno=1 because it is the
word that follows AND.

```
        if (next.start < end &&
            strncasecmp(next.start, "not", next.len) == 0)
        {
          s = get_word(&next, s, end);
          next.yesno = -1;
        }
        else
          next.yesno = 1;
      }
      else
```

If the next (after the current) word was not AND but OR we simply ignore it.
Remember that OR has the same effect as no Boolean operator at all:

```
      if (next.start < end &&
          strncasecmp(next.start, "or", next.len) == 0)
        s = get_word(&next, s, end);
```

At this moment we have read the word (in word), the Boolean operator that follows
it, if any, and the word after the Boolean operator (in next). We can now set up
bool_info appropriately and pass the word down to MySQL.

```
        bool_info.type = FT_TOKEN_WORD;
        bool_info.yesno = word.yesno;
      }
      param->mysql_add_word(param, word.start, word.len,
                            &bool_info);
```

Now, if there was an AND before the current word and no AND after it (which we can
find out by looking at the yesno of the current and next words) we need to end the
subexpression that we started for this AND group:

```
      if (word.yesno && !next.yesno)
      {
        bool_info.type = FT_TOKEN_RIGHT_PAREN;
        param->mysql_add_word(param, 0, 0, &bool_info);
      }
    }
  }
```

This is it. Together with the plugin declaration, which we have done previously, this makes a complete plugin. We can build and install it to see:

```
mysql> create table toc (chapter int, title varchar(255), fulltext(title)
with parser andor) engine=myisam;
Query OK, 0 rows affected (0.01 sec)
```

```
mysql> insert toc values (0, 'Preface'), (1, 'Compiling and Using
MySQL Plugins'), (2, 'User Defined Functions'), (3, 'Daemon Plugins'),
(4, 'Information Schema Plugins'), (5, 'Advanced Information Schema
Plugins'), (6, 'Full-Text Parser Plugins'), (7, 'Practical Full-Text
Parsers'), (8, 'Storage Engine Plugins'), (9, 'HTML Storage Engine -
reads and writes'), (10, 'TOCAB Storage Engine - implementing indexes'),
(11, 'Appendix: Beyond MySQL 5.1');
Query OK, 12 rows affected (0.02 sec)
Records: 12  Duplicates: 0  Warnings: 0
```

```
mysql> select * from toc;
+---------+-------------------------------------------------+
| chapter | title                                           |
+---------+-------------------------------------------------+
|       0 | Preface                                         |
|       1 | Compiling and Using MySQL Plugins               |
|       2 | User Defined Functions                          |
|       3 | Daemon Plugins                                  |
|       4 | Information Schema Plugins                       |
|       5 | Advanced Information Schema Plugins              |
|       6 | Full-Text Parser Plugins                        |
|       7 | Practical Full-Text Parsers                     |
|       8 | Storage Engine Plugins                          |
|       9 | HTML Storage Engine - reads and writes          |
|      10 | TOCAB Storage Engine - implementing indexes     |
|      11 | Appendix: Beyond MySQL 5.1                      |
+---------+-------------------------------------------------+
12 rows in set (0.00 sec)
```

You have probably noticed that this is the table of contents of this very book. Now the searches:

```
mysql> select * from toc where match title against('full');
+---------+------------------------------+
| chapter | title                        |
+---------+------------------------------+
|       6 | Full-Text Parser Plugins     |
|       7 | Practical Full-Text Parsers  |
+---------+------------------------------+
```

```
2 rows in set (0.00 sec)

mysql> select * from toc where match title against('using mysql');
+---------+---------------------------------+
| chapter | title                           |
+---------+---------------------------------+
|       1 | Compiling and Using MySQL Plugins |
|      11 | Appendix: Beyond MySQL 5.1      |
+---------+---------------------------------+
2 rows in set (0.00 sec)
```

Natural language queries work as before, no surprises here.

```
mysql> select * from toc where match title against('using mysql' in
boolean mode);
+---------+---------------------------------+
| chapter | title                           |
+---------+---------------------------------+
|       1 | Compiling and Using MySQL Plugins |
|      11 | Appendix: Beyond MySQL 5.1      |
+---------+---------------------------------+
2 rows in set (0.01 sec)
```

Nothing interesting happens in Boolean mode if we use no Boolean operators. But if we do, we see:

```
mysql> select * from toc where match title against('using and mysql' in
boolean mode);
+---------+---------------------------------+
| chapter | title                           |
+---------+---------------------------------+
|       1 | Compiling and Using MySQL Plugins |
+---------+---------------------------------+
1 row in set (0.00 sec)
```

It works! We asked for a row that contains both "using" and "mysql" and this is exactly what was found. More complex queries work too:

```
mysql> select * from toc where match title against('using and mysql
or full and practical or storage and engine and not plugins' in
boolean mode);
```

```
+----------+------------------------------------------+
| chapter  | title                                    |
+----------+------------------------------------------+
|        1 | Compiling and Using MySQL Plugins        |
|        7 | Practical Full-Text Parsers              |
|        9 | HTML Storage Engine - reads and writes   |
|       10 | TOCAB Storage Engine - implementing indexes |
+----------+------------------------------------------+
4 rows in set (0.00 sec)
```

An Image Metadata processor

In the previous examples we have discussed full-text parser plugins that were actually doing the parsing—extracting words from a text. But as we have seen in Chapter 6, a full-text parser plugin does not necessarily have to do that. Only "tokenizer" plugins do. In this example we will create an "extractor" plugin—a plugin that merely converts the data to plain text and lets MySQL parse it with a built-in parser.

As many know, digital cameras store inside an image file the metadata that contains various details about the photo. It is stored using a format called Exif (Exchangeable image file format).

This full-text parser plugin will take the image filenames from the database, parse the Exif data, and allow MySQL to index it. In other words, one can INSERT rows with filenames in the table, but MATCH ... AGAINST() will search in the Exif metadata of these images!

How to access Exif data

To extract the image metadata we will use the *libexif* library. It is included in most Linux distributions, and it has also been ported to Mac OS X, Windows, FreeBSD, Solaris, and other operating systems. The binaries and the source code can be found at http://libexif.sourceforge.net/. We will need to tell the compiler to link our plugin with this library. For gcc this is done by adding -lexif to the command line.

The libexif library has many different objects and types, and a lot of different functions that manipulate them. But we are only interested in reading (not writing) all (not selected) values of Exif tags. For this very limited task we need to know just a few libexif functions:

Function	Description
exif_data_new_from_file(const char *path)	Creates an ExifData object and fills it with the data from an image file.

Function	Description

exif_data_foreach_content(
  ExifData *data,
  ExifDataForeachContentFunc func,
  void * user_data)
	Exif data inside a file is organized in data structures called IFD (Image File Directory). There can be many of them, and this function iterates over them all and invokes a user defined callback func for every IDF in turn.

exif_content_foreach_entry(
  ExifContent *content,
  ExifContentForeachEntryFunc func,
  void *user_data)
	Exif data are stored in tags inside an IDF. Similar to the previous function, this one iterates over all tags in a given IDF and invokes a user defined callback func for every tag.

exif_entry_get_value(
  ExifEntry *entry,
  char *buf,
  unsigned int buflen)
	And, finally this function takes an Exif tag, represented by an ExifEntry object, and stores a textual representation of its value in the supplied buffer. It is this textual representation that we will feed to the MySQL parser.

According to the above, we need to call exif_data_new_from_file() and then call exif_data_foreach_content(). From its callback function we call exif_content_foreach_entry() and from its callback we invoke exif_entry_get_value(), that returns us the data to parse.

There is also one tag, Maker Notes, which contains other tags in a manufacturer-specific binary format. The format is proprietary, but some of the manufacturer formats have been decoded and libexif understands them. To access Maker Notes one needs to extract them with the exif_data_get_mnote_data() function, which returns the ExifMnoteData object, and get individual tag values with the exif_mnote_data_get_value() function.

Writing the plugin

Headers first, as always. Note the libexif header below:

```
#include <mysql/plugin.h>
#include <libexif/exif-data.h>
#include <stdio.h>
#include <string.h>
```

For convenience we will introduce a system variable with the path to the images. So that we, or end users of our plugin, can then simply store filenames in the table, and the path will be added automatically:

```
static char *exif_path;
static MYSQL_SYSVAR_STR(path, exif_path,
            PLUGIN_VAR_RQCMDARG | PLUGIN_VAR_MEMALLOC,
            "The path to image files", NULL, NULL, "");
```

And let's write a plugin declaration now, while we're at it:

```
static struct st_mysql_ftparser ft_exif =
{
  MYSQL_FTPARSER_INTERFACE_VERSION,
  exif_parse,
  NULL,
  NULL
};

static struct st_mysql_sys_var* exif_system_var[] =
{
  MYSQL_SYSVAR(path),
  NULL
};

mysql_declare_plugin(ftexif)
{
  MYSQL_FTPARSER_PLUGIN,
  &ft_exif,
  "exif",
  "Andrew Hutchings <Andrew.Hutchings@Sun.COM>",
  "A graphic file EXIF Full-Text Parser",
  PLUGIN_LICENSE_GPL,
  NULL,
  NULL,
  0x0100,
  NULL,
  exif_system_var,
  NULL
}
mysql_declare_plugin_end;
```

Now, the real thing — the parsing function. In fact, it will not parse anything, but we will call it `exif_parse()` anyway. Just to remember, it needs to generate a full path to the image file, load Exif data from it, iterate the tags with two "foreach" functions, and invoke `mysql_parse()` for every extracted piece of data. Additionally, it needs to extract Maker Notes, iterate them, and again invoke `mysql_parse()`, as appropriate.

```
static int exif_parse(MYSQL_FTPARSER_PARAM *param)
{
  ExifData *exif_data;
  ExifMnoteData *maker_notes;
  char buf[4096];
  int path_len, i, mnote_count;
```

Local variable declarations are not interesting, apart from the buffer. It is worth an explanation. What do we need a buffer for? We need to create a full path to an image file, to concatenate an `exif_path` and a filename. It may require up to PATH_MAX bytes, which is 4096 on my system — in any case, a few kilobytes. We need to use a buffer to store Exif tag values; `exif_entry_get_value()` takes a buffer as an argument. Examples that come with libexif use a buffer of 1024 bytes, so presumably one kilobyte is enough. And we need a buffer for the values of Maker Notes, which can be also 1024 bytes. There is little reason to allocate these buffers with `malloc()` — they are only needed until we call `mysql_parse()` so we can safely allocate them on the stack. But remember, MySQL is a multi-threaded program. It is used to run a lot of threads simultaneously, and stacks of all threads will exist at the same time. To save memory MySQL sets the thread-stack size to a relatively low value. There are many tricks we can use to not allocate all multi-kilobyte buffers on the stack at the same time. For example, we could split the code in different functions, one function per buffer. Or we could simply allocate only one buffer and reuse it. In our plugin we do the latter.

Having decided on the buffer, we use it immediately to concatenate the image path and a filename. As we store filenames in the table, it is the filename, from the MySQL point of view, which is the data, and we get it in `param->doc`. To create a full file path we simply append `param->doc` to `exif_path`.

```
path_len = snprintf(buf, sizeof(buf), "%s/%.*s", exif_path,
                    param->length, param->doc);

if (path_len == sizeof(buf) || path_len < 0)
  exif_data = 0;
else
  exif_data = exif_data_new_from_file(buf);
```

It is an interesting detail—what should we do if we fail to open the file? The parsing function is called not only for indexing, but also for searching. As our previous Boolean example very well shows, the parser is used to parse the query string as well as the table data. Practically it means that if someone writes `MATCH col AGAINST("taken with sony and flash")` our parser plugin will get `param->doc="taken with sony and flash"` and not a filename. And when we concatenate it with a path and try to open the result, it will certainly fail. In short, if we cannot open `param->doc` as a file, we have to treat it as a query string:

```
if (!exif_data)
  return param->mysql_parse(param,
                          param->doc, param->length);
```

But if we did open a file, we're in. We extract the Exif tag values and parse them. As they will all be extracted into the same buffer, overwriting each other, we need to tell MySQL to copy the parsed words to a safe place:

```
param->flags |= MYSQL_FTFLAGS_NEED_COPY;
param->doc = buf;
param->length = sizeof(buf);
```

We have also stored a pointer to our buffer in `param->doc` to be able to access it and reuse the buffer in our callback function. Now we are ready to go:

```
exif_data_foreach_content(exif_data, get_exif_content,
                          param);
```

The `get_exif_content()` is our callback function that will be called for every IFD (Image File Directory) section from our file. This function is very simple:

```
static void get_exif_content(ExifContent *content, void *arg)
{
    exif_content_foreach_entry(content, get_exif_entry, arg);
}
```

It only invokes another libexif iterator function that goes over all tags in a given IFD. The iterator will call yet another callback, `get_exif_entry()`, which is also quite simple:

```
static void get_exif_entry(ExifEntry *entry, void *arg)
{
    MYSQL_FTPARSER_PARAM *param = arg;
    exif_entry_get_value(entry, param->doc, param->length);
    param->mysql_parse(param, param->doc, strlen(param->doc));
}
```

It extracts the Exif tag value into our buffer, as `param->doc` points to our buffer now, and calls the built-in MySQL parser via the `mysql_parse()` function. This is exactly how "extractor" plugins work; they convert `param->doc` to a text that needs to be indexed and invoke the MySQL built-in parser. This technique allows us, plugin writers, to concentrate on the main plugin functionality and not waste time on implementing something that MySQL already can do on its own.

Now, let's get back to the `exif_parse()` function. We interrupted it in the middle to look at the callbacks, but now we can continue. Now that all of the Exif tags are parsed, it's time to do Maker Notes. It is very straightforward—obtain the corresponding `ExifMnoteData` object, iterate over all Maker Notes, get the note value into our buffer, and parse it:

```
ExifMnoteData  maker_notes = exif_data_get_mnote_data(exif_data);
mnote_count = exif_mnote_data_count(maker_notes);
for (i = 0; i < mnote_count; i++)
{
  if (exif_mnote_data_get_value(maker_notes, i,
                                buf, sizeof(buf)))
    param->mysql_parse(param, buf, strlen(buf));
}
return 0;
}
```

That's all. Now we naturally want to see whether it works.

Test run

First we compile the plugin, with `-lexif` of course, and install it.

We will use the following four images for testing:

They are included in the code bundle and can be downloaded from the Packt website.

We need to create a table, configure the path to the image files, and insert the data. We insert only filenames, but we will search within file contents!

```
mysql> create table test (jpeg text, fulltext(jpeg) with parser exif)
engine=myisam;
Query OK, 0 rows affected (0.00 sec)

mysql> set global exif_path='/opt/images';
Query OK, 0 rows affected (0.00 sec)

mysql> insert test values ('2688188166_c1be338744_o.jpg'),
('3439686345_6bfcd62538_o.jpg'),('3881772447_d957742a33_o.jpg'),
('3999772754_b433240fce_b.jpg');
Query OK, 4 rows affected (0.09 sec)
Records: 4  Duplicates: 0  Warnings: 0
```

This is how the search works:

```
mysql> select * from test where match jpeg against('bookend');
+----------------------------+
| jpeg                       |
+----------------------------+
| 3999772754_b433240fce_b.jpg |
+----------------------------+
1 row in set (0.00 sec)
```

This picture has bookends on it. But, of course, our plugin did not look at the picture, it found the file because it has the matching description tag (as shown by the `exiftool` command-line utility):

```
shell$ exiftool -UserComment 3999772754_b433240fce_b.jpg
User Comment    : Bookend spiral art
```

Our parser does no image recognition. It is only as good as the image description is. Other tags are filled in automatically by the camera, they thus have a better chance of being set correctly. We can search, for example, by camera model:

```
mysql> select * from test where match jpeg against('sony');
+----------------------------+
| jpeg                       |
+----------------------------+
| 3881772447_d957742a33_o.jpg |
+----------------------------+
1 row in set (0.01 sec)
```

And indeed:

```
shell$ exiftool -Make 3881772447_d957742a33_o.jpg
Make                             : SONY
```

We can even search from the command line and display the found image at once:

```
shell$ display `mysql -N -e 'select * from test where match jpeg
against("easy street")'`
```

If *ImageMagick* is installed, the above command will show the corresponding image. Alternatively, you can use any other image viewer instead of display. To make these searches really convenient we can create a shell script, like this:

```
#!/bin/sh
display  `mysql -N -e "select concat(@@exif_path, \
                      '/', jpeg) from test \
                      where match jpeg against('$*')"`
```

If called show, it can be used as:

```
shell$ show spiral art
```

or

```
shell$ show flower
```

A Soundex full-text parser

We have seen the "tokenizer" and "extractor" plugins. We finish this chapter with a "post-processor" plugin. Such a plugin is interested in doing something with the individual words of the text, but not in splitting the text into words. It puts itself after the mysql_parse() function, but before mysql_add_word(). In this position it can see every word and modify it if needed, but it will be MySQL that will do the parsing job. Again, just as in the case of "extractor" plugins, this technique allows us to implement only the main functionality of the plugin, only what makes it unique, and not repeat the parsing code that already exists in the server. As an example of a "post-processor" plugin we will create a Soundex plugin—a plugin that replaces every word with its Soundex code, making the full-text search insensitive to typos.

The Soundex algorithm

The Soundex algorithm was patented in 1918. It is a phonetic algorithm that converts words to codes, which mainly corresponds to the word pronunciation, and much less to the word spelling. Using this algorithm, words can be often matched even in the presence of misspellings. There are many variations and improvements of the original Soundex algorithm that are mostly aimed at increasing the accuracy of the algorithm. We will use the original Soundex algorithm—it is the same one that MySQL uses for its SOUNDEX function.

In this original Soundex version the code is computed according to the following rules:

1. Keep the first letter of the word

2. Replace all other letters with numbers as follows:
   - b, f, p, v = 1
   - c, g, j, k, q, s, x, z = 2
   - d, t = 3
   - l = 4
   - m, n = 5
   - r = 6

3. Remove all other letters

4. Collapse adjacent duplicate numbers

5. Right-pad with zeros if the result has less than three digits

6. Return the first letter of the word and the first three code digits

The built-in MySQL SOUNDEX function differs in the last step—it does not truncate the result and may return more than four characters. But we will stick to the original algorithm.

According to the above rules the word "blast" has a Soundex code of B423, as well as the word "blacked", while the word "hello" becomes H400.

The plugin

We need our plugin to work after the MySQL parser has split the text into words, but before these words were inserted into the index or used for searching. We can do that by replacing the `param->mysql_add_word` pointer. If we change it to point to our function and invoke `param->mysql_parse()`, MySQL's built-in parser will do the parsing and, naturally, it will call `param->mysql_add_word()` for every word. And this is exactly what we need — we can calculate the Soundex code of the word and invoke the original `mysql_add_word()` function. This way we will not need to implement the parsing and only do the Soundex processing of words.

```
#include <mysql/plugin.h>
#include <stdio.h>
#include <ctype.h>
```

As in previous examples, we start with the simple stuff — the end of the file. A plugin declaration here is no different from all the other plugin declarations we have done:

```
static struct st_mysql_ftparser ft_soundex =
{
  MYSQL_FTPARSER_INTERFACE_VERSION,
  soundex_parse,
  NULL,
  NULL
};

mysql_declare_plugin(ftsoundex)
{
  MYSQL_FTPARSER_PLUGIN,
  &ft_soundex,
  "soundex",
  "Andrew Hutchings <Andrew.Hutchings@Sun.COM>",
  "A Full-Text Soundex parser",
  PLUGIN_LICENSE_GPL,
  NULL,
  NULL,
  0x0100,
  NULL,
  NULL,
  NULL
}
mysql_declare_plugin_end;
```

A parsing function is new to us, but completely predictable. The only detail to keep in mind is to remember the old value of `param->mysql_add_word` to be able to invoke it at the end:

```
static int soundex_parse(MYSQL_FTPARSER_PARAM *param)
{
  param->ftparser_state = param->mysql_add_word;
  param->mysql_add_word = soundex_add_word;
  return param->mysql_parse(param, param->doc, param->length);
}
```

Now, let's create the main functionality of our plugin, which in this case is not the `soundex_parse()` but the `soundex_add_word()` function.

```
                            /* ABCDEFGHIJKLMNOPQRSTUVWXYZ */
static const char *codemap = "-123-12--22455-12623-1-2-2";
```

This is our letter to number map, starting with "A" and ending in "Z".

```
static int soundex_add_word(MYSQL_FTPARSER_PARAM *param,
                            char *word, int len,
                            MYSQL_FTPARSER_BOOLEAN_INFO *info)
{
  char soundex[4];
  int  soundex_len = 0;
  char ch, prev = 0;
  char *word_end = word+len;
  int (*real_add_word)(MYSQL_FTPARSER_PARAM *, char *, int,
                       MYSQL_FTPARSER_BOOLEAN_INFO *);
  real_add_word = param->ftparser_state;
```

We declare a function pointer of the same type as `mysql_add_word`, and assign the old value of `param->mysql_add_word` to it. Note that our own `soundex_add_word()` also has exactly the same prototype.

Now we iterate the characters of the word:

```
  for (; word < word_end; word++)
  {
```

Convert to uppercase, skip if not a letter:

```
    ch = toupper(*word);
    if (ch < 'A' || ch > 'Z')
      continue;
```

If it's a first letter, copy it to the result buffer verbatim, otherwise map it to a digit:

```
if (soundex_len == 0)
{
  soundex[soundex_len++] = ch;
  continue;
}
ch = codemap[ch - 'A'];
```

If there is no digit for this letter or if it is the same as the previous digit, we skip it (see steps 3 and 4 in the Soundex algorithm mentioned previously), otherwise append it to the output buffer:

```
if (ch == '-' || ch == prev)
  continue;
else
  soundex[soundex_len++] = ch;
```

We can stop if the Soundex code has four characters:

```
if (soundex_len == 4)
  break;
prev = ch;
}
```

If the word was too short and did not generate a four-character code, we pad the output buffer with zeros:

```
while (soundex_len < 4)
  soundex[soundex_len++] = '0';
```

Remember to set the "need copy" flag, because all words (really, Soundex codes) are generated in the same buffer, overwriting each other. And the last step — we call the original `mysql_add_word()` function to let MySQL process the word:

```
param->flags |= MYSQL_FTFLAGS_NEED_COPY;
return real_add_word(param, soundex, soundex_len, info);
}
```

Ready. Now we can try it out.

Trying it out

We build and install the plugin as usual. Then we create a table and populate it with data:

```
mysql> create table test (t text, fulltext(t) with parser soundex)
engine=myisam;

Query OK, 0 rows affected (0.01 sec)

mysql> insert test values ('The Soundex algorithm was patented in
1918.'), ('It is a phonetic algorithm'), ('that converts words to
codes.'), ('Codes mainly correspond to the word pronunciation,'),
('and much less to the word spelling.');

Query OK, 5 rows affected (0.01 sec)

Records: 5  Duplicates: 0  Warnings: 0


mysql> select * from test;
+----------------------------------------------------+
| t                                                  |
+----------------------------------------------------+
| The Soundex algorithm was patented in 1918.        |
| It is a phonetic algorithm                         |
| that converts words to codes.                      |
| Codes mainly correspond to the word pronunciation, |
| and much less to the word spelling.                |
+----------------------------------------------------+
5 rows in set (0.00 sec)
```

Simple searches work as usual:

```
mysql> select * from test where match t against ('algorithm');
+---------------------------------------------+
| t                                           |
+---------------------------------------------+
| It is a phonetic algorithm                  |
| The Soundex algorithm was patented in 1918. |
+---------------------------------------------+
2 rows in set (0.00 sec)
```

Even if badly misspelled, the word can be found:

```
mysql> select * from test where match t against ('alkareetm');

+------------------------------------------+
| t                                        |
+------------------------------------------+
| It is a phonetic algorithm               |
| The Soundex algorithm was patented in 1918. |
+------------------------------------------+
2 rows in set (0.00 sec)
```

As we have used the built-in MySQL parser, all of its features are available; for example, Boolean searches:

```
mysql> select * from test where match t against ('+word' in boolean
mode);

+-------------------------------------------------------+
| t                                                     |
+-------------------------------------------------------+
| Codes mainly correspond to the word pronunciation,    |
| and much less to the word spelling.                   |
+-------------------------------------------------------+
2 rows in set (0.00 sec)
```

```
mysql> select * from test where match t against ('+word -pronansiashn' in
boolean mode);

+-----------------------------------+
| t                                 |
+-----------------------------------+
| and much less to the word spelling. |
+-----------------------------------+
1 row in set (0.00 sec)
```

But Soundex has its limitations, for example:

```
mysql> select * from test where match t against ('kodezz');

Empty set (0.00 sec)
```

The above did not find lines with the word "codes". Why? This is because Soundex code unconditionally starts from the first letter of the word, not a mapped letter. We can see it in MySQL:

```
mysql> select soundex('codes'),soundex('kodezz');
+------------------+------------------+
| soundex('codes') | soundex('kodez') |
+------------------+------------------+
| C320             | K320             |
+------------------+------------------+
1 row in set (0.00 sec)
```

Using a more complex phonetic algorithm, for example, *Metaphone*, would solve this particular problem; Metaphone code for both "Codes" and "Kodezz" is KTS.

Summary

In this chapter we have learned how to write parsers that support searches in Boolean mode. We have developed three parser plugins that show different ways of using a full-text parser plugin API—"extractor", "tokenizer", and "post-processor" approaches. We have seen how full-text parser plugins can be used to implement searches within image metadata, and how to create search-enabled applications that are insensitive to typos and misspelled words.

This chapter is the last one dedicated to full-text parser plugins. The next chapter starts with the topic of the most complex and broad MySQL plugin type of all—the Storage Engine plugins.

8

Storage Engine Plugins

One of the great strengths of MySQL and one of the main features which sets it apart from other RDBMSs is its ability to use different storage engines for different tables. These different storage engines can control where and how the data is stored and retrieved. Every storage engine has strengths and weaknesses, which means that MySQL can be tailored to the user's need through its use of storage engines.

In this chapter, we will outline everything you need to create your own storage engine. We will then finish off the chapter with an example of a simple read-only storage engine plugin.

Introducing storage engines

Earlier in this book we covered Information Schema plugins. Although very differently defined, these plugins work a little like partially implemented read-only storage engines. We just have to provide the table layout and fill the rows when queried. With a basic storage engine plugin we have to do exactly the same, but there are many other methods which can be implemented to cover indexes, updates, inserts, and so on.

The storage engine plugins are implemented using two main structures:

- A class, inherited from a MySQL class, called `handler`
- A structure called `handlerton`

The `handler` class provides the methods that work on a single table such as `open()`, `index_read()`, `write_row()`, and so on. There can be many objects of the `handler` class. The `handlerton` object is created only once per storage engine (it is a singleton, thus the name) and provides methods that affect the whole storage engine, such as `commit()`, `savepoint_rollback()`, `show_status()`, and so on. There are roughly 150 methods in the `handler` class and about 30 methods in `handlerton`, which we can implement in our storage engine plugins covering many of the functions that MySQL can provide, but most of these are not required. We will cover the commonly used ones in this chapter, but for further reading, the `sql/handler.h` and `sql/handler.cc` files in the MySQL source could be looked into.

A read-only storage engine

This simple storage engine plugin, called `STATIC_TEXT`, supports only read-only tables. It defines two system variables, which we use to change its behavior. The first variable is `@@static_text_text`, which specifies the text returned in VARCHAR fields ("Hello world!" by default) and the second variable is `@@static_text_rows`, which specifies the number of rows to return (the default is 3). When a table in this storage engine is queried, any VARCHAR field will contain the contents of `@@static_text_text` and any integer field will contain the current row number:

```
mysql> install plugin STATIC_TEXT soname 'ha_text.so';
Query OK, 0 rows affected (0.03 sec)


mysql> create table t1 (a int, b varchar(50)) engine=static_text;
Query OK, 0 rows affected (0.37 sec)


mysql> select * from t1;
+------+--------------+
| a    | b            |
+------+--------------+
|    1 | Hello World! |
|    2 | Hello World! |
|    3 | Hello World! |
+------+--------------+
3 rows in set (0.00 sec)
```

The number of rows and the contents of the VARCHAR column can be modified by assigning new values to the system variables:

```
mysql> show variables like 'static%';
+-------------------+--------------+
| Variable_name     | Value        |
+-------------------+--------------+
| static_text_rows  | 3            |
| static_text_text  | Hello World! |
+-------------------+--------------+
2 rows in set (0.00 sec)


mysql> set global static_text_rows = 5;
Query OK, 0 rows affected (0.00 sec)


mysql> set global static_text_text = 'This is a test!';
Query OK, 0 rows affected (0.00 sec)


mysql> select * from t1;
+------+-----------------+
| a    | b               |
+------+-----------------+
|    1 | This is a test! |
|    2 | This is a test! |
|    3 | This is a test! |
|    4 | This is a test! |
|    5 | This is a test! |
+------+-----------------+
5 rows in set (0.00 sec)
```

More complex queries should work too:

```
mysql> select * from t1 where a > 3 order by a desc;
+------+-----------------+
| a    | b               |
+------+-----------------+
|    5 | This is a test! |
|    4 | This is a test! |
+------+-----------------+
2 rows in set (0.00 sec)
```

Looking at the data directory for this database we see a t1.frm file. This is the MySQL internal file that stores the table's definition. Without it MySQL will not know the table exists.

Now, let us look at how such a storage engine can be implemented. Typically, a storage engine plugin consists of at least two files, ha_xxx.h and ha_xxx.cc, "xxx" being the engine name. For more complex engines these two files define only the interface code between MySQL and the actual storage library, which occupies its own set of files. In the case of our simple engine, though, one file, ha_text.cc, is all that is needed.

ha_text.cc

As always, it starts by including the obligatory header file. Despite the historical priv (private) in the name, this header is needed for storage engine plugins, providing declarations for all interface data structures and functions:

```
#include <mysql_priv.h>
```

We want to declare two system variables. As we remember from the preceding chapters, it is done as follows:

```
static char *static_text_varchar;
static ulong static_text_rows;

static MYSQL_SYSVAR_STR(text, static_text_varchar,
   PLUGIN_VAR_MEMALLOC,
   "The value of VARCHAR columns in the static engine tables",
   NULL, NULL, "Hello World!");

static MYSQL_SYSVAR_ULONG(rows, static_text_rows, 0,
   "Number of rows in the static engine tables",
   NULL, NULL, 3, 0, 0, 0);

static struct st_mysql_sys_var* static_text_sys_var[] = {
   MYSQL_SYSVAR(text),
   MYSQL_SYSVAR(rows),
   NULL
};
```

These declarations create two system variables:

- @@static_text_text: String variable of a global scope with the default value of "Hello World!"

- @@static_text_rows: Integer variable (based on C++ unsigned long type) of a global scope that has a default value of 3

Both variables are recognized on the command line too, as `--static-text-text` and `--static-text-rows` accordingly. Note that we have specified variable names simply as `text` and `rows` because MySQL will add the plugin name as a prefix automatically.

Similar to other plugin types, when defining a storage engine plugin, we need the following incantation:

```
struct st_mysql_storage_engine static_text_storage_engine =
{ MYSQL_HANDLERTON_INTERFACE_VERSION };

mysql_declare_plugin(static_text)
{
  MYSQL_STORAGE_ENGINE_PLUGIN,
  &static_text_storage_engine,
  "STATIC_TEXT",
  "Andrew Hutchings (Andrew.Hutchings@Sun.COM)",
  "An example static text storage engine",
  PLUGIN_LICENSE_GPL,"
  static_text_init,
  NULL,
  0x0001,
  NULL,
  static_text_sys_var,
  NULL
}
mysql_declare_plugin_end;
```

The main job of the plugin initialization function is to set up the `handlerton` structure. For an engine as simple as ours, we only need to provide the `create()` method. This is a `handlerton` method that creates a new `handler` object, more precisely, a new instance of our `ha_static_text` class that inherits from the `handler` class:

```
static int static_text_init(void *p)
{
  handlerton *static_text_hton = (handlerton *)p;
  static_text_hton->create = static_text_create_handler;
  return 0;
}

static handler* static_text_create_handler(handlerton *hton,
                   TABLE_SHARE *table, MEM_ROOT *mem_root)
{
  return new (mem_root) ha_static_text(hton, table);
}
```

The `ha_static_text` class that implements interfaces defined by the `handler` class is the heart of our storage engine. The `handler` class itself is quite big and has many virtual methods that we can implement in `ha_static_text`. But luckily only a few are defined as abstract—and it is only these methods that we are absolutely required to implement. They are:

Method name	Description
`table_type`	This method simply returns the name of a storage engine, `STATIC_TEXT` in our case.
`bas_ext`	When an engine puts different tables in different files, like MyISAM does, this method returns a list of filename extensions that the engine uses. Otherwise it is an empty list.
`table_flags`	A combination of flags that define table capabilities. It is a `handler` method, not a `handlerton` method, as different tables are allowed to have different capabilities.
`index_flags`	A combination of flags that define index capabilities. It does not matter what we return here; this method will never be called, as our engine does not support indexes.
`create`	This method is invoked to create a new table in the storage engine. It will be empty in our case, because our engine does not need to do anything on table creation, but we still have to provide this method.
`store_lock`	Another method that every engine is required to implement. It is used by the MySQL locking subsystem. This method takes two arguments, lock level and a pointer to a variable, and stores a lock of this (or modified) lock level in this variable. That is where the name of the method comes from. Engines that rely on MySQL table level locking store the unaltered lock level, while engines that support a higher lock granularity—page or row-level locking—downgrade the lock to allow concurrent write access to the tables.
`open`	This method opens an existing table.
`close`	The opposite of `open()`—to close an open table.
`rnd_init`	This method is called before random reads or sequential table scans (but not before an index lookup or traversal). It should prepare the table for this kind of access.
`rnd_next`	In sequential table scans this method returns the next record of the table. When invoked in a loop it works like an iterator, advancing the cursor, and returning the next record on each invocation until the end of table is reached.
`position`	This method remembers a current record *position* in the internal handler variable. A *position* is whatever the engine uses to uniquely identify the record; for example, a primary key value, a row ID, an address in memory, or an offset in the data file.

Method name	Description
rnd_pos	The opposite of position() — this method takes a *position* as an argument and returns a record identified by it.
info	MySQL invokes this method to query various information about the table, such as approximate number of records, the date of the last modification, the average record length, index cardinalities, and so on.
ha_static_text	The constructor is not abstract, of course, but it still needs to be implemented. At least to pass the arguments to the constructor of the parent class.

Keeping the above table in mind, this is how we can start declaring the ha_static_text class:

```
class ha_static_text: public handler
{
public:
  ha_static_text(handlerton *hton, TABLE_SHARE *table_arg)
    : handler(hton, table_arg) { }
  const char *table_type() const { return "STATIC_TEXT"; }
  const char **bas_ext() const {
    static const char *exts[] = { 0 };
    return exts;
  }
  ulonglong table_flags() const;
  ulong index_flags(uint inx, uint part, bool all_parts) const
  { return 0; }
  int create(const char *name, TABLE *table_arg,
             HA_CREATE_INFO *create_info) { return 0; }
  THR_LOCK_DATA **store_lock(THD *thd, THR_LOCK_DATA **to,
                             enum thr_lock_type lock_type);
  int open(const char *name, int mode, uint test_if_locked);
  int close(void);
  int rnd_init(bool scan);
  int rnd_next(unsigned char *buf);
  void position(const uchar *record);
  int rnd_pos(uchar * buf, uchar *pos);
  int info(uint flag);
};
```

We have defined all the simple methods inline. Now let us consider more complex methods one by one.

```
int ha_static_text::open(const char *name, int mode,
                         uint test_if_locked)
{
  share = find_or_create_share(name, table);
  if (share->use_count++ == 0)
    thr_lock_init(&share->lock);
  thr_lock_data_init(&share->lock,&lock,NULL);

  return 0;
}
```

There was no table to create in the `create()` method, and there is nothing to open here. The only thing we need to do is to initialize the THR_LOCK and THR_LOCK_DATA objects. They are used by the MySQL locking subsystem and every storage engine must provide them.

As we remember, there can be many instances of the `handler` class. If a table is used in one query more than once, for example, in a self-join, or a table is accessed in many connections simultaneously, MySQL will create many `handler` objects for this table, and each of them will need to have its very own THR_LOCK_DATA object. Still, all of these `handler` objects refer to the same table and they must use the same THR_LOCK object. To repeat, for MySQL locking code to work there should be one THR_LOCK object per table and one THR_LOCK_DATA object per table opening. The latter is easy — we add a new member `lock` of the THR_LOCK_DATA type to the `ha_static_text` class and initialize it in the `open()` method with the `thr_lock_data_init()` function.

However, the former needs more work, as it requires us to have some kind of a shared object — we will call it STATIC_SHARE — to put THR_LOCK in. Two `handler` objects that refer to a same table should use the same STATIC_SHARE object, otherwise they should use different STATIC_SHARE objects. The function `find_or_create_share()`, used previously, finds a corresponding STATIC_SHARE or creates a new one, if this is the first time a given table is being opened. Let us see how it can be implemented.

When we need to find a STATIC_SHARE object for a specific table, we are given a MySQL TABLE object and a table name. The first and obvious solution is to use a hash to create a mapping from table names to their corresponding STATIC_SHARE objects and protect it from concurrent accesses with a mutex. Indeed, many storage engines use this approach. But perhaps we can do better—simpler, faster, and with less concurrency overhead? Note that besides a table name we are given a TABLE object. The MySQL TABLE object, just like a handler, is created as many times as the table is used. In fact, with few exceptions, there are as many TABLE objects as there are handler objects. But MySQL also has a TABLE_SHARE object which, as we can expect, is created only once per table. If table is a pointer to TABLE, then table->s is its TABLE_SHARE pointer, and table->s->ha_data is an unused void* pointer in the TABLE_SHARE that a storage engine can use for any purpose. It would be easy for us to store our STATIC_SHARE in the table->s->ha_data, and make the find_or_create_share() function as simple as return table->s->ha_data. In fact, it would be too easy to be true. When a table is partitioned, all partitions share the same TABLE object, and, of course, the same TABLE_SHARE. However, partitions are different tables from the storage engine point of view, and the only way to distinguish them is by a "table name", which in this case will have a partition (and a subpartition, if any) number embedded in it. To solve this problem we will link all STATIC_SHARE objects for a given TABLE_SHARE in a linked list and will search the list to find the matching table name:

```
typedef struct st_static_text {
  const char *name;
  THR_LOCK lock;
  uint use_count;
  struct st_static_text *next;
} STATIC_SHARE;

static STATIC_SHARE *find_or_create_share(
                      const char *table_name, TABLE *table)
{
  STATIC_SHARE *share;
  for (share = (STATIC_SHARE*)table->s->ha_data;
       share; share = share->next)

    if (my_strcasecmp(table_alias_charset,
                      table_name, share->name) == 0)
      return share;
```

Note the detail—we use `table_alias_charset` to compare table names. It
will give a case-sensitive or case-insensitive comparison, depending on the
`lower_case_table_names` MySQL configuration variable. To avoid bugs it is
important to use exactly the same case sensitivity rules as elsewhere in the server.

```
    share = (STATIC_SHARE*)alloc_root(&table->s->mem_root,
                                      sizeof(*share));
    bzero(share, sizeof(*share));
    share->name = strdup_root(&table->s->mem_root, table_name);
    share->next = (STATIC_SHARE*)table->s->ha_data;
    table->s->ha_data = share;
    return share;
  }
```

If no matching `STATIC_SHARE` is found in the list, we create a new one and link it
in. As all memory is allocated in the `TABLE_SHARE` memory root, it will be freed
automatically along with `TABLE_SHARE`. Very handy.

> A thought about locking and concurrent accesses: In MySQL 5.1 a
> table is opened under a mutex. We can safely access and modify
> `table->s->ha_data` and not worry about other threads. In later MySQL
> versions this mutex is removed. It has improved the concurrency, but
> our code is no longer correct. There is an easy fix though—these MySQL
> versions provide a dedicated mutex `table->s->LOCK_ha_data` that we
> will need to use to protect `table->s->ha_data`.

It seems logical to initialize `share->lock` directly in `find_or_create_share()`,
when a new `STATIC_SHARE` is created, but unfortunately MySQL will not give us a
chance to destroy it before freeing `STATIC_SHARE` along with `TABLE_SHARE`. Hence,
we have no choice but to maintain a usage counter for `STATIC_SHARE` and call the
initialization and destruction functions accordingly.

```
    int ha_static_text::close(void)
    {
      if (--share->use_count == 0)
        thr_lock_delete(&share->lock);
      return 0;
    }
```

The `close()` method does the opposite of `open()`. It decrements the `STATIC_SHARE` usage counter and destroys its `THR_LOCK` object if necessary. The `THR_LOCK_DATA` object does not need to be destroyed.

```
ulonglong ha_static_text::table_flags() const
{
  return HA_NO_TRANSACTIONS | HA_STATS_RECORDS_IS_EXACT |
         HA_REC_NOT_IN_SEQ;
}
```

This method returns the capabilities of the particular table. In MySQL-5.1 there are 35 different capability flags. The complete list is as follows:

Flag	Description
HA_NO_TRANSACTIONS	The table is not transactional.
HA_PARTIAL_COLUMN_READ	The table that does not have this capability bit set can only read complete rows. In any row image returned by such a table all field values will be known. If this capability flag is set, MySQL will use the read_set bitmap in the TABLE object to specify which fields must be present in the row image.
HA_TABLE_SCAN_ON_INDEX	Usually, MySQL prefers a full table scan over a large index scan, because sequential disk I/O is many times faster than random disk I/O. If the data storage is index based and any "sequential table scan" means an index scan internally, the above optimization strategy will not work as expected. The flag tells MySQL to disable this optimization.
HA_REC_NOT_IN_SEQ	If this flag is set, MySQL will always call position() to get a value for a later rnd_pos() call. If it is not set, in sequential table scans a *position* will be increased by table->s->db_record_offset per row, starting from 0. In this case, remember to initialize table->s->db_record_offset to the correct value in the info() method.
HA_CAN_GEOMETRY	The engine supports spatial data types. This only means that the engine can store and retrieve spatial data. It does not mean that the engine knows how to index them.
HA_CAN_RTREEKEYS	The engine supports indexes over spatial data types.

Flag	Description
HA_FAST_KEY_READ	MySQL tries to use sequential disk I/O if possible. When looking up a set of values in the index it sorts them first to make the I/O pattern more sequential. If random index lookups are as fast as sequential lookups, for example, if the index is completely in memory, then MySQL will not sort the values before looking them up in the index.
HA_REQUIRES_KEY_ COLUMNS_FOR_DELETE HA_PRIMARY_KEY_ REQUIRED_FOR_DELETE	The delete() method takes a previously read row as an argument. Storage engine can tell MySQL what fields should have values in this row for deletion to work, and MySQL will configure the read_set bitmap accordingly. For example, the engine may need primary key fields to be present— to be able to identify the row, or all indexed fields to be present—to make removing their values from indexes easier. Or it may need no field values at all—as a deletion is always performed for the last read row, the engine can simply delete the row at the cursor position. Of course, if HA_PARTIAL_COLUMN_READ is not set, all field values will be present in the row anyway.
HA_NULL_IN_KEY	The engine can index fields that store NULL values. If unset, all indexed fields will have to be declared NOT NULL.
HA_DUPLICATE_POS	If set, on a duplicate key error in INSERT or UPDATE, MySQL will read the *position* of the other row that caused the conflict (not the row that was inserted/updated) from the dup_pos member of the handler object (after the info(HA_STATUS_ERRKEY) method call—see below). If not set, MySQL will do an extra index lookup to find the conflicting row.
HA_NO_BLOBS	BLOB columns are not supported.
HA_CAN_INDEX_BLOBS	BLOB columns can be indexed.
HA_AUTO_PART_KEY	Auto-increment column does not have to be the first column in the index.
HA_REQUIRE_PRIMARY_KEY	The table is required to have a primary key, CREATE TABLE will fail otherwise.

Flag	Description
HA_STATS_RECORDS_IS_EXACT	Number of records returned in stats.records by the info() method is exact, not an estimate, and can be used as a result for SELECT COUNT(*). If this flag is not set, the value will only be used as an estimate when choosing a best query execution plan. But note that if stats.records is 0, MySQL considers the table to be completely empty. In other words, the value of 0 is always exact. Only when stats.records is 1 or larger and HA_STATS_RECORDS_IS_EXACT is not set, the number is treated as an inexact estimate.
HA_HAS_RECORDS	This flag tells MySQL that the record() method returns an exact number of rows in the table. It is only used when HA_STATS_RECORDS_IS_EXACT is not set.
	The logic is as follows: certain engines maintain the live row counter, and at any time they know the number of rows in a table. These engines return this number in stats.records using the info() method and have the flag HA_STATS_RECORDS_IS_EXACT set. Other engines do not maintain a row counter, but they can calculate it reasonably fast (although slower than simply consulting stats.records). They implement this calculation in the records() method and set the HA_HAS_RECORDS flag. If neither flag is set, to get an exact record counter, MySQL will have to resort to the slowest possible approach—full table scan.
HA_CAN_INSERT_DELAYED	INSERT DELAYED works correctly with this engine.
HA_PRIMARY_KEY_IN_READ_INDEX	This tells MySQL that any row returned as a result of an index lookup or an index scan will always have values in primary key fields, independent of read_set. In other words, any index access returns primary key values too, for free, without increasing the cost of the query.
HA_PRIMARY_KEY_REQUIRED_FOR_POSITION	A storage engine needs to know the value of the primary key to execute the position() method. If primary key fields are not part of the read_set, the position() method will not work.
HA_NOT_DELETE_WITH_CACHE	Obsolete. No engine has used it since 2001.
HA_NO_PREFIX_CHAR_KEYS	The engine does not support indexes over a prefix of a CHAR or VARCHAR column (created using the KEY (col_name(length)) syntax).
HA_CAN_FULLTEXT	The engine supports FULLTEXT indexes. Only MyISAM does.

Flag	Description
HA_CAN_SQL_HANDLER	The HANDLER statement works correctly with this table.
HA_NO_AUTO_INCREMENT	AUTO_INCREMENT columns are not supported.
HA_HAS_CHECKSUM	If this flag is set, CHECKSUM TABLE will use the checksum() method of the handler object to get a live table checksum. If this flag is not set, CHECKSUM TABLE will do a full table scan to calculate the checksum. Of course, the live checksum, if supported, should use exactly the same algorithm as CHECKSUM TABLE does.
HA_FILE_BASED	This flag means that tables are stored in files, filename being the table name. In other words, table name searching and matching is done by the file system (table names are treated case sensitively or case insensitively depending on the file system case sensitivity).
HA_NO_VARCHAR	VARCHAR columns are not supported. MySQL will convert them to CHAR automatically.
HA_CAN_BIT_FIELD	BIT fields can be stored in the row image in one of the two ways—either as a part of the NULL bitmap in the beginning of the row or as a separate VARCHAR column. If this flag is set, MySQL uses the first approach, otherwise the second.
HA_NEED_READ_RANGE_ BUFFER	This is used by the optional multi-read-range optimization. In MySQL 5.1 only NDBCluster has this flag on.
HA_ANY_INDEX_MAY_BE_ UNIQUE	Only MERGE tables need this; it enables a special workaround for MERGE tables with differently defined underlying MyISAM tables.
HA_NO_COPY_ON_ALTER	Only MERGE tables need this; it is used to avoid rebuilding the MERGE table in ALTER TABLE ... UNION=(...)
HA_HAS_OWN_BINLOGGING	This flag means that in row-based binary logging the server will not log operations on this table. The engine is supposed to do that itself, using a special binary log injector. Only NDBCluster uses that. See the *MySQL Cluster Replication* section in the MySQL manual for details.
HA_BINLOG_ROW_CAPABLE	Changes to the table can be logged in the row-based replication mode.
HA_BINLOG_STMT_CAPABLE	Changes to the table can be logged in the statement-based replication mode. A transactional table may need to disable this flag conditionally, depending on the isolation level.

We have set our table flags in the `ha_static_text::table_flags()` method to specify the table is not transactional, the number of rows in the `stats.records` is exact, and that the server should always call the `position()` method to calculate the *position*.

```
THR_LOCK_DATA **ha_static_text::store_lock(THD *thd,
        THR_LOCK_DATA **to, enum thr_lock_type lock_type)
{
  if (lock_type != TL_IGNORE && lock.type == TL_UNLOCK)
    lock.type = lock_type;
  *to ++= &lock;
  return to;
}
```

As we remember, this method stores the `lock` of the level `lock_type` (or possibly of different lock level, as the primary purpose of this method is to give the engine a possibility to modify the lock level) in `*to`. Using unmodified lock level will give us a standard MySQL table-level locking. Downgrading the lock will result in a higher concurrency and put the burden of maintaining the data protection and correctness on the engine itself. We do not want to complicate our engine by adding a lock manager to it, so we will use MySQL table-level locking. The function `store_lock()`, as above, is identical in all table-level locking engines.

Now, let us look at the functions that return rows. MySQL uses its own row format internally. There are storage engines (for example, MyISAM) that natively read and write rows in this format, but most engines need to do the conversion. Fields, represented as objects of the `Field` class, and available via the `TABLE` object, know how to store and convert themselves. We have seen how to use the `Field` classes in the Information Schema chapters; storage engines use them similarly. This is how one can use them to fill in a row buffer:

```
static void fill_record(TABLE *table, unsigned char *buf,
                        ulong row_num)
```

Our engine shows the row number in integer columns, so this function needs to know it.

```
{
  my_bitmap_map *old_map =
        dbug_tmp_use_all_columns(table, table->write_set);
```

MySQL tries to ensure that only the fields listed in the `table->write_set` bitmap are modified in a query. The check is in the `Field::store()` method – presumably, MySQL should never call this method for any field that is not in the `write_set`. Unfortunately, this logic is flawed, because this method can be also used to fill in the row inside a storage engine. As a workaround, to be able to use the `Field::store()` method without triggering an assert we have to temporarily reset the `table->write_set` bitmap.

```
for (uint i = 0; i < table->s->fields; i++)
{
  Field *field = table->field[i];
  my_ptrdiff_t offset;
  offset = (my_ptrdiff_t) (buf - table->record[0]);
  field->move_field_offset(offset);
```

Fields always operate with the row image at `table->record[0]`. If we want to write our data elsewhere we need to move the field pointer there and restore it later.

```
  field->set_notnull();
  if (field->type() == MYSQL_TYPE_VARCHAR)
    field->store(static_text_varchar,
                 strlen(static_text_varchar),
                 system_charset_info);
  else if (field->type() == MYSQL_TYPE_LONG)
    field->store(row_num, false);
```

As mentioned before, we store the value of the `@@static_text_varchar` variable in the VARCHAR field and a row number in the integer field.

```
  field->move_field_offset(-offset);
}
  dbug_tmp_restore_column_map(table->write_set, old_map);
}
```

At the end we restore the field pointers and the `table->write_set` bitmap.

Having this function ready we can finish the remaining handler methods. As all integer fields contain the current row number we will need a counter, `returned_data`, which will be stored in these fields. Thus, we extend the `ha_static_text` class with the following:

```
private:
  THR_LOCK_DATA lock;
  STATIC_SHARE *share;
  ulong returned_data;
```

To start a new table scan we initialize the row counter:

```
int ha_static_text::rnd_init(bool scan)
{
  returned_data = 0;
  return 0;
}
```

Returning the next row is easy too:

```
int ha_static_text::rnd_next(unsigned char *buf)
{
  if (returned_data >= static_text_rows)
    return HA_ERR_END_OF_FILE;

  fill_record(table, buf, ++returned_data);
  return 0;
}
```

As a *position*, to identify the row, we can simply use the row number:

```
void ha_static_text::position(const uchar *record)
{
  *(ulong*)ref = returned_data;
}
```

Given a *position*, we can easily return the corresponding row. There is a fine detail though, before using the *position* we copy it to a local variable. This is done for better portability – pos pointer is not necessarily aligned in memory and dereferencing an unaligned pointer as *(ulong*)pos will cause a crash on some architectures (for example, on Sparc).

```
int ha_static_text::rnd_pos(uchar * buf, uchar *pos)
{
  ulong row_num;
  memcpy(&row_num, pos, sizeof(row_num));
  fill_record(table, buf, row_num);
  return 0;
}
```

The last method we implement is `info()`. It can return a lot of different information about the table, depending on the argument. The argument is a bitmap of flags; the server requests the storage engine to update different data by setting different flags:

Flag	Description
HA_STATUS_CONST	Update the "constant" part of the information—constant, because it does not change after a table is opened. It includes `stats.max_data_file_length`, `stats.max_index_file_length`, `stats.create_time`, `stats.block_size`, `table->s->db_options_in_use`, `table->s->keys_in_use` (a bitmap that shows what indexes are enabled, usually all indexes are), `table->s->keys_for_keyread` (a bitmap of indexes usable as covering indexes), `table->s->db_record_offset`, (see the description of HA_REC_NOT_IN_SEQ table flag), `table->key_info[].rec_per_key` (inverted index cardinalities), `data_file_name`, and `index_file_name`.
HA_STATUS_VARIABLE	Update the "variable" part of the information, in particular `stats.records`, `stats.deleted`, `stats.data_file_length`, `stats.index_file_length`, `stats.delete_length`, `stats.check_time`, `stats.mean_rec_length`.
HA_STATUS_ERRKEY	MySQL uses this `info()` flag after a duplicate key error. The engine is supposed to put the number of the key that has caused a conflict in the `errkey` and the *position* of the conflicting row, if the HA_DUPLICATE_POS table flag is set, in the `dup_ref`.
HA_STATUS_TIME	Update the value of `stats.update_time`.
HA_STATUS_AUTO	Update the value of `stats.auto_increment_value`.
HA_STATUS_NO_LOCK	This is not a request for information, but a hint to the engine that the engine can provide possibly outdated information from a local cache (if the engine caches it, that is) and avoid taking the lock to access the actual shared objects that store the up-to-date engine information. An engine is free to ignore this hint and most engines do.

From all of the above we provide only one piece of "variable" information—a number of rows in the table:

```
int ha_static_text::info(uint flag)
{
  if (flag & HA_STATUS_VARIABLE)
    stats.records = static_text_rows;
  return 0;
}
```

That's it! Our first storage engine plugin is complete. Now we can compile it, install it, and start playing with it.

This example could be easily extended to generate random data. We could then populate another table by creating a similar schema, setting the number of rows required, and doing:

```
mysql> insert into t1 select * from t2;
```

where t1 is a normal table and t2 is using our random data generator table.

Summary

In this chapter, we have seen the basics of creating a new storage engine plugin and have written a simple read-only engine. We will use this knowledge as a basis for more advanced engines in the following chapters.

9
HTML Storage Engine— Reads and Writes

In the previous chapter, we created a simple read-only MySQL storage engine. Now, we will consider a more complex example, a complete read-write storage engine, but with no support for indexes. Let's say, it will be an "html" engine—an engine that stores tables in HTML files. Such a file can be later loaded in a web browser and the table will be shown as an HTML table.

An idea of the HTML engine

Ever thought about what your tables might *look* like? Why not represent a table as a <TABLE>? You would be able to *see* it, visually, in any browser. Sounds cool. But how could we make it work?

We want a simple engine, not an all-purpose Swiss Army Knife HTML-to-SQL converter, which means we will not need any existing universal HTML or XML parsers, but can rely on a fixed file format. For example, something like this:

```
<html><head><title>t1</title></head><body><table border=1>
<tr><th>col1</th><th>other col</th><th>more cols</th></tr>
<tr><td>data</td><td>more data</td><td>more data</td></tr>
<!-- this row was deleted ...                           -->
<tr><td>data</td><td>more data</td><td>more data</td></tr>
```
... and so on ...
```
</table></body></html>
```

But even then this engine is way more complex than the previous example, and it makes sense to split the code. The engine could stay, as usual, in the `ha_html.cc` file, the declarations in `ha_html.h`, and if we need any utility functions to work with HTML we can put them in the `htmlutils.cc` file.

Flashback

As we have seen in a previous chapter, a storage engine needs to declare a plugin and an initialization function that fills a `handlerton` structure. Again, the only `handlerton` method that we need here is a `create()` method.

```
#include "ha_html.h"

static handler* html_create_handler(handlerton *hton,
                    TABLE_SHARE *table, MEM_ROOT *mem_root)
{
  return new (mem_root) ha_html(hton, table);
}

static int html_init(void *p)
{
  handlerton *html_hton = (handlerton *)p;
  html_hton->create = html_create_handler;
  return 0;
}

struct st_mysql_storage_engine html_storage_engine =
{ MYSQL_HANDLERTON_INTERFACE_VERSION };

mysql_declare_plugin(html)
{
  MYSQL_STORAGE_ENGINE_PLUGIN,
  &html_storage_engine,
  "HTML",
  "Sergei Golubchik",
  "An example HTML storage engine",
  PLUGIN_LICENSE_GPL,
  html_init,
  NULL,
  0x0001,
  NULL,
  NULL,
  NULL
}
mysql_declare_plugin_end;
```

Now we need to implement all of the required `handler` class methods, as described in the previous chapter. Let's start with simple ones:

```
const char *ha_html::table_type() const
{
  return "HTML";
}

const char **ha_html::bas_ext() const
{
  static const char *exts[] = { ".html", 0 };
  return exts;
}

ulong ha_html::index_flags(uint inx, uint part, bool all_parts) const
{
  return 0;
}

ulonglong ha_html::table_flags() const
{
  return HA_NO_TRANSACTIONS | HA_REC_NOT_IN_SEQ | HA_NO_BLOBS;
}

THR_LOCK_DATA **ha_html::store_lock(THD *thd,
          THR_LOCK_DATA **to, enum thr_lock_type lock_type)
{
  if (lock_type != TL_IGNORE && lock.type == TL_UNLOCK)
    lock.type = lock_type;
  *to ++= &lock;
  return to;
}
```

These methods are familiar to us. They say that the engine is called "HTML", it stores the table data in files with the `.html` extension, the tables are not transactional, the position for `ha_html::rnd_pos()` is obtained by calling `ha_html::position()`, and that it does not support BLOBs. Also, as we have seen in the previous chapter, we need a function to create and initialize an `HTML_SHARE` structure:

```
static HTML_SHARE *find_or_create_share(
                      const char *table_name, TABLE *table)
{
  HTML_SHARE *share;
  for (share = (HTML_SHARE*)table->s->ha_data;
```

```
            share; share = share->next)

      if (my_strcasecmp(table_alias_charset,
                        table_name, share->name) == 0)
         return share;
   share = (HTML_SHARE*)alloc_root(&table->s->mem_root,
                                     sizeof(*share));
   bzero(share, sizeof(*share));
   share->name = strdup_root(&table->s->mem_root, table_name);
   share->next = (HTML_SHARE*)table->s->ha_data;
   table->s->ha_data = share;
   return share;
}
```

It is exactly the same function, only the structure is now called HTML_SHARE, not STATIC_SHARE.

Creating, opening, and closing the table

Having done the basics, we can start working with the tables. The first operation, of course, is the table creation. To be able to read, update, or even open the table we need to create it first, right? Now, the table is just an HTML file and to create a table we only need to create an HTML file with our header and footer, but with no data between them. Just like in the previous chapter, we do not need to create any TABLE or Field objects, or anything else—MySQL does it automatically. To avoid repeating the same HTML tags over and over we will define the header and the footer in the ha_html.h file as follows:

```
#define HEADER1 "<html><head><title>"
#define HEADER2 "</title></head><body><table border=1>\n"
#define FOOTER "</table></body></html>"
#define FOOTER_LEN ((int)(sizeof(FOOTER)-1))
```

As we want a header to include a table name we have split it in two parts. Now, we can create our table:

```
int ha_html::create(const char *name, TABLE *table_arg,
                    HA_CREATE_INFO *create_info)
{
   char buf[FN_REFLEN+10];
   strcpy(buf, name);
   strcat(buf, *bas_ext());
```

We start by generating a filename. The "table name" that the storage engine gets is not the original table name, it is converted to be a safe filename. All "troublesome" characters are encoded, and the database name is included and separated from the table name with a slash. It means we can safely use name as the filename and all we need to do is to append an extension. Having the filename, we open it and write our data:

```
FILE *f = fopen(buf, "w");
if (f == 0)
   return errno;
fprintf(f, HEADER1);
write_html(f, table_arg->s->table_name.str);
fprintf(f, HEADER2 "<tr>");
```

First, we write the header and the table name. Note that we did not write the value of the name argument into the header, but took the table name from the TABLE_SHARE structure (as table_arg->s->table_name.str), because name is mangled to be a safe filename, and we would like to see the original table name in the HTML page title. Also, we did not just write it into the file, we used a write_html() function— this is our utility method that performs the necessary entity encoding to get a well-formed HTML. But let's not think about it too much now, just remember that we need to write it, it can be done later.

Now, we iterate over all fields and write their names wrapped in <th>...</th> tags. Again, we rely on our write_html() function here:

```
for (uint i = 0; i < table_arg->s->fields; i++) {
   fprintf(f, "<th>");
   write_html(f, table_arg->field[i]->field_name);
   fprintf(f, "</th>");
}
fprintf(f, "</tr>");
fprintf(f, FOOTER);
fclose(f);
return 0;
}
```

Done, an empty table is created.

Opening it is easy too. We generate the filename and open the file just as in the `create()` method. The only difference is that we need to remember the `FILE` pointer to be able to read the data later, and we store it in `fhtml`, which has to be a member of the `ha_html` object:

```
int ha_html::open(const char *name, int mode,
                  uint test_if_locked)
{
  char buf[FN_REFLEN+10];
  strcpy(buf, name);
  strcat(buf, *bas_ext());
  fhtml = fopen(buf, "r+");
  if (fhtml == 0)
    return errno;
```

When parsing an HTML file we will often need to skip over known patterns in the text. Instead of using a special library or a custom pattern parser for that, let's try to use `scanf()` — it exists everywhere, has a built-in pattern matching language, and it is powerful enough for our purposes. For convenience, we will wrap it in a `skip_html()` function that takes a `scanf()` format and returns the number of bytes skipped. Assuming we have such a function, we can finish opening the table:

```
skip_html(fhtml, HEADER1 "%*[^<]" HEADER2 "<tr>");
for (uint i = 0; i < table->s->fields; i++) {
  skip_html(fhtml, "<th>%*[^<]</th>");
}
skip_html(fhtml, "</tr>");

data_start = ftell(fhtml);
```

We skip the first part of the header, then "everything up to the opening angle bracket", which eats up the table name, and the second part of the header. Then we skip individual row headers in a loop and the end of row `</tr>` tag. In order not to repeat this parsing again we remember the offset where the row data starts. At the end we allocate an `HTML_SHARE` and initialize lock objects:

```
share = find_or_create_share(name, table);
if (share->use_count++ == 0)
  thr_lock_init(&share->lock);
thr_lock_data_init(&share->lock,&lock,NULL);
return 0;
}
```

Closing the table is simple, and should not come as a surprise to us. It is almost the same as `ha_static_text::close()` from the previous chapter:

```
int ha_html::close(void)
{
  fclose(fhtml);
  if (--share->use_count == 0)
    thr_lock_delete(&share->lock);
  return 0;
}
```

Reading data

As we have learned in the previous chapter, an indexless table can be read using two access patterns—either sequential, with `rnd_init()` and `rnd_next()` methods, or a random one with `position()` and `rnd_pos()` methods. Let's start with the former:

```
int ha_html::rnd_next(unsigned char *buf)
{
  fseek(fhtml, current_row_end, SEEK_SET);
  for (;;) {
```

This is one of the most complex methods in our storage engine. Let's analyze it line by line. We started by positioning the stream at the end of the last read row, and will be looking for the first non-deleted row (remember that a row starts with a `<tr>` tag, while a deleted row starts with `<!--`).

But first we save the offset of the row that we will read, as it may be needed for `position()`, and check it against the end of data offset:

```
        current_row_start= ftell(fhtml);
        if (current_row_start >= data_end)
          return HA_ERR_END_OF_FILE;
```

This check allows us to skip any processing and return an error at once if we have read all of the rows. It is a minor optimization for a read-only table, but for an updatable table it is of paramount importance. Imagine that we are doing a table scan and the same SQL statement adds new data at the end of the table (which can easily happen in an UPDATE statement). Our table scan should ignore all of the rows that were added in the same statement, and if we remember where the row data ends in the file, we can stop reading at that offset. For this to work, data_end needs to be recalculated at the beginning of every statement. Indeed, as the table may be growing, it is not enough to do it in the open() method. We will talk about statement boundaries later. On the other hand, data_start can never change, we can determine it only once.

```
if (skip_html(fhtml, "<tr>") == 4)
  break;
```

Now, we can start reading the data. First, we read and skip over the <tr> tag. If it was successful, and we have skipped over four characters, we have found our row, and can break out of the loop.

```
if (skip_html(fhtml, "!--%*[^-]-->\n") >=7)
  continue;
```

Otherwise we try to match a deleted row. As the opening angle bracket was already matched and consumed by the previous skip_html() we omit it from the pattern. If there was a match, we restart the loop.

```
    return HA_ERR_CRASHED;
}
```

Otherwise we return an error, complaining that the table is corrupted.

```
my_bitmap_map *old_map =
        dbug_tmp_use_all_columns(table, table->write_set);
my_ptrdiff_t offset = (my_ptrdiff_t)(buf-table->record[0]);

for (uint i = 0; i < table->s->fields; i++) {
  Field *field = table->field[i];
  field->move_field_offset(offset);
```

This loop over all fields and the two assignments before it are the same as in the previous chapter.

```
if (skip_html(fhtml, "<%*[td/]>") == 5)
  field->set_null();
else {
```

Here we skip "an angle bracket, any sequence of characters t, d, /, and a closing angle bracket". If we have skipped five characters, it was a `<td/>` tag, which stands for a NULL value, otherwise it was an opening `<td>` tag, and we need to read the value of the field:

```
char *buf = (char*)
                malloc(field->max_display_length() + 1);
int buf_len = read_html(fhtml, buf);
field->set_notnull();
field->store(buf, buf_len, &my_charset_bin);
skip_html(fhtml, "</td>");
free(buf);
```

To read the value we allocate a buffer, big enough to hold the string representation of the field value, and read the value using our `read_html()` function—a counterpart of `write_html()` that converts HTML entities back into characters. Then we mark the field as holding a NOT NULL value, and store the string value in the field. As we have seen in the Information Schema chapters, the field—an object of the Field class—automatically performs all of the necessary conversion from a string to a number, a date, or whatever the field type is. Then we skip the closing `</td>` tag and free the buffer.

An inquisitive reader may have noticed that calling `malloc()` and `free()` for every field in every row during a table scan does not indicate performance-conscious programming. He would be right—it would be better to allocate the buffer once, big enough to hold a value of any field. It could have been done in the `ha_html::open()` method, because field lengths cannot change after a table is opened. We will do this optimization in the next chapter.

```
    }
    field->move_field_offset(-offset);
  }
  skip_html(fhtml, "</tr>\n");
  dbug_tmp_restore_column_map(table->write_set, old_map);
  current_row_end = ftell(fhtml);
  return 0;
}
```

We finish reading a row by restoring field offsets and a `write_set` bitmap, skipping the closing `</tr>` tag, and remembering the offset where the row ended.

```
int ha_html::rnd_init(bool scan)
{
  current_row_start = 0;
  current_row_end = data_start;
  return 0;
}
```

In this function, we need to prepare for a sequential table scan. All we need to do is to initialize `current_row_start` and `current_row_end`. As we start reading a new row from the `current_row_end` offset, we should set it here to the `data_start` offset, that is to the beginning of the very first row. Additionally, we reset `current_row_start` to indicate that no row has been read yet.

```
void ha_html::position(const uchar *record)
{
  *(ulong*)ref = current_row_start;
}
```

This method is very simple. A unique row identifier, in our case, is the file offset to the row data. That is, all we need to do here is to store the offset of the current row at the `ref` pointer.

```
int ha_html::rnd_pos(uchar * buf, uchar *pos)
{
  memcpy(&current_row_end, pos, sizeof(current_row_end));
  return rnd_next(buf);
}
```

Reading a row at the given *position* is easy too. We only restore the position into `current_row_end` and let our `rnd_next()` method to do the rest of the job.

Updating the table

There are three primary methods that modify the table data. They are `write_row()`, `delete_row()`, and `update_row()`, which are used by the INSERT, DELETE, and UPDATE statements accordingly. In our engine, `write_row()` is the most complex one.

```
int ha_html::write_row(uchar *buf)
{
  if (table->timestamp_field_type &
      TIMESTAMP_AUTO_SET_ON_INSERT)
    table->timestamp_field->set_time();
  if (table->next_number_field && buf == table->record[0]) {
    int error;
    if ((error= update_auto_increment()))
      return error;
  }
```

Almost every engine's `write_row()` method starts with these lines. They update the values of the TIMESTAMP and AUTO_INCREMENT fields, if necessary. Strictly speaking, the second — AUTO_INCREMENT — block is not needed here. Our engine does not support indexes, that is, it can never have an AUTO_INCREMENT field.

```
fseek(fhtml, -FOOTER_LEN, SEEK_END);
fprintf(fhtml, "<tr>");
```

We write a new row at the end of the file. That is, we position the stream at the end, just before the footer, and start a new row with an opening `<tr>` tag.

```
my_bitmap_map *old_map =
            dbug_tmp_use_all_columns(table, table->read_set);
my_ptrdiff_t offset = (my_ptrdiff_t)(buf-table->record[0]);

for (uint i = 0; i < table->s->fields; i++) {
  Field *field = table->field[i];
  field->move_field_offset(offset);
```

Now we iterate over the fields in a loop very similar to the one in `rnd_next()`, only it modifies the `read_set` bitmap, not the `write_set`.

```
if (field->is_null())
  fprintf(fhtml, "<td/>");
```

If the field value is NULL we write it down as `<td/>` to be able to distinguish it from the empty string (which is written as `<td></td>`), otherwise we take the field value and write it to the file:

```
else {
  char tmp_buf[1024];
  String tmp(tmp_buf, sizeof(tmp_buf), &my_charset_bin);
  String *val = field->val_str(&tmp, &tmp);
```

The `val_*` family of `Field` methods — `val_str()`, `val_int()`, `val_real()`, and `val_decimal()` return the value of the `Field`, converted to a corresponding type. To store it in the HTML file, obviously, we want the value converted to a string, that is, we need to use `val_str()`. This method takes two arguments, pointers to `String` objects. The `Field::val_str()` method may use either the first or a second, depending on whether it needs a memory buffer or not. However, as a caller we can simply pass the same `String` in both arguments.

To recall the Information Schema chapter, the class String is a utility class for working, well, with strings. An object of the String class represents a string as a pointer, string length in bytes, and string character set. It knows whether the string was allocated or not. It can reallocate it as the string grows and as expected, it will free the allocated memory on destruction. What is important for us is that it can start off from a fixed buffer and allocate the memory automatically if the string value does not fit. It means that if we create a buffer on the stack we can hope to avoid memory allocations in most cases. Indeed, the above declarations with tmp_buf and String tmp show a typical String usage pattern that can be seen everywhere in the MySQL code.

```
fprintf(fhtml, "<td>");
write_html(fhtml, val->c_ptr());
fprintf(fhtml, "</td>");
```

Here we have used the String::c_ptr() method. It returns the string value as a zero terminated string, appropriate for passing to the fprintf() function.

```
  }
  field->move_field_offset(-offset);
}
dbug_tmp_restore_column_map(table->read_set, old_map);
if (fprintf(fhtml, "</tr>\n" FOOTER) < 6 + FOOTER_LEN)
  return errno;
else
  return 0;
}
```

Having written all of the fields, we restore field offsets and read_set, write the closing </tr> tag and the file footer, and return. Just in case the disk was full we verify that the footer was written in whole.

```
int ha_html::delete_row(const uchar *buf)
{
  assert(current_row_start);
  fseek(fhtml, current_row_start, SEEK_SET);
  fprintf(fhtml, "<!--");
  fseek(fhtml, current_row_end-4, SEEK_SET);
  fprintf(fhtml, "-->\n");
  return 0;
}
```

Compared to `write_row()`, our `delete_row()` method is much simpler. MySQL can only call `delete_row()` for the current row. And because we know where it starts — at the `current_row_start` offset, we can even assert this fact — and we know where it ends, we can easily comment the complete row out, "deleting" it from the HTML table.

```
int ha_html::update_row(const uchar *old_data,
                        uchar *new_data)
{
  assert(current_row_start);
  if (table->timestamp_field_type &
      TIMESTAMP_AUTO_SET_ON_UPDATE)
    table->timestamp_field->set_time();

  delete_row(old_data);
  table->timestamp_field_type = (timestamp_auto_set_type)
    (table->timestamp_field_type &
      ~TIMESTAMP_AUTO_SET_ON_INSERT);

  return write_row(new_data);
}
```

The `update_row()` method is simple too. Just like `write_row()` it starts by updating the `TIMESTAMP` field, but after that we can simply delete the old row and insert the new one at the end of the table. We just need to remember to remove the `TIMESTAMP_AUTO_SET_ON_INSERT` bit to avoid unnecessary `TIMESTAMP` updates; MySQL will restore it for the next statement automatically. Because we have remembered the original "end of table" offset at the beginning of the statement, we do not need to worry that our table scan will read newly inserted data.

Optimizing and analyzing

In our storage engine, even deleted rows take space, and if the table is regularly updated, it will grow even if the number of rows does not increase. It would be nice to implement `OPTIMIZE TABLE` so that users could have a simple tool to reclaim the unused space. Luckily, there is a very easy shortcut, we almost do not need to do anything:

```
int ha_html::optimize(THD* thd, HA_CHECK_OPT* check_opt)
{
  return HA_ADMIN_TRY_ALTER;
}
```

This tells MySQL that for our engine, OPTIMIZE TABLE xxx should be mapped to ALTER TABLE xxx ENGINE=HTML. That is, to optimize our table MySQL will create a new table with the same structure, copy all data over to it, and replace the old table with the new one. Nice, isn't it? Unfortunately, at least in MySQL 5.1.47 there is a bug that will cause our OPTIMIZE TABLE to fail unless our engine can do ANALYZE TABLE too. As a workaround we implement a dummy analyze() that succeeds without actually doing anything:

```
int ha_html::analyze(THD* thd, HA_CHECK_OPT* check_opt)
{
  return 0;
}
```

What's left

Not much. The obligatory info() method – although we cannot do much here, we do not even know the number of rows in the table. Let's just return something – MySQL will not take this value too seriously, because we do not have the HA_STATS_RECORDS_IS_EXACT flag in table_flags():

```
int ha_html::info(uint flag)
{
  if (flag & HA_STATUS_VARIABLE)
    stats.records = 10;
  return 0;
}
```

Then, there is the external_lock() method. It is an important method – with a few exceptions MySQL calls it at the beginning and at the end of every statement. The name is historical, MyISAM and pre-MyISAM engines stored tables in files – just like our engine does – but used file locking to prevent multiple processes from modifying the same table file in parallel. The method "external lock" was designed to allow the engine to take this (external for MySQL) lock, after MySQL has taken its own "internal" table lock. The second argument of external_lock() is either F_UNLCK (at the end of the statement) or F_RDLCK or F_WRLCK (at the beginning of the statement). We can use this method to remember the data_end offset, as discussed before:

```
int ha_html::external_lock(THD *thd, int lock_type)
{
  if (lock_type != F_UNLCK) {
    fseek(fhtml, -FOOTER_LEN, SEEK_END);
    data_end = ftell(fhtml);
  }
```

```
        else
          fflush(fhtml);
        return 0;
}
```

See how we flush the write buffer at the end of the statement? When the statement ends, MySQL removes its table lock from our table and another thread may start using it. If that thread opens the file and starts reading it, it needs to see all of the data — we cannot allow half of the inserted rows to sit in the write buffer after the statement ends.

So far so good, but there is one problem — under LOCK TABLES the method external_lock() is *not* called at the beginning of every statement. Because external_lock() has already locked its file during the LOCK TABLES statement, MySQL does not see a reason to call external_lock() again as the file is still locked. It may be fine for file locking and MyISAM, but we need to know when the statement starts even under LOCK TABLES! For this very reason MySQL developers have introduced a separate method, start_stmt(), which is called at the beginning of every statement under LOCK TABLES. For our engine we can simply call external_lock() here, to save the data_end offset.

```
    int ha_html::start_stmt(THD *thd, thr_lock_type lock_type)
    {
        return external_lock(thd, F_WRLCK);
    }
```

There is no end_stmt() method, but we do not need one anyway — we do not have to flush the write buffer at the end of every statement under LOCK TABLES, because while LOCK TABLES is in effect no other thread can read the table we are writing to.

ha_html.h

Having written all of the methods, we can complete the class declaration. This is what our ha_html.h header should look like:

```
    #include <mysql_priv.h>

    #define HEADER1 "<html><head><title>"
    #define HEADER2 "</title></head><body><table border=1>\n"
    #define FOOTER  "</table></body></html>"
    #define FOOTER_LEN  ((int)(sizeof(FOOTER)-1))

    typedef struct st_html_share {
      const char *name;
      THR_LOCK lock;
```

```
    uint use_count;
    struct st_html_share *next;
} HTML_SHARE;

class ha_html: public handler
{
private:
    THR_LOCK_DATA lock;
    HTML_SHARE *share;
    FILE *fhtml;
    off_t data_start, data_end;
    off_t current_row_start, current_row_end;

public:
    ha_html(handlerton *hton, TABLE_SHARE *table_arg)
        handler(hton, table_arg) { }

    const char *table_type() const;
    const char **bas_ext() const;
    ulong index_flags(uint inx,
                              uint part, bool all_parts) const;
    ulonglong table_flags() const;
    THR_LOCK_DATA **store_lock(THD *thd,
            THR_LOCK_DATA **to, enum thr_lock_type lock_type);
    int create(const char *name, TABLE *table_arg,
               HA_CREATE_INFO *create_info);
    int open(const char *name, int mode,
            uint test_if_locked);
    int close(void);
    int rnd_next(unsigned char *buf);
    int rnd_init(bool scan);
    void position(const uchar *record);
    int rnd_pos(uchar * buf, uchar *pos);
    int write_row(uchar *buf);
    int delete_row(const uchar *buf);
    int update_row(const uchar *old_data,
                     uchar *new_data);
    int optimize(THD* thd, HA_CHECK_OPT* check_opt);
    int analyze(THD* thd, HA_CHECK_OPT* check_opt);
    int info(uint flag);
    int external_lock(THD *thd, int lock_type);
    int start_stmt(THD *thd, thr_lock_type lock_type);
};

void write_html(FILE *f, char *str);
int read_html(FILE *f, char *buf);
int skip_html(FILE *f, const char *pattern);
```

htmlutils.cc

Implementing the utility functions that we used—`write_html()`, `read_html()`, and `skip_html()`—is straightforward:

```cpp
#include "ha_html.h"

void write_html(FILE *f, char *str)
{
  for (; *str; str++)
  {
    switch (*str) {
    case '<': fputs("&lt;", f); break;
    case '>': fputs("&gt;", f); break;
    case '&': fputs("&amp;", f); break;
    case '-': fputs("&ndash;", f); break;
    default: fputc(*str, f); break;
    }
  }
}
```

This function writes a string to an HTML file, encoding "unsafe" characters. As a bonus it also encodes a hyphen (-), because it allows us to skip deleted rows—HTML comments—very easily. As no row can ever contain a hyphen, we skip "from `<!--` and up to the next hyphen".

```cpp
int read_html(FILE *f, char *buf)
{
  int c;
  char *start = buf;
  while ((c = fgetc(f)) != '<') {
    if (c == '&') {
      char entity[21];
      fscanf(f, "%20[^;];", entity);
      if (strcmp(entity, "lt") == 0) { c = '<'; }
      else
      if (strcmp(entity, "gt") == 0) { c = '>'; }
      else
      if (strcmp(entity, "amp") == 0) { c = '&'; }
      else
      if (strcmp(entity, "ndash") == 0) { c = '-'; }
    }
    *buf++ = c;
  }
  ungetc(c, f);
  *buf=0;
  return buf - start;
}
```

This function does the opposite to `write_html()` — it reads the data from the HTML file up to the angle bracket, replacing entities with characters.

```
int skip_html(FILE *f, const char *pattern)
{
  long old=ftell(f);
  fscanf(f, pattern);
  return ftell(f) - old;
}
```

This is our `fscanf()` wrapper that parses a text using a `scanf()` pattern and returns the number of skipped characters. Of course, when we call it we should take extra care to use only "skipping" (`%*`) patterns, that mean "parse the input and discard it", and not any of the "normal" patterns, that mean "parse the input and store it in the supplied variable".

Compiling and linking

Our engine from the previous chapter and all other plugins had to be built manually — anybody wanting to use them needed to invoke the compiler with the correct options. This is error prone and if we were to distribute a storage engine like this our users certainly would not appreciate this manual building process. For this engine, we will try to automate the building as described in the first chapter. We will need to create three files — `plug.in`, `Makefile.am`, and `CMakeLists.txt`.

We can copy the `plug.in` file from the first chapter almost verbatim. Our new engine will only work with HTML files of a predefined fixed structure. It will not use a general purpose HTML parser, and thus we will not need to check for any libraries in `MYSQL_PLUGIN_ACTIONS`. Our `plug.in` file can be just:

```
MYSQL_PLUGIN(html,[HTML Storage Engine],
                  [Storage Engine that writes an HTML file], [max])
MYSQL_PLUGIN_STATIC(html, [libha_html.a])
MYSQL_PLUGIN_DYNAMIC(html, [ha_html.la])
```

Similarly we create a `Makefile.am` file from the example in the first chapter:

```
pkgplugindir = $(pkglibdir)/plugin

INCLUDES = -I$(top_srcdir)/include   \
           -I$(top_builddir)/include \
           -I$(top_srcdir)/sql

pkgplugin_LTLIBRARIES = @plugin_html_shared_target@
ha_html_la_LDFLAGS = -module -rpath $(pkgplugindir)
ha_html_la_CXXFLAGS= -DMYSQL_DYNAMIC_PLUGIN
```

```
ha_html_la_SOURCES = ha_html.cc htmlutils.cc

noinst_LIBRARIES = @plugin_html_static_target@
libha_html_a_SOURCES= ha_html.cc htmlutils.cc

EXTRA_LTLIBRARIES = ha_html.la
EXTRA_LIBRARIES = libha_html.a

EXTRA_DIST = CMakeLists.txt plug.in
noinst_HEADERS = ha_html.h
```

The only new line is the one with `noinst_HEADERS`. This variable lists all header files that should not be installed, but should be included in a source distribution, our `ha_html.h` being such a file.

As with the two previous files, we copy `CMakeLists.txt` from the first chapter:

```
INCLUDE(
    "${PROJECT_SOURCE_DIR}/storage/mysql_storage_engine.cmake")
SET(HTML_SOURCES ha_html.cc htmlutils.cc)
MYSQL_STORAGE_ENGINE(HTML)
```

All files in place, we need to re-run autotools — `autoreconf -f` — configure the source — simply `./configure` for a dynamically built plugin, or `./configure --with-plugin-html` for a statically built plugin (while `./configure --without-plugin-html` will prevent the plugin from being built at all) — build the MySQL together with our plugin — `make` — and install it — `make install`.

Putting it all together

Let's install the plugin and see how it works:

```
mysql> install plugin html soname 'ha_html.so';

Query OK, 0 rows affected (0.00 sec)
```

Keep in mind that if a plugin was built statically into the server, it does not need to be installed.

```
mysql> create table test (number int, timestamp timestamp, string
varchar(50)) engine=html;

Query OK, 0 rows affected (0.01 sec)


mysql> insert test values (1,null,"foo"), (2, "2010-01-02 03:04:05",
"barbarbar"), (5,0,NULL);

Query OK, 3 rows affected (0.00 sec)

Records: 3  Duplicates: 0  Warnings: 0
```

```
mysql> select * from test;

+--------+---------------------+-----------+
| number | timestamp           | string    |
+--------+---------------------+-----------+
|      1 | 2010-06-29 18:23:18 | foo       |
|      2 | 2010-01-02 03:04:05 | barbarbar |
|      5 | 0000-00-00 00:00:00 | NULL      |
+--------+---------------------+-----------+

3 rows in set (0.00 sec)
```

It looks like it works. INSERT works, SELECT works, NULL values can be stored, and the TIMESTAMP column is automatically updated.

```
mysql> update test set number=10 where string="foo";

Query OK, 1 row affected (0.00 sec)

Rows matched: 1  Changed: 1  Warnings: 0


mysql> delete from test where string is null;

Query OK, 1 row affected (0.00 sec)


mysql> select * from test;

+--------+---------------------+-----------+
| number | timestamp           | string    |
+--------+---------------------+-----------+
|      2 | 2010-01-02 03:04:05 | barbarbar |
|     10 | 2010-06-29 18:23:18 | foo       |
+--------+---------------------+-----------+

2 rows in set (0.00 sec)


mysql> optimize table test\G

*************************** 1. row ***************************

   Table: test.test

      Op: optimize

Msg_type: note

Msg_text: Table does not support optimize, doing recreate + analyze
instead

*************************** 2. row ***************************

   Table: test.test

      Op: optimize

Msg_type: status
```

```
Msg_text: OK
2 rows in set (0.01 sec)


mysql> insert test values (100,"2001-09-08 07:06:05", "a row"), (101,
"2020-03-14 17:18:28", "one more row");
Query OK, 2 rows affected (0.00 sec)
Records: 2  Duplicates: 0  Warnings: 0
```

Everything works! And this is what our table *looks* like:

Summary

In this chapter, we have learned the methods needed to create a storage engine with a full read/write support, and created an example engine that stores the data in HTML files.

In the next, the last in the storage engine series, chapter, we will see what it takes to write a storage engine that supports indexes.

10
TOCAB Storage Engine— Implementing Indexes

In this chapter, we will implement the most complex plugin of the book. Indexes are crucial for the performance of the storage engine and a big part of Storage Engine API deals with indexes, different types of indexes, various ways of using them, and numerous index-related optimizations. We will inevitably have to cut corners to keep the size of this chapter in bounds. Although the plugin that we will develop here will be a fully working storage engine, it will be by no means feature complete. At the end of the chapter, we will discuss what this engine is missing and what features it could get to become a usable general purpose storage engine.

B-tree library

There are many different data structures that can be used as "indexes". Most popular are those of the B-tree family and hash tables. However, discussing details of different B-tree or hash table implementations is beyond the scope of this book. For our purposes, we will simply take an existing B-tree implementation. There are many libraries providing that or another implementation of some of the B-tree variant. We will build a MySQL storage engine on top of the LGPL licensed *Tokyo Cabinet* library (`http://1978th.net/tokyocabinet/`) by Mikio Hirabayashi. It is fast, simple to use, and reasonably portable. Unfortunately, it does not fit exactly into the MySQL Storage Engine API model—indeed, probably no third-party library does it out of the box—we will need to work around their differences. But first, let's see what the Tokyo Cabinet API looks like.

The library provides different types of storage. It can do hash tables (in memory and on disk), B+ trees (a variant of B-trees), and other, more specialized types. In our engine we will only use the B+tree API of Tokyo Cabinet, although an advanced storage engine could have used them all, selecting the most appropriate storage automatically, depending on the table structure.

A Tokyo Cabinet library supports multi-threaded access to data, but any table file can be opened only once in any process and all threads should access the same open TCBDB (which apparently stands for "Tokyo Cabinet B+tree Data-Base") handle. All records are identified by the corresponding keys. Tokyo Cabinet supports unique as well as non-unique B+tree indexes. It has a notion of cursors, and can use them for scanning and updating the tree. It supports transparent data compression. It allows the caller to specify a custom comparison function for index entries. Any single Tokyo Cabinet data file can have only one index—for example, only one B+tree or one hash table.

What does that mean for us? The table can be opened once and its handle is shared between threads—that is, logically, the TCBDB handle belongs to our TOCAB_SHARE structure, not to the ha_tocab class. Cursors and compression—great, we can use them. Custom comparison function—perfect, no external library would do string comparison in the same way as MySQL does, using all MySQL collations and character sets. In fact, most probably, any B-tree library without the ability to use a custom comparison function would be unusable for us. One index per file—not good, because in MySQL tables may have many indexes, and we need to support it. It is not too difficult though. We could simply create as many files as there are indexes in the table. For example, a table t1 with three indexes would generate at least four files—t1.frm, t1.index1, t1.index2, and t1.index3. An alternative solution would be to put all indexes in one B-tree, prefixing all index values with the index number to be able to distinguish them. This second approach looks cleaner from the end user point of view—only one file per table—and we will give it a try.

We put all indexes in one file, but where do we put the row data? There are two basic approaches—MyISAM stores row data in a separate file, uses an offset in a file as a row *position* and all indexes refer to a row by its *position*. InnoDB and NDB identify a row by its primary key—rows are stored in the index tree of primary keys, and all secondary keys refer to a row by its primary key. In the previous chapter, we saw how to use file offset as a *position*, so let's try the primary key approach here. As a primary key is an index too, it will naturally go into the same B+tree with all other indexes, and our table will nicely fit in one file, all indexes and row data together.

Storage engine API for indexes

There are quite a few methods in the `handler` class that deal with indexes. Luckily, we do not have to implement every single one of them. Still, it is good to know what methods exist and what possibilities we have. The table below lists most of the `handler` methods related to indexes:

Name	Description
index_type	This is a purely informational method, similar to the `table_type()` method, and it returns a string with the index type. Often, it is either "HASH" or "BTREE", but it can be just anything. For example, Federated engine returns "REMOTE" here. This method takes an index number as an argument, as different indexes may be of different types.
index_flags	This is, too, similar to the `table_flags()` method. It returns a bitmap defining index capabilities that, depending on arguments, describe a whole index, a specific key part (one column in a multi-column index), or an index prefix up to and including a given key part. Index capability flags are listed in the next table.
max_supported_keys max_supported_key_parts max_supported_key_length max_supported_key_part_length	These methods tell MySQL about the engine limits— how many keys per table and key parts per key it supports, and what is the maximal supported key and key part length. MySQL will allow `CREATE` and `ALTER TABLE` statements only if the resulting table will stay within these limits. Most have reasonable defaults, but `max_supported_keys()` has to be overridden. In the base class it returns zero, meaning the engine cannot do indexing.
index_init	This method is called before starting index lookups or traversals. It takes the index number as an argument, and allows the engine to prepare the table for index-based access. The base class implementation simply saves the index number in the `active_index` member
index_end	This is the opposite of `index_init()`. It is called when MySQL has finished accessing the index.
index_read	This is the method that MySQL uses to search in the index. It takes a key to search for, its length, a `find_flag`, and a result buffer as arguments. The index number is specified in the preceding `index_init()`.

Name	Description
index_read_map	Certain index search functions exist in two flavors — one that takes a key and *key length* as arguments, and another that takes a key and a *bitmap of used key parts* as arguments. For example, if a key is created over five columns: **KEY(a,b,c,d,e,f)** and MySQL searches for a key prefix that has only the first three columns set: **WHERE a=1 AND b=2 AND c=3** the bitmap will be 00111 in binary; that is, 7.
index_read_idx_map	The only difference between the index_read_idx_map() method and the index_read_map() method is that it takes the index number as an argument, and does not use index_start() or index_end(). The implementation of this method in the base class simply converts it into a sequence of index_init()... index_read_map()... index_end().
index_read_last index_read_last_map	This is similar to the index_read() method, but asks for the last matching key. MySQL can use it, for example, in ORDER BY ... DESC queries.
index_next	This method can be called after index_read(), when MySQL wants to get the next value in the index order after the last found. This is used in index scans or for getting all matching values from a non-unique index.
index_prev	This is just like index_next(), but asks for a previous key in the index order. It can be used in ORDER BY ... DESC.
index_first	This asks for the very first value in the index, or, more precisely, for a row that corresponds to the very first key in the index. MySQL may do that in case of a full index scan or a range query with an upper bound, but without a lower bound.
index_last	This is similar, but asks for the very last value in the index.

Name	Description
index_next_same	It works just like index_next(), but the engine is only expected to return the next row if it has *exactly the same* key as the one that was searched for. On the other hand, index_next() returns the next row independent of its key. This method is implemented in the base handler class by calling index_next() and comparing the key of the returned row.
records_in_range	This method is used by the optimizer. It takes a range (a pair or keys—lower and upper bounds of a range; either one can be unset, meaning an open range) and returns an approximate number of rows that fit into this range. This method does not need to be precise, but it is expected to be fast—the optimizer may call it many times for different indexes and ranges, before it decides which one to use to resolve the query.
read_range_first read_range_next	These two methods work not with individual keys, but with ranges. The first method takes a range, finds a matching row and stores it in table->record[0]. The second method finds another matched row. Just like index_next() it is usually called in a loop until no more rows are found. Only engines that benefit from knowing both range ends in advance will benefit from implementing these methods; others can rely on the base class implementation that converts them into a sequence of index_read() and index_next() calls.
read_multi_range_first read_multi_range_next	This is an even higher level of batching. The methods work with an array of ranges. This can be useful for a clustered storage—the engine can feed all ranges to the appropriate nodes and start receiving the data in parallel, instead of requesting one row at time, wasting a network round-trip per row. Most engines do not implement these methods—the base class implementation turns them into a sequence of read_range_first() and read_range_next().
preload_keys	This is called when a user runs the LOAD INDEX INTO CACHE statement. The engine can use it to read index pages into the memory cache to speed up future index reads. This is only used by MyISAM.

Describing the engine

We already know a great deal about storage engine plugins and can write the basic skeleton fairly quickly:

```c
#include "ha_tocab.h"

static handler* tocab_create_handler(handlerton *hton,
                    TABLE_SHARE *table, MEM_ROOT *mem_root)
{
  return new (mem_root) ha_tocab(hton, table);
}

static int tocab_init(void *p)
{
  handlerton *tocab_hton = (handlerton *)p;
  tocab_hton->create = tocab_create_handler;
  return 0;
}

struct st_mysql_storage_engine tocab_storage_engine =
{MYSQL_HANDLERTON_INTERFACE_VERSION };

mysql_declare_plugin(tocab)
{
  MYSQL_STORAGE_ENGINE_PLUGIN,
  &tocab_storage_engine,
  "TOCAB",
  "Sergei Golubchik",
  "An example storage engine that uses Tokyo Cabinet library",
  PLUGIN_LICENSE_GPL,
  tocab_init,
  NULL,
  0x0001,
  NULL,
  NULL,
  NULL
}
mysql_declare_plugin_end;
```

This declares a plugin and provides an initialization function. As usual, we need a function to create a share:

```
static TOCAB_SHARE *find_or_create_share(
                        const char *table_name, TABLE *table)
{
  TOCAB_SHARE *share;
  for (share = (TOCAB_SHARE*)table->s->ha_data;
         share; share = share->next)
    if (my_strcasecmp(table_alias_charset,
                       table_name, share->name) == 0)
      return share;
  share = (TOCAB_SHARE*)alloc_root(&table->s->mem_root,
                                   sizeof(*share));
  bzero(share, sizeof(*share));
  share->name = strdup_root(&table->s->mem_root, table_name);
  share->next = (TOCAB_SHARE*)table->s->ha_data;
  table->s->ha_data = share;
  return share;
}
```

This looks exactly as in previous chapters. The same applies to the `store_lock()` method — it has not changed at all either:

```
THR_LOCK_DATA **ha_tocab::store_lock(THD *thd,
          THR_LOCK_DATA **to, enum thr_lock_type lock_type)
{
  if (lock_type != TL_IGNORE && lock.type == TL_UNLOCK)
    lock.type = lock_type;
  *to ++= &lock;
  return to;
}
```

Our `table_type()` and `bas_ext()` methods, although not completely identical, are still very similar to what we have seen earlier:

```
const char *ha_tocab::table_type() const { return "TOCAB"; }

const char **ha_tocab::bas_ext() const {
  static const char *exts[] = { ".tocab", 0 };
  return exts;
}
```

Unfortunately, we cannot copy the rest of the engine from the previous chapter. Everything else here needs to be written anew, and, simple things first, we start with the `index_type()` and `max_supported_keys()` methods:

```
const char *ha_tocab::index_type(uint key_number)
{
  return "BTREE";
}
```

```
uint ha_tocab::max_supported_keys() const { return 128; }
```

We say that our indexes are of the "BTREE" type (ignoring the detail that they will be, in fact, B+trees), and we say that our engine supports up to 128 indexes per table. The limit comes from using seven bits—one byte minus one bit that will be needed later—to store the index number in the key prefix. We could have used more bytes or implemented a variable length encoding here and supported more indexes, but let's keep things simple. Besides, MySQL by default only supports 64 indexes per table, and no engine will be allowed to use more than that.

Now, let's do the `index_flags()` method. It is not completely unfamiliar, we had it in previous chapters too, as an abstract method of the base `handler` class, defined in every descendant class. But, until now, we did not really care what it returned, it was never expected to be called, as `max_supported_keys()` was always returning zero. In this chapter, we changed `max_supported_keys()` and we need to use `index_flags()` to tell MySQL what our indexes can do out of the following:

Flag	Description
HA_READ_NEXT	It is supposed to mean that the table supports the `index_next()` method for this index. But in fact, this flag is never checked; MySQL assumes that `index_next()` is always supported.
HA_READ_PREV	This flag means that `index_prev()` is supported. Unlike HA_READ_NEXT, MySQL actually checks this capability and will not invoke `index_prev()` unless this flag is set.
HA_READ_ORDER	Traversing the index with `index_next()` or `index_prev()` will return values in the sort order. For example, MySQL can read rows from the index and avoid sorting them for an ORDER BY clause. This is usually true for B-tree based indexes, and usually not true for hash-based indexes.

Flag	Description
HA_READ_RANGE	The index can be used to find all records in a range. If an index returns values in the sort order, it can do ranges too, automatically. Indexes that do not preserve sort order sometimes can do ranges anyway, but they will need the special read_range_first() and read_range_next() methods, the default implementation will not work correctly for them.
HA_ONLY_WHOLE_INDEX	The index cannot search for a prefix of a key, say, when only the first two columns out of a three-column index have values. Hash indexes usually have this flag set.
HA_KEYREAD_ONLY	The index supports a so called *keyread* optimization. MySQL gives a HA_EXTRA_KEYREAD hint to an engine for a query when it decides to use an index and this index is *covering* – all columns that this query uses are part of the index. For example:
	`SELECT a FROM tbl WHERE a > 5;`
	assuming the column a is indexed. In such a case, the engine does not need to return the complete row, but can only restore the columns that are part of the key; in a sense, "unpack" the key into a row. The HA_KEYREAD_ONLY flag tells MySQL that the engine can do that and it will be faster than reading the whole row.

Now, we can write our very own `index_flags()` method. Our indexes are B-tree like, and they can do pretty much everything from the previous table:

```
ulong ha_tocab::index_flags(uint inx, uint part,
                            bool all_parts) const
{
  return HA_READ_NEXT | HA_READ_PREV | HA_READ_ORDER |
    HA_READ_RANGE | (inx ? HA_KEYREAD_ONLY : 0);
}
```

The `index_flags()` method returns a bitmap of flags describing the capabilities of the key part `part` of the index `inx`. If `all_parts` is set, the bitmap describes capabilities of the index prefix from the first and up to the key part `part` (including all of the intermediate key parts, that is), otherwise it describes only the key part `part`. However, in our engine the capabilities do not depend on the key part, they are always the same — a B+tree in Tokyo Cabinet can be traversed either forward, using `tcbdbcurnext()`, or backward, using `tcbdbcurprev()`. All keys in B+tree are naturally ordered according to our custom comparison functions, and thus can do ranges too. Since we will store column values in their original form, we will be able to copy them from the key back into the row buffer, thus supporting the *keyread* optimization.

Let's talk a bit more about *keyread*. Remember that our *position* is the primary key and all secondary keys refer to a row by its primary key. It means that for every search by a secondary key we need to perform *two* B+tree lookups — first, we look up this secondary key and find a corresponding primary key, then we look up the primary key to find the actual row data. But if this secondary key is *covering*, we do not need to do a second lookup, we can restore key columns in the row buffer from the key. Other columns' values will be undefined, but that is fine, MySQL does not need them. It looks like not only our engine can do *keyread*, but it will also get twice the speed with this optimization! But this is only for secondary keys. For a primary key, this brings no benefits — that is, we should enable `HA_KEYREAD_ONLY` only for secondary keys in our `index_flags()` method. A primary key in MySQL is always the first, key number 0, and we disable *keyread* for it.

And note another fine detail — when we read from a secondary index we know not only the secondary key, but also a corresponding primary key. That is, in the *keyread* optimization we know values for all columns that are part of this secondary key and all columns that are part of the primary key — and after just one index lookup, not two! We can convey this information to MySQL in `table_flags()`:

```
ulonglong ha_tocab::table_flags() const
{
  return HA_NO_TRANSACTIONS |
         HA_TABLE_SCAN_ON_INDEX |
         HA_REC_NOT_IN_SEQ |
         HA_NULL_IN_KEY |
         HA_STATS_RECORDS_IS_EXACT |
         HA_CAN_INDEX_BLOBS |
         HA_AUTO_PART_KEY |
         HA_PRIMARY_KEY_IN_READ_INDEX |
         HA_REQUIRE_PRIMARY_KEY ;
}
```

Recalling the table from *Chapter 8, Storage Engine Plugins*, we see that:

- The tables of the TOCAB engine are not transactional
- Any "sequential table scan" means a random disk access anyway, the optimizer should not assume that sequential table access is much faster than random
- MySQL should use the position() method to obtain the *position*
- NULL values in indexes are supported
- The number of records that the info() method provides is exact, not approximate
- Our engine supports indexes over BLOB fields
- An auto-increment column does not need to be at the beginning of the key
- In the *keyread* optimization the primary key columns are always included no matter what index is selected
- Our engine expects a primary key to exist in all tables

The last requirement is not very user friendly. Most other engines that need a primary key, such as InnoDB, do not force a user to specify it, but generate a hidden primary key automatically, if necessary. However, for simplicity, we will require the end user to create a primary key explicitly — when HA_REQUIRE_PRIMARY_KEY flag is set the CREATE TABLE statement will fail if no primary key is present.

Creating, opening, and closing the table

To open a table in a Tokyo Cabinet one needs to create a new handle with tcbdbnew() and actually open a file with tcbdbopen(). Before opening, one can prepare the handle for multi-threaded use with tcbdbsetmutex(), set a custom comparison function with tcbdbsetcmpfunc(), and set various tuning parameters with tcbdbtune(). MySQL is multi-threaded, so we will use that handle concurrently, and, of course, we will need our comparison function, but we won't do any tuning in our example. There is no special function to create a Tokyo Cabinet file, it is created by opening. That is, both ha_tocab::open() and ha_tocab::create() will open a Tokyo Cabinet file, and we can factor out this functionality in a helper function:

```
static TCBDB *open_tcdb(const char *name, TABLE *table,
                        int *error)
{
  char fname[FN_REFLEN+10];
  strcpy(fname, name);
  strcat(fname, ".tocab");
  *error = 0;
```

```
  TCBDB *dbh = tcbdbnew();
  if (!dbh) {
    *error = HA_ERR_OUT_OF_MEM;
    return 0;
  }
  if (tcbdbsetmutex(dbh) &&
      tcbdbsetcmpfunc(dbh, tocab_compare, table->s) &&
      tcbdbopen(dbh, fname, BDBOWRITER|BDBOCREAT))
    return dbh;
  *error = tc_error(dbh);
  tcbdbdel(dbh);
  return 0;
}
```

This function is not very complex. We generate a filename just like in the previous chapter, create a new `TCBDB` handle, and call other necessary functions listed earlier. In Tokyo Cabinet most functions return `true` to indicate a success and `false` to signal a failure (which can be very confusing if you are used to MySQL conventions, where 0 is returned for a success). The third argument of `tcbdbsetcmpfunc()` is an arbitrary `void*` pointer that Tokyo Cabinet will give to the custom comparison function. We use the `TABLE_SHARE` pointer there, so that in `tocab_compare()` we see the table structure. It must be `TABLE_SHARE`, not a `TABLE` or `ha_tocab` object, because the `TCBDB` handler is shared between all threads, it is stored in the `TABLE_SHARE` structure, and `TABLE_SHARE` may live longer than any individual `TABLE` or `ha_tocab` object. In the case of a failure, we remember the error code and destroy the `TCBDB` handle.

With this helper function, a `create()` method looks almost trivial:

```
int ha_tocab::create(const char *name, TABLE *table_arg,
                 HA_CREATE_INFO *create_info)
{
  int err;
  TCBDB *dbh = open_tcdb(name, table_arg, &err);
  if (dbh) {
    tcbdbclose(dbh);
    tcbdbdel(dbh);
  }
  return err;
}
```

We open a table, which creates it as a side-effect, and close it at once because this method should not leave open tables around, the job of opening in the `handler` class is delegated to the `open()` method. We do not need to worry that this may overwrite an existing table, MySQL does this check for us using its `.frm` files.

The `open()` method is a bit more complex. First of all, it does not necessarily need to open anything, as we decided to put the `TCBDB` handle in `TOCAB_SHARE`, it may as well find the table file already opened. But it will need to create a `BDBCUR` cursor handle as we need a cursor to iterate the table, to allocate memory for a key buffer, and set `ref_length` correctly, and… let's just look at it:

```
int ha_tocab::open(const char *name, int mode,
                    uint test_if_locked)
{
  int err;
  ref_length = table->key_info[0].key_length + 1;
```

First, we set `ref_length` — the length of the *position* — as explained in previous chapters. In this case, our *position* is the primary key. Conveniently, MySQL orders all indexes in a table, putting `UNIQUE` indexes before non-`UNIQUE`, and `PRIMARY KEY` before all others. This means that the primary key is always the key number 0, the first element of the `table->key_info[]` array. We add 1 to the primary key length, because — remember? — we prefix every key with one byte containing the index number to be able to put all indexes in one B+tree.

Later, we will need a buffer to hold one key — for example, in `write_row()` we generate a key based on the row data and insert this key in the index — we can allocate this key buffer now, once, instead of doing it in `write_row()` every time:

```
int max_key_len = 0;
for (int i = 1; i < table->s->keys; i++)
  if (max_key_len < table->key_info[i].key_length)
    max_key_len = table->key_info[i].key_length;
key_buffer = (uchar*)malloc(max_key_len + 1 + ref_length);
```

First, we iterate over all secondary keys (as we start from 1, not from 0) to find the longest one. We want the buffer to be big enough to hold any possible key. But note that we allocate a buffer of `max_key_len + 1 + ref_length`, that is, the length of the longest secondary key plus the prefix byte plus the length of the primary key. It is a trick, and to understand it, we need to look at how the keys will be stored.

Tokyo Cabinet provides an API for storing and retrieving key/value pairs, for example, `tcbdbput()` takes a pointer to a key, this key length, a pointer to a value, and this value length. The API supports both unique and non-unique keys. What it does not support is SQL `NULL` values. The comparison function returns -1, 0, or 1, and one can expect that if `compare(a,b) > 0` then, logically, `compare(b,a) < 0`. But, if both `a` and `b` are `NULL`, we can only say that they are not equal, not which one is larger. And if we return 1, just arbitrarily, to indicate non-equality, how could we know to return -1 when our comparison function is called with exactly the same two arguments (`NULL` and `NULL`), but swapped?

What we need here is to make these two NULL values unique in some way, to be able to distinguish between them and provide a stable sorting order. The trick we use in our engine is to use combined keys. Remember that the task of secondary key indexes is to map a secondary key to a corresponding primary key? NULL is not a problem for primary keys, as all primary key columns are always NOT NULL. But, for every secondary key, instead of using {secondary key, primary key} as a key/value pair in the Tokyo Cabinet B+trees, we will use {secondary key concatenated with primary key, empty string} as a key/value pair. This immediately solves our problem—if two secondary keys are exactly identical, but should be reported as different because they are both NULL, we return -1 or 1 depending on the corresponding primary keys, which are guaranteed to be unique. But the key buffer needs to be big enough to hold the largest secondary key and the primary key together. It is exactly how we allocated it above.

```
if (key_buffer == 0)
  return HA_ERR_OUT_OF_MEM;
share = find_or_create_share(name, table);
if (share->use_count == 0) {
  share->dbh = open_tcdb(name, table, &err);
  if (err) {
    free(key_buffer);
    key_buffer = 0;
    return err;
  }
  thr_lock_init(&share->lock);
}
```

As usual, in the open() method we find (or create) a TOCAB_SHARE structure, and if this share was created we initialize its THR_LOCK member. But we also open our .tocab table file here, because we decided to store its handle in the share.

```
share->use_count++;
thr_lock_data_init(&share->lock,&lock,NULL);
dbcur = tcbdbcurnew(share->dbh);
if (!dbcur) {
  close();
  return HA_ERR_OUT_OF_MEM;
}
keyread = false;
return 0;
}
```

At the end, we create a cursor using the `tcbdbcurnew()` function, initialize the *keyread* optimization indicator, and return. The cursor should be in the handler, not in the share, as there may be many threads reading the table in parallel, all using their own private cursors.

For a change, the `close()` method is very simple—it frees the buffer, destroys the cursor, and, if necessary, closes and destroys the TCBDB handler:

```
int ha_tocab::close(void)
{
  free(key_buffer);
  key_buffer = 0;
  tcbdbcurdel(dbcur);
  dbcur = 0;
  if (--share->use_count == 0) {
    thr_lock_delete(&share->lock);
    tcbdbclose(share->dbh);
    tcbdbdel(share->dbh);
  }
  return 0;
}
```

Searching in the index

`index_read()` is, perhaps, the most complex function in our engine. Not because it is difficult to look up a key in the B+tree, but because there are too many "search modes" in MySQL. But let's get started:

```
int ha_tocab::index_read(uchar *buf, const uchar *key,
              uint key_len, enum ha_rkey_function find_flag)
{
```

Just like `rnd_next()`, from the previous chapter this method takes a pointer to a row buffer as an argument. The row that we will find should be written there. Not surprisingly, two other arguments of this method are key and key length—it is what we will need to search for. But the last argument—what is it? It is this very "search mode" that makes our lives complicated. It can take one of the following values:

Value	Description
HA_READ_KEY_EXACT	In this mode, `index_read()` should find a first row with the key exactly matching the key argument. If no such row exists, it should return HA_ERR_KEY_NOT_FOUND.

Value	Description
HA_READ_AFTER_KEY	In this mode, `index_read()` should find a row with the key that follows the `key` in the index, in other words, the smallest key that is larger than the `key` argument.
HA_READ_KEY_OR_NEXT	Here it should find a smallest key that is larger than or equal to the `key`. That is, if the row with the key of `key` exists, this mode behaves exactly as HA_READ_KEY_EXACT, but if such a row does not exist it behaves as HA_READ_AFTER_KEY.
HA_READ_PREFIX	In this mode, the `key` should match the prefix of the key of the found row. Although in all search modes MySQL can search for a prefix of a key (for example, for a specific value of the `a` field in a KEY (a,b) index), only in this mode can it search for a prefix of a field (first 5 characters in the 20-character string key). This search mode is never used in MySQL 5.1.
HA_READ_KEY_OR_PREV	This is similar to HA_READ_KEY_OR_NEXT— MySQL wants a row with the key, which is smaller than or equal to `key`. In other words, when looking for a key, if we find it, we return it at once. If we do not find it, we take the previous key in the index, the key that had been directly preceding to our key if it would have been in the index. Only the HANDLER statement may use this search mode.
HA_READ_BEFORE_KEY	Similar to HA_READ_AFTER_KEY, this means a request for a largest key which is less than the value of the `key` argument.
HA_READ_PREFIX_LAST	This means a search for a last (in the index order) key that starts from the `key`.
HA_READ_PREFIX_LAST_OR_PREV	This means, not surprisingly, a search for a last key that starts from the `key` or a previous key if a matching key was not found.
HA_READ_MBR_CONTAIN HA_READ_MBR_INTERSECT HA_READ_MBR_WITHIN HA_READ_MBR_DISJOINT HA_READ_MBR_EQUAL	These modes are only used for spatial indexes and we will not discuss them in this book.

These are eight different search modes, all packed in one `index_read()` function. And, of course, Tokyo Cabinet does not support them all natively, we have to implement them in our engine. But fear not, we will do it, one by one.

```
int reclen;
const void *rec;
table->status = STATUS_NOT_FOUND;
```

There are places in the MySQL storage engine API that exist for obscure historical reasons and have no logical explanation these days. One of them is an oh-not-so-easy way of marking the beginning and end of a statement. As we remember, `external_lock()` is invoked at the beginning and at the end of the statement, but not under LOCK TABLES, where `start_stmt()` is called at the beginning of the statement and not at the end, and it is even more difficult in case of nested statements (for example, statements that are part of the trigger that is invoked in the context of another statement). Another is `table->status`. In the early days old MySQL storage engines used the `status` member of the TABLE structure to communicate the result of a search back to the SQL layer. It was never changed and our engine still needs to set `table->status` appropriately, as if the return value of `index_read()` was not enough. The only two values of the `table->status` that we are interested in are STATUS_NOT_FOUND, which should be set when nothing was found and the return value is HA_ERR_KEY_NOT_FOUND, and 0 when the search was successful and the return value is also 0. To satisfy that requirement we start our `index_read()` method from setting `table->status` to STATUS_NOT_FOUND — it will allow us to return any time without a second thought.

```
key_buffer[0] = active_index;
memcpy(key_buffer+1, key, key_len);
key_len++;
```

The next thing we do is generate a key to search for. Our internal search key is the MySQL search key with a one-byte prefix that contains the key number. We take the key number from the `active_index` member of the `handler` class where the `index_init()` method put it.

```
switch (find_flag) {
```

Now, having the key buffer ready, we are fully equipped to perform the search as instructed by the `find_flag` argument. The Tokyo Cabinet API has two sets of functions to search in the B+tree. Functions of the `tcbdbget*` family return the value corresponding to the given key. Functions of the `tcbdbcurjump*` family position the cursor. As after an `index_read()` search MySQL may decide to continue scanning with `index_next()` or `index_prev()` we need to use functions that work with cursors.

We can start with the simple one. `tcbdbcurjump()` has the semantics that matches exactly the `HA_READ_KEY_OR_NEXT` mode. That is, in this mode all we need to do is to call `tcbdbcurjump()`:

```
case HA_READ_KEY_OR_NEXT:
  if (!tcbdbcurjump(dbcur, key_buffer, key_len))
    return tc_error(share->dbh);
  break;
```

Similarly, `tcbdbcurjumpback()` does almost exactly what we need for the `HA_READ_PREFIX_LAST_OR_PREV` mode, but only when we work with complete keys. Prefix searches are difficult, though.

Let's consider an example:

```
CREATE TABLE t (a int, b int, key (a,b));
INSERT INTO t VALUES (1,2),(2,3),(2,3),(3,4);
SELECT * FROM t WHERE a>=2;
```

In such a query MySQL will use `HA_READ_KEY_OR_NEXT`. The index will have four two-part keys: {1,2}, {2,3}, {2,3}, {3,4}, sorted in this order. We are looking for the first key that starts from {2}, and the only way to influence Tokyo Cabinet is by the return value of our `tocab_compare()` function. There are only three ways we can compare a key {2,3} with a key prefix {2}. We can say that the prefix is *less than* a key, that it is *equal* to a key, or that it is *greater than* a key, returning -1, 0, or 1 accordingly. We cannot say that a prefix is equal to a key, in this case Tokyo Cabinet will decide that a match is found and it will return that key. If it is doing a binary search in the sorted list of keys, we can get any of the matching keys returned; if there were a hundred matching keys, any arbitrary one from that hundred. We simply have to say that a prefix is less than or greater than a key, otherwise we will never get stable results. Now think of it — if we need a *first* matching key, like in the `HA_READ_KEY_OR_NEXT` mode, we have to say that the prefix is *less than* a key. But if we want the *last* matching key, for example, for `HA_READ_PREFIX_LAST_OR_PREV`, we want to pretend that the prefix is *greater than* a key! The logic of the prefix comparison depends on the search mode! Unfortunately, Tokyo Cabinet does not allow us to pass the search mode information to the comparison function. We cannot use `TABLE_SHARE` for that because it is shared between threads, and many threads could be searching the index in parallel. We work around this problem, by passing the necessary information to the search function embedded in the key we are searching for. As the `max_supported_keys()` function returns 128, the largest index number that is stored in the `key_buffer[0]` is 127, and we can use the highest bit of the first byte of the key to say that we want a prefix to be larger than a key.

Our implementation of the HA_READ_PREFIX_LAST_OR_PREV mode simply calls
tcbdbcurjumpback() (as this function does almost exactly what we need here), but
sets the first bit of the key, to indicate that we need the last key with a given prefix:

```
case HA_READ_PREFIX_LAST_OR_PREV:
  key_buffer[0] |= 0x80;
  if (!tcbdbcurjumpback(dbcur, key_buffer, key_len))
    return tc_error(share->dbh);
  break;
```

Now let's try something more complex — HA_READ_KEY_EXACT mode. As
tcbdbcurjump() finds either the matching or the next key, to make sure we have
the exactly matching key, we simply need to retrieve the key at the cursor position
with the tcbdbcurkey3() function and compare it with the requested key using our
tocab_compare() comparison function:

```
case HA_READ_KEY_EXACT:
  if (!tcbdbcurjump(dbcur, key_buffer, key_len))
    return tc_error(share->dbh);
  rec = tcbdbcurkey3(dbcur, &reclen);
  if (tocab_compare((char*)rec, key_len,
      (char*)key_buffer, key_len, table->s))
    return HA_ERR_KEY_NOT_FOUND;
  break;
```

In HA_READ_AFTER_KEY mode we are interested in the first key that is greater than
the key argument. We can find it by calling tcbdbcurjump() and then moving
the cursor forward until we find a non-matching key or reach the end of the
index. But it would be much better to jump to the last matching key using the
tcbdbcurjumpback() function — it would allow us to avoid a loop over all matching
keys, as there can be thousands of them:

```
case HA_READ_AFTER_KEY:
  key_buffer[0] |= 0x80;
  if (!tcbdbcurjumpback(dbcur, key_buffer, key_len)) {
    if (!tcbdbcurjump(dbcur, key_buffer, key_len))
      return HA_ERR_KEY_NOT_FOUND;
  }
  else
    if (!tcbdbcurnext(dbcur))
      return HA_ERR_KEY_NOT_FOUND;
  break;
```

To understand this, let's look at our example—{1,2}, {2,3}, {2,3}, {3,4}—again. After the first `tcbdbcurjumpback()` the cursor will point to the last matching key or to a previous key if the exact matching key cannot be found. It means that if we are looking for {2}, or {2,3}, or {3,1}, in all of these cases the cursor will be at the last {2,3} key. In this case we call `tcbdbcurnext()`, the cursor is moved to the next key, and we get what is needed for HA_READ_AFTER_KEY. On the other hand, if the first `tcbdbcurjumpback()` fails, it can only mean that neither exact matching nor any lesser key exists. For example, if we searching for the {0,1} key; in this case, we can simply position the cursor on the next larger key with `tcbdbcurjump()` and it will be the key we want. We do not even need to reset the bit in the `key_buffer[0]` for a forward search, as it only affects how a prefix is compared with a *matching* key, and at that line we know that no matching key exists.

HA_READ_BEFORE_KEY mode is, in a sense, a reverse of HA_READ_AFTER_KEY. We can expect that the reverse code of HA_READ_AFTER_KEY will work for it:

```
case HA_READ_BEFORE_KEY:
  if (!tcbdbcurjump(dbcur, key_buffer, key_len)) {
    if (!tcbdbcurjumpback(dbcur, key_buffer, key_len))
      return HA_ERR_KEY_NOT_FOUND;
  }
  else
    if (!tcbdbcurprev(dbcur))
      return HA_ERR_KEY_NOT_FOUND;
  break;
```

Just as HA_READ_BEFORE_KEY is a reverse of HA_READ_AFTER_KEY, HA_READ_PREFIX_LAST is the reverse of HA_READ_KEY_EXACT:

```
case HA_READ_PREFIX_LAST:
  key_buffer[0] |= 0x80;
  if (!tcbdbcurjumpback(dbcur, key_buffer, key_len))
    return tc_error(share->dbh);
  rec = tcbdbcurkey3(dbcur, &reclen);
  if (tocab_compare((char*)rec, key_len,
              (char*)key_buffer, key_len, table->s))
    return HA_ERR_KEY_NOT_FOUND;
  break;
```

MySQL should never use any other search mode with our engine, but just in case:

```
default: return HA_ERR_WRONG_COMMAND;
}
```

Having positioned the cursor on the right row we read it into a buffer and return:

```
    return get_cursor_row(active_index, buf);
}
```

Now, we can easily implement the rest of the index searching functions. For example, `index_first()` is just a search for an empty prefix with `HA_READ_KEY_OR_NEXT`, while `index_last()` searches for an empty prefix with `HA_READ_PREFIX_LAST`, and `index_read_last()` can also be implemented in terms of `HA_READ_PREFIX_LAST`:

```
int ha_tocab::index_first(uchar *buf)
{
  return index_read(buf, 0, 0, HA_READ_KEY_OR_NEXT);
}

int ha_tocab::index_last(uchar *buf)
{
  return index_read(buf, 0, 0, HA_READ_PREFIX_LAST);
}

int ha_tocab::index_read_last(uchar *buf,
                              const uchar *key, uint key_len)
{
  return index_read(buf, key, key_len, HA_READ_PREFIX_LAST);
}
```

Only two functions are left — `index_next()` and `index_prev()` — and they are quite straightforward to implement:

```
int ha_tocab::index_next(uchar *buf)
{
  table->status = STATUS_NOT_FOUND;
  if (!tcbdbcurnext(dbcur))
    return HA_ERR_END_OF_FILE;
  return get_cursor_row(active_index, buf);
}

int ha_tocab::index_prev(uchar *buf)
{
  table->status = STATUS_NOT_FOUND;
  if (!tcbdbcurprev(dbcur))
    return HA_ERR_END_OF_FILE;
  return get_cursor_row(active_index, buf);
}
```

Rows and keys

Now we discuss the row and key formats. The naive approach would be to store rows in a MySQL format—what is passed to the write_row() function is written to disk. Thus retrieval would be easy too. Unfortunately, this does not work. For example, this format has all CHAR and VARCHAR fields space padded to their full length. Storing them that way would waste a lot of space. But the main reason why this simple approach is fundamentally flawed is the BLOB type. In memory, all BLOB (and TEXT) fields are kept outside of the row buffer; the row buffer only keeps a pointer to the actual BLOB field content. This is why we use a special packed row format, which makes our code only slightly more complex, as MySQL conveniently provides a Field::pack() method that will do all of the packing job. First, we need a buffer for a packed row. A growing String object (briefly discussed in the previous chapter) would be very handy here. As we do not need more than one row buffer per table, we can put it in the ha_tocab object:

```
bool ha_tocab::pack_row(const uchar *from)
{
  uint max_length = table->s->reclength;
  for (int i = 0; i < table->s->blob_fields ; i++) {
    Field_blob *blob = (Field_blob*)
                table->field[table->s->blob_field[i]];
    max_length += blob->get_packed_size(from +
                        blob->offset(table->record[0]),
                          table->s->db_low_byte_first);
  }
```

We start by calculating the required buffer size. The row length without BLOB fields is table->s->reclength, and for all BLOB fields we add up the sizes of their packed values to get the buffer size that we need. MySQL has a blob_field[] array in TABLE_SHARE, it is an array of field numbers—indexes in the table->field[] array of Field objects—for all BLOB fields. We simply iterate over this array, find the corresponding Field_blob object, and use its get_packed_size() method, which returns the number of bytes that the packed image of the actual BLOB field value will need. Unlike table>s->reclength, which is a fixed length of the row, and does not depend on the row content, we need to use a sizes of an actual BLOB field content, unless we want to allocate 4 GB of memory for every BLOB field in the table up front.

```
  if (row_buf.realloc(max_length))
    return 1;
```

Knowing the row size, we increase the size of the buffer, if necessary. The `String::realloc()` method never decreases the size of the `String` object buffer. It means we only need to allocate memory when a new row has larger BLOB values than all rows this `ha_tocab` object has seen so far.

```
uchar *to = (uchar*)row_buf.ptr();
memcpy(to, from, table->s->null_bytes);
to += table->s->null_bytes;
```

Having the row buffer ready, we copy the NULL bitmap first—MySQL row format starts with a bitmap that shows which fields are NULL; it has one bit per any field that can be NULL. Its length is in the `null_bytes` member of TABLE_SHARE, and we copy this bitmap verbatim into our packed row.

```
for (Field **field = table->field ; *field ; field++)
  if (!((*field)->is_null()))
    to = (*field)->pack(to,
               from + (*field)->offset(table->record[0]));
  row_buf.length(to - (uchar*)row_buf.ptr());
  return 0;
}
```

After the NULL bitmap we simply invoke the `pack()` method of every field that is not NULL, packing them one after another in the row buffer, and update the `String` length accordingly. We have our packed row now.

The unpacking procedure, as expected, does the reverse of packing. In our case it is even simpler than that, as we do not need to allocate a buffer for BLOB fields:

```
void ha_tocab::unpack_row(const uchar *from, uchar *to)
{
  memcpy(to, from, table->s->null_bytes);
  from += table->s->null_bytes;
  for (Field **field = table->field ; *field ; field++)
    if (!((*field)->is_null()))
      from = (*field)->unpack(to +
                  (*field)->offset(table->record[0]), from);
}
```

In this `unpack_row()` method we copy the NULL bitmap, and invoke the `unpack()` method of all fields that are not NULL. Note that a field knows whether it is NULL by consulting the NULL bitmap. That is why we have to copy the NULL bitmap first, before using the `Field::is_null()` method.

Now, the key format. We should be able to construct a key from the row buffer, that is, given values for all columns, create a corresponding key. We need it, for example, when inserting new rows into the table. We will need the reverse procedure too — reconstructing the column values in the row buffer from a key; this is the *keyread* optimization that we have discussed before.

There could be many key formats one can think of, but just as with rows, we will use MySQL help to simplify our example. We have used the `Field::pack()` method for our row format; we will use MySQL's `key_copy()` function for our key format. This function, defined in the `sql/key.cc` file, generates a key in the MySQL key format from a row buffer. It comes with a companion function, `key_restore()`, which fills in a row buffer from a MySQL key. As prototypes of both functions are not visible to plugins, we need to declare them in our engine:

```
void key_copy(uchar *to_key, uchar *from_record,
             KEY *key_info, uint key_length);
void key_restore(uchar *to_record, uchar *from_key,
             KEY *key_info, uint key_length);
```

Equipped with these two helpers we can easily write our methods. To generate a key from the row buffer we start by writing the first byte with the key number, then invoking `key_copy()` to put the key into the output buffer. After that, if we are generating a secondary key (not a key number 0), we append a primary key, again using `key_copy()`, to the key buffer:

```
int ha_tocab::pack_key(uchar *key, int key_num,
                       const uchar *record)
{
  *key++ = key_num;
  key_copy(key, const_cast<uchar*>(record),
          &table->key_info[key_num], 0);
  if (key_num == 0)
    return ref_length;
  key+= table->key_info[key_num].key_length;
  *key++ = 0;
  key_copy(key, const_cast<uchar*>(record),
          &table->key_info[0], 0);
  return table->key_info[key_num].key_length + 1 + ref_length;
}
```

We have already used our helper function `get_cursor_row()` a few times. Now, having decided on the key and row format, we can actually implement it:

```
int ha_tocab::get_cursor_row(int key, uchar *buf)
{
  int reclen;
  const void *rec;
  rec = tcbdbcurkey3(dbcur, &reclen);
  if (*(uchar*)rec != key)
    return HA_ERR_END_OF_FILE;
```

First, we need to retrieve the key at the cursor position and verify that this is the key that we need. Indeed, because we have put all indexes in one B+tree sorted by the index number, `tcbdbcurnext()` can move from the last key of the index N to the first key of the index N+1. For Tokyo Cabinet it is still the same index, but we know that the index N (the one we are interested in) has no more values, and it is `HA_ERR_END_OF_FILE`.

```
  table->status = 0;
```

At this moment, we know that the row is found, and we can reset `table->status`.

```
  if (key == 0) {
    rec = tcbdbcurval3(dbcur, &reclen);
    unpack_row((uchar*)rec, buf);
    return 0;
  }
```

If the current index is the primary key, the value corresponding to it is the row data; all we need is to unpack it. Otherwise, we try to use the *keyread* optimization:

```
  int klen = table->key_info[key].key_length;
  if (keyread) {
    key_restore(buf, (uchar*)rec + 1,
                &table->key_info[key], klen);
    key_restore(buf, (uchar*)rec + klen + 2,
                &table->key_info[0], ref_length - 1);
    return 0;
  }
```

If MySQL has allowed us to use *keyread*, we simply invoke the MySQL `key_restore()` function to fill in the row buffer from the current key (retrieved previously with the `tcbdbcurkey3()` function). We restore both the secondary key (number `key`) and the primary key (number 0) as we have both in the key buffer. Otherwise, we need to use the primary key (the *position*) to find the corresponding row data. Remembering that reading the row by its *position* is precisely what the `rnd_pos()` method does, we can end our `get_cursor_row()` function with:

```
    return rnd_pos(buf, (uchar*)rec + klen + 1);
}
```

The last and very important function that needs intimate knowledge of the key format, and thus belongs to this section, is our custom comparison function, `tocab_compare()`. It is a callback function that we give to Tokyo Cabinet using the `tcbdbsetcmpfunc()` call, and Tokyo Cabinet invokes it when it needs to compare two keys. That is, the number and type of the arguments of this function are defined by the Tokyo Cabinet API.

```
    static int tocab_compare(const char *aptr, int asiz,
                             const char *bptr, int bsiz,
                             void *op)
    {
       TABLE_SHARE *table = (TABLE_SHARE*)op;
```

The callback comparison function in Tokyo Cabinet takes five arguments — the first key and its length, the second key and its length, and a pointer that was passed to the `tcbdbsetcmpfunc()` function. The caller can use it to pass any information down to the comparison function, and we use the opportunity to pass TABLE_SHARE, the structure that has all of the information about the table structure, field types, and keys of the table in question.

We start by deciding how to compare key prefixes — the first bit of the key is responsible for that:

```
        int prefix_retval = -1;
        if (*aptr & 0x80 || *bptr & 0x80)
          prefix_retval = 1;
```

Having done that, we start the comparison. The first byte of every key is the index number. If two keys belong to different indexes, we can stop immediately:

```
        int keynum = *aptr & 0x7F;
        int keynumb = *bptr & 0x7F;
        if (keynum != keynumb)
          return keynum - keynumb;
```

Otherwise, we scan both keys, and compare them, part by part:

```
int null_found = 0;
const char *aend = aptr+asiz;
const char *bend = bptr+bsiz;
for (;;) {
  aptr++;
  bptr++;
  KEY *key_info = &table->key_info[keynum];
  for (int i = 0; i < key_info->key_parts; i++) {
    if (aptr >= aend)
      return bptr >= bend ? 0 : prefix_retval;
    if (bptr >= bend)
      return -prefix_retval;
```

We need to make sure that we are not comparing past the end of the key prefix. If we have reached the end of one of the keys, we return `prefix_retval`, which was set to be -1 or 1 depending on the first bit, exactly the way we wanted it.

```
KEY_PART_INFO *key_part = & key_info->key_part[i];
int off = 0;
if (key_part->null_bit) {
  if (*aptr != *bptr) return *bptr - *aptr;
  null_found |= *aptr;
  off = 1;
}
```

If the key part value can be NULL, the first byte of the key part value in the MySQL key format will be 1 or 0, depending on whether the key part value is NULL or not. If one of the compared keys is NULL and the other is not, we can stop comparing; otherwise we go on, remembering whether we have compared two NULL values.

```
int cmp = key_part->field->key_cmp((uchar*)aptr + off,
                                   (uchar*)bptr + off);
if (cmp) return cmp;
```

To perform the actual value comparison we use the `Field::key_cmp()` method. It will compare the values correctly, taking their type, character set, collation, and other such details into account.

```
aptr += key_part->store_length;
bptr += key_part->store_length;
```

And if everything is equal so far we move to the next key part.

```
  }
  if ((key_info->flags & HA_NOSAME) && !null_found)
    return 0;
  keynum = 0;
```

We reach these lines if we have successfully compared all key parts of the index `keynum` and found no differences so far. What do we do now? If the index `keynum` was declared `UNIQUE` — we see that by looking at the `HA_NOSAME` flag — we can report the equality right now, and let Tokyo Cabinet propagate the unique constraint violation error up the stack. But only if we have not seen any `NULL` values! According to the SQL standard and the `NULL` value semantics, one can store many `NULL` values even in the `UNIQUE` index. For all practical purposes, it means that the `UNIQUE` index is only unique unless the key contains `NULL`. And this is exactly what we have done. If the index is `UNIQUE` and no `NULL` values have contaminated our comparison, we report the equality. Otherwise, we repeat the whole comparison again, for the key number 0, that is for the primary key, which we append to any secondary key for this very reason.

```
  }
  return 0;
}
```

Table scan and random access

Compared to indexes, sequential and random table access (`rnd_*` methods) are much simpler. We have discussed them extensively in previous chapters. In our engine there is no way to scan all of the rows in a sequential order — Tokyo Cabinet has no API for that. Like other engines that store the row data in the index by primary key, we convert the table scan into the primary key index scan.

There is only one detail worth mentioning. As we remember, the call sequence for the sequential table scan is `rnd_init()`, `rnd_next()` many times, and `rnd_end()`. While for the index scan it is `index_init()`, `index_first()`, `index_next()` many times, and `index_end()`. See? In the indexed case, MySQL calls a special method to retrieve the first row in the sequence. In the table scan case, the same method is used to get the first and all subsequent rows. The indexed call sequence fits the Tokyo Cabinet logic pretty well, as we have seen already. The table scan does not; we need to know whether MySQL asks for the first or any of the subsequent rows. We will use a Boolean member in the `ha_tocab` object to solve this problem:

```
  int ha_tocab::rnd_init(bool scan)
  {
    first_row = true;
```

```
    active_index = 0;
    return 0;
  }

  int ha_tocab::rnd_next(uchar *buf)
  {
    if (first_row) {
      first_row = false;
      return index_first(buf);
    }
    else
      return index_next(buf);
  }
```

In the `rnd_init()` method we set `first_row` to be `true`, and in `rnd_next()` we either call `index_first()` or `index_next()`, depending on the `first_row` property. As `active_index` is 0, `index_*` methods will use the primary key, as desired.

```
  void ha_tocab::position(const uchar *record)
  {
    pack_key(ref, 0, record);
  }

  int ha_tocab::rnd_pos(uchar *buf, uchar *pos)
  {
    int reclen;
    const void *rec = tcbdbget3(share->dbh, pos,
                                 ref_length, &reclen);
    table->status = 0;
    unpack_row((uchar*)rec, buf);
    return 0;
  }
```

Both methods for the random table access are just as simple. As our *position* is the primary key, and we need to store it in the buffer pointed to by `ref`, the position method is reduced to a single `pack_key()` call. To retrieve the row by its position we use the `tcbdbget3()` function. It does not affect the cursor position, and directly returns the value corresponding to a key.

Inserting rows

We have done almost everything MySQL needs to read the table data. But we do not know yet how to populate the table. No problem, we will do our `write_row()` method now.

```
int ha_tocab::write_row(uchar *buf)
{
  if (table->timestamp_field_type &
      TIMESTAMP_AUTO_SET_ON_INSERT)
    table->timestamp_field->set_time();
  if (table->next_number_field && buf == table->record[0]) {
    int error;
    if ((error= update_auto_increment()))
      return error;
  }
```

As we know from previous chapters, the `write_row()` method starts with the obligatory incantation that sets values for the TIMESTAMP and AUTO_INCREMENT columns.

```
  if (pack_row(buf))
    return HA_ERR_OUT_OF_MEM;
  int key_len = pack_key(ref, 0, buf);
```

Then we prepare the packed row and the primary key in the `ref` buffer, and use Tokyo Cabinet's transactional features to simplify our `write_row()` method significantly.

Even in non-transactional engines, MySQL expects the `write_row()` method to be atomic. However, it performs a set of table updates that can fail the operation in the middle, that is, it needs to insert the row data into the table, and for any index insert the corresponding key/value pair in the appropriate index. Having many UNIQUE indexes in the table, it is possible that after a few indexes are updated the next UNIQUE index will report a constraint violation. In such a case, the engine needs to undo all of the effects of `write_row()`, and most non-transactional engines do it by explicitly deleting all of the already inserted keys from their indexes. But with Tokyo Cabinet transactions we can simply wrap the complete update operation in a transaction and roll it back in case of a failure:

```
  tcbdbtranbegin(share->dbh);
  last_key = 0;
  if (!tcbdbputkeep(share->dbh, ref, key_len,
                    row_buf.ptr(), row_buf.length()))
    goto error;
```

We start our update operation by inserting the primary key with the packed row data into the B+tree. The `tcbdbputkeep()` function tries to "put" the key/value pair into the index, but "keep" the old value for this key if it already exists in the index. In other words, it is the function to use when inserting into a `UNIQUE` index, and we abort the operation if we get a duplicate primary key. Before modifying the index, we remember what index is to be modified in `last_key` to be able to report the index of conflict back to MySQL.

```
for (int idx=1; idx < table->s->keys; idx++) {
  int key_len = pack_key(key_buffer, last_key = idx, buf);
  if (!tcbdbputkeep(share->dbh, key_buffer, key_len, "", 0))
    goto error;
}
```

After the primary key, we insert all secondary indexes one by one. The value has zero length here, as everything is in the key itself.

```
  tcbdbtrancommit(share->dbh);
  return 0;
error:
  int err=tc_error(share->dbh);
  tcbdbtranabort(share->dbh);
  return err;
}
```

At the end, we commit the Tokyo Cabinet transaction and return 0, which means success, or abort the transaction and return an error code.

Because of space constraints we will not implement `delete_row()` or `update_row()` in this example. But there is one more method that MySQL may use to delete rows from a table. For the `DELETE` statement without a `WHERE` clause and for the `TRUNCATE` statement MySQL first tries to delete all rows at once using the `delete_all_rows()` method. If it is not implemented, MySQL resorts to deleting rows one by one with the `delete_row()` method. We will implement `delete_all_rows()` in our engine, because Tokyo Cabinet provides a function, `tcbdbvanish()` that does just that:

```
int ha_tocab::delete_all_rows()
{
  if (tcbdbvanish(share->dbh))
    return 0;
  return tc_error(share->dbh);
}
```

What's left

Not much. We need to know when to use the *keyread* optimization. MySQL tells it using the HA_EXTRA_KEYREAD hint. The extra() method is used by MySQL to give various hints to the engine that are safe to ignore. In other words, this method is completely optional. In our case, though, we are interested in the *keyread* optimization hint:

```
int ha_tocab::extra(enum ha_extra_function hint)
{
  if (hint == HA_EXTRA_KEYREAD)
    keyread=true;
  if (hint == HA_EXTRA_NO_KEYREAD)
    keyread=false;
  return 0;
}
```

In table_flags() we had the HA_STATS_RECORDS_IS_EXACT flag, that is, we need to return the exact number of records in stats.records. On a unique constraint violation we need to tell MySQL what index has caused the failure. The method info() is used for both purposes:

```
int ha_tocab::info(uint flag)
{
  if (flag & HA_STATUS_VARIABLE)
    stats.records = tcbdbrnum(share->dbh) / table->s->keys;
  if (flag & HA_STATUS_ERRKEY)
    errkey = last_key;
  return 0;
}
```

When optimizing, MySQL uses the records_in_range() method to get an estimate for a number of records that fall into a certain range of values for a given key inx. These estimates are used to choose the best query execution plan, for example, the range with the least number of records. Unfortunately, the Tokyo Cabinet API does not provide a way of obtaining this estimate. We could traverse the index from the lower to the upper range limits and count keys, but this method would be too slow if the range contains, say, many millions of keys. It is not too difficult to add this feature to Tokyo Cabinet, but for the purpose of this example, we will just return a fixed number, because we do not know better:

```
ha_rows ha_tocab::records_in_range(uint inx,
                                   key_range *min_key,
                                   key_range *max_key)
{
  return 10;
}
```

In many of the previous methods we used the `tc_error()` function — it is our utility function that maps the Tokyo Cabinet error code to the MySQL error code:

```
static int tc_error(TCBDB *dbh)
{
  int err;
  switch(err = tcbdbecode(dbh)) {
  case TCESUCCESS: return 0;
  case TCEKEEP:    return HA_ERR_FOUND_DUPP_KEY;
  case TCENOREC:   return HA_ERR_KEY_NOT_FOUND;
  case TCENOFILE:  return HA_ERR_NO_SUCH_TABLE;
  case TCENOPERM:  return HA_ERR_TABLE_READONLY;
  case TCEMETA:    return HA_ERR_NOT_A_TABLE;
  case TCERHEAD:   return HA_ERR_CRASHED;
  default:         return err+10000;
  }
}
```

The `tcbdbecode()` function returns the error code from the last failed operation. If there is no mapping for any particular error code, we return it plus a big number to make sure it never matches an existing MySQL error number. Although such a collision would not cause any bugs, it would be confusing for the user.

As an extra bit of user-friendliness, we implement the `get_error_message()` method. MySQL calls it to turn the unknown (read: engine specific) error code to a string. Without it a user may see, for example:

Got error 10014 from storage engine

But with it, the error will be:

Got error 10014 'write error' from TOCAB

The method takes an error number as an argument, and needs to store the message in the supplied `String` buffer. It returns `false` for the error message as above, and `true` for a transient error. The error message in this case would have been:

Got temporary error 10014 'write error' from TOCAB

MySQL does not do anything special for transient errors besides using a slightly different error message.

```
bool ha_tocab::get_error_message(int error, String *buf)
{
  const char *msg=tcbdberrmsg(error-10000);
  buf->set(msg, strlen(msg), &my_charset_bin);
  return false;
}
```

Compiling and linking

We will need a `Makefile.am` file, which looks almost exactly as in the previous chapter:

```
pkgplugindir =     $(pkglibdir)/plugin
INCLUDES =         -I$(top_srcdir)/include \
                   -I$(top_builddir)/include \
                   -I$(top_srcdir)/sql

noinst_HEADERS = ha_tocab.h

EXTRA_LTLIBRARIES = ha_tocab.la
pkgplugin_LTLIBRARIES= @plugin_tocab_shared_target@
ha_tocab_la_LDFLAGS = -module -rpath $(pkgplugindir)
ha_tocab_la_CXXFLAGS= -DMYSQL_DYNAMIC_PLUGIN
ha_tocab_la_SOURCES = ha_tocab.cc

EXTRA_LIBRARIES = libha_tocab.a

noinst_LIBRARIES = @plugin_tocab_static_target@
libha_tocab_a_SOURCES= ha_tocab.cc

EXTRA_DIST =   plug.in
```

We will also require a `plug.in` file that has two new lines:

```
MYSQL_PLUGIN(tocab, [TOCAB Storage Engine],
    [Storage Engine that uses Tokyo Cabinet storage library],
    [max,max-no-ndb])
MYSQL_PLUGIN_STATIC(tocab, [libha_tocab.a])
MYSQL_PLUGIN_DYNAMIC(tocab, [ha_tocab.la])

AC_CHECK_HEADER([tctdb.h],,[with_plugin_tocab=no])
AC_CHECK_LIB(tokyocabinet,tcbdbopen,,[with_plugin_tocab=no])
```

Besides declaring a storage engine plugin and specifying that it supports both static and dynamic linking with the server, we check for the installed Tokyo Cabinet library. If it is not installed, we disable our plugin and it will not be built. If a Tokyo Cabinet is installed, it will be detected and a plugin will be built, dynamically by default, or statically, if a user said so. Of course, a user may decide to disable the plugin nevertheless. We just do what we can to gracefully handle the situation when a Tokyo Cabinet library is not present, to avoid failing the build with an unsightly compilation error.

Putting it all together

It was a long and exhausting chapter with lots of code and lots of details. We deserve to see what we have created:

```
mysql> create table t (a int primary key, b int, c int, d int, e blob,
key bcd_key (b,c,d)) engine=tocab;
Query OK, 0 rows affected (0.01 sec)
```

```
mysql> insert t values (1,2,3,4,"foo"),(2,3,4,5,"bar"),(3,4,5,6,"abc"),(
4,5,6,7,"serg"),(5,6,7,8,"andrew"),(6,7,8,9,"mysql"),(0,4,6,7,"tocab"),
(7,5,6,7,"something");
Query OK, 8 rows affected (0.01 sec)
Records: 8  Duplicates: 0  Warnings: 0
```

```
mysql> insert t values (7,5,6,7,"this will fail");
ERROR 1062 (23000): Duplicate entry '7' for key 'PRIMARY'
```

Yes, this has worked, the error message is correct.

```
mysql> select * from t;
+---+------+------+------+-----------+
| a | b    | c    | d    | e         |
+---+------+------+------+-----------+
| 0 |    4 |    6 |    7 | tocab     |
| 1 |    2 |    3 |    4 | foo       |
| 2 |    3 |    4 |    5 | bar       |
| 3 |    4 |    5 |    6 | abc       |
| 4 |    5 |    6 |    7 | serg      |
| 5 |    6 |    7 |    8 | andrew    |
| 6 |    7 |    8 |    9 | mysql     |
| 7 |    5 |    6 |    7 | something |
+---+------+------+------+-----------+
8 rows in set (0.00 sec)
```

```
mysql> explain select a,b,c,d from t\G
*************************** 1. row ***************************
           id: 1
  select_type: SIMPLE
        table: t
         type: index
possible_keys: NULL
          key: bcd_key
      key_len: 15
          ref: NULL
         rows: 8
        Extra: Using index
1 row in set (0.00 sec)
```

This is interesting. See how EXPLAIN shows "Using index" (it means *keyread* optimization) on the bcd_key index? But bcd_key is not covering! We have selected columns a, b, c, and d while bcd_key only covers b, c, and d. Could that be a bug in MySQL? No, column a is part of the primary key, and MySQL knows that any of our indexes includes a primary key implicitly, because in our table_flags() method we have used the HA_PRIMARY_KEY_IN_READ_INDEX flag. This allows MySQL to allow the *keyread* optimization even in cases when a key is not covering according to the table definition.

```
mysql> select * from t force index (b) where b < 5 order by b desc;
+---+------+------+------+-------+
| a | b    | c    | d    | e     |
+---+------+------+------+-------+
| 0 |    4 |    6 |    7 | tocab |
| 3 |    4 |    5 |    6 | abc   |
| 2 |    3 |    4 |    5 | bar   |
| 1 |    2 |    3 |    4 | foo   |
+---+------+------+------+-------+
4 rows in set (0.00 sec)
```

This is one of the cases when MySQL uses the HA_READ_BEFORE_KEY search mode. As the example shows, this mode, as well as the index_prev() method, seem to work correctly. We need to use the FORCE INDEX hint in the query, otherwise the MySQL optimizer would prefer to use a table scan, not an index scan. The table has only 8 rows, and a table scan would need to touch only 8 rows, while an index range would contain 10 rows (that's what our fake records_in_range() method says), and MySQL prefers a cheaper table scan. If the table had few times more rows, the FORCE INDEX hint would not be needed.

More queries that provide almost complete coverage of our example engine source code can be found in the `tocab.test` file that is a part of the code bundle for this book and can be downloaded from the Packt website.

Possible extensions

Our TOCAB engine, although fully functional, is still missing few features, before it can be truly called a general purpose storage engine for MySQL. For example:

- Working `delete_row()` and `update_row()` methods.
- Auto-increment implemented in the engine — this is the only way to make sure that auto-increment numbers are not reused. If it is implemented in the server, as is the case with our engine, every new auto-increment number is the largest auto-increment number in the table plus one. Obviously, when we delete the row with the largest auto-increment number and insert a new row we get the same auto-increment number.
- A working `records_in_range()` method. Most probably it would require some modifications in the Tokyo Cabinet source code.
- Our engine should not require the user to specify a primary key, but needs to generate a hidden primary key automatically, if necessary.
- Working `optimize()` and `analyze()` methods (there is the `tcbdboptimize()` method that can be used here).
- Make use of the `tcbdbtune()` method — with tuning parameters available as MySQL server variables (`MYSQL_SYSVAR_*` macros) or as `CREATE TABLE` attributes (see *Appendix*).
- Tokyo Cabinet supports hash indexes too. In MySQL a user can specify whether an index should use a B-tree or hash algorithm with the `USING BTREE` or `USING HASH` clause. If our engine used hash indexes provided by Tokyo Cabinet, it could support this clause, allowing a user to use the algorithm that is best suited for any given index.

Summary

In this chapter we have studied, in excruciating detail, the inner workings of a MySQL storage engine that supports B-tree indexes. We have seen how to implement a translation layer between the MySQL storage engine API and a third-party B-tree storage library API, and how to work around their incompatibilities.

This chapter concludes the storage engine part of the book.

Beyond MySQL 5.1

In the Appendix, we will briefly look at changes in the Plugin API that you may expect to see in MySQL versions after MySQL 5.1.

Server services

Over the years, MySQL developers have implemented a lot of functionality for the server to use. There are wrappers over the system functions such as `my_open()`, `my_sync()`, and `my_malloc()` that add additional features such as error checking and reporting. Compatibility wrappers such as `my_snprintf()` and `pthread_mutex_lock()` behave identically on all platforms and add additional features too. There are also various useful data structures such as red-black binary trees, dynamically growing hash tables, priority queues, and so on. Useful utility functions such as connection local memory allocator and character set support were developed specifically for the MySQL server run-time environment.

In many cases, plugins would like to use all of this and not reinvent the wheel. But how can they do that? Just calling any of these functions directly will create an additional dependency on the server—a dependency not covered by the Plugin API. Although not always possible, it is wise to avoid dependencies like that. MySQL developers can change internal details of the server implementation anytime—it is only the API that they promised to keep stable. If our plugin depends on such internal details, and they are changed, the best we can hope for is that the plugin will not load. However, it could cause a crash on load, or it may appear to work but produce incorrect results. There is no way to know in advance.

A safe, though time consuming, solution would be to ask MySQL developers to add functions we need to the `plugin.h` header. By doing this they add these functions to the Plugin API and promise to keep them stable. Or at least protected them with an API version number, as sometimes changes are unavoidable. If such an unavoidable change happens, the Plugin API version is incremented and old plugins stop loading. There will be no crash or incorrect results, MySQL will simply complain that the plugin requires an incompatible API version and will refuse to load a plugin.

This approach is safe, no crash, but not perfect. There is only one version number—the Plugin API version—but there can be hundreds of utility functions. An incompatible change of any single one of them requires the version to be incremented, and all plugins are invalidated—although most, if not all, plugins do not need or use this particular utility function and are not affected by the change. But MySQL does not know it, because there is one global version number that covers everything.

What is really needed is a fine-grained version control, to track interface changes on a function level, one version per function, or at least per a group of related functions. A plugin stores version numbers for all of the functions it uses and MySQL checks them when it loads a plugin. Ideally, it should be completely automatic—we do not want to maintain a list of all functions (and their versions) that our plugin needs.

This is exactly what Server Services are. Fine-grained version control—one version per service, that is a group of functions (a group can be as small as one function though). Automatic dependency tracking—we do not need to think about it, it just works; the versions for all services that we have used in our plugin are automatically recorded in the plugin binary (`.dll` or `.so` file). They are automatically checked when a plugin is loaded to guarantee complete API compatibility. Changes in functions that *our* plugin does not use will not affect the compatibility of *our* plugin, even if they may affect other plugins. It is completely transparent and does not require any changes in the plugin source code—calling a function from a service is as simple as calling a normal function. We can simply write:

```
my_snprintf(buf, sizeof(buf), "string=%s", str);
```

This will call an appropriate function from an appropriate service.

What are the drawbacks? It is almost automatic and transparent, but not quite. There is one manual step—we need to link our plugin with `libmysqlservices.a`. Usually, it means adding `-lmysqlservices` to `LDFLAGS` in the `Makefile.am` file. In Windows, there is no need to do even that.

Another issue is that services do not cover all MySQL internal functionality yet. Their number is growing, we can expect more services to appear. Eventually, everything that MySQL developers want to make accessible for plugins will be available via services. But at the time of writing, there are only two services in the MySQL 5.5 source tree: *my_snprintf* and *thd_alloc*.

my_snprintf

This service provides two functions: `my_snprintf()` and `my_vsnprintf()`. They are roughly equivalent to the system `snprintf()` and `vsnprintf()` (leaving aside the fact that not all systems provide them) with the following differences:

- They do not support all `printf()` format features. For example, left-padding is not implemented.

- They produce identical results on all operating systems, compilers, and architectures — passing a null pointer for `%s` prints `(null)` (while system `printf()` either does that or crashes). Floating point numbers are printed identically everywhere as they use MySQL internal routines for conversion. Printing a pointer with `%p` always adds the `0x` prefix (a system `printf()` either does it or not).

- They support a few non-standard extensions, such as printing a string with embedded null bytes (using `%b` format) or quoting identifiers with backticks according to MySQL quoting rules (using `%`s` format).

The complete documentation for this service is in the `mysql/service_my_snprintf.h` file.

thd_alloc

This service gives us a specialized memory allocation function `thd_alloc()` as well as helper functions `thd_calloc()`, `thd_strdup()`, `thd_strmake()`, and `thd_memdup()`.

There are two main differences between `malloc()` and `thd_alloc()`:

- The system `malloc()` typically allocates memory from a global memory pool. It means that when many threads want to allocate memory in parallel, `malloc()` needs to protect its shared data structures, which causes mutex locks and reduces concurrency. The `thd_alloc()` function takes memory from a thread local memory pool, and as different threads use different pools the concurrency overhead disappears. In other words, `thd_alloc()` is much faster than `malloc()` when MySQL is serving many connections at the same time.

- There is no need to free the memory. All memory allocated with `thd_alloc()` is automatically freed when the processing of the current SQL statement ends. It significantly simplifies plugin memory management as we do not need to worry about memory leaks anymore.

It all means that this service is perfect for small and medium-sized allocations that we need only for a short time, otherwise we are better off with a good old `malloc()`.

The complete documentation for this service is in the `mysql/service_thd_alloc.h` file.

Audit plugins

Besides many other features, MySQL 5.5 adds a new plugin type—Audit plugin. As the name suggests, it allows us to do auditing and logging of whatever happens in the server. At certain points, the MySQL server emits *audit events*. An audit plugin can subscribe to receive them, all or only a subset, for further processing. Let's look at what the audit event looks like:

```
struct mysql_event
{
  unsigned int event_class;
};
```

Every audit event is characterized by its class. The event structure may have more members, but what they are depends on the event class.

Now, what makes the audit plugin API different from all other plugin type APIs—it is not feature complete. It does not try to anticipate all possible audit use cases and generate all possible audit events for everything that anyone may want to audit some day. Instead, MySQL developers (including one of the authors of this book) have only implemented one audit event class—general—as new audit classes can be added later, when they will be needed for real, not hypothetical, plugins. The event of the general audit class is defined as:

```
#define MYSQL_AUDIT_GENERAL_LOG     0
#define MYSQL_AUDIT_GENERAL_ERROR   1
#define MYSQL_AUDIT_GENERAL_RESULT 2

struct mysql_event_general
{
  unsigned int event_class;
  unsigned int event_subclass;
  int general_error_code;
  unsigned long general_thread_id;
```

```
        const char *general_user;
        unsigned int general_user_length;
        const char *general_command;
        unsigned int general_command_length;
        const char *general_query;
        unsigned int general_query_length;
        struct charset_info_st *general_charset;
        unsigned long long general_time;
        unsigned long long general_rows;
    };
```

All events of the general class are sorted into one of the three subclasses — log, error, and result. Events of the log subclass are emitted when a statement is received by the MySQL server, but before its execution starts. It is also the point when logging into the MySQL general query log takes place. Events of the error subclass are emitted when an error happens during the execution of the SQL statements. The `general_error_code` member of the `mysql_event_general` structure is non-zero only for the events of this subclass. Finally, events of the result subclass are emitted when the execution of the SQL statement is finished, almost where logging into the slow query log takes place. The `general_time` and `general_rows` members are defined only for events of this subclass.

Let's look at a simple audit plugin to understand the API better:

```
    mysql_declare_plugin(securlog)
    {
      MYSQL_AUDIT_PLUGIN,
      &securlog_struct,
      "SecurLog",
      "Sergei Golubchik",
      "Log Security Violations",
      PLUGIN_LICENSE_GPL,
      NULL,
      NULL,
      0x0001,
      NULL,
      NULL,
      NULL
    }
    mysql_declare_plugin_end;
```

The audit plugin, like any other plugin, must be declared with the help of the `mysql_declare_plugin` macro. The only element specific to auditing here is the pointer to the `securlog_struct` structure — the descriptor of our audit plugin:

```
static struct st_mysql_audit securlog_struct =
{
  MYSQL_AUDIT_INTERFACE_VERSION,
  NULL,
  securlog_log,
  { MYSQL_AUDIT_GENERAL_CLASSMASK }
};
```

The audit plugin descriptor starts from the API version number — any plugin descriptor structure starts from that, independently from the plugin type. The last member in the structure is the bitmap of the event classes we are interested in. In this way we declare what events we want to see, and MySQL will do the filtering for us. Of course, there is only one event class for now, so there is not much to filter. We specify that we want to see events in the general class.

The third member is the most important one — it is a pointer to the function that will be called for every event, a *notification* function, `securlog_log()`. This function takes two arguments, the calling `THD` and the event descriptor of the `mysql_event` type. The second member is a pointer to the *release* function — the function that should remove any dependency that exists between `THD` and the plugin, as if the `THD` would be destroyed the very next moment. For example, if our notification function wants to cache data in the `THD`, it needs to invalidate the cache here. If we ever allocate the memory and store the pointer in `THD`, we would have to free it now. And if we use the `thd_alloc` service to allocate memory in the current thread memory pool, we should consider this memory to be gone after the release function is called.

However, we are not going to do anything like that in this example, and our release function pointer is `NULL`. We just want to log all of the attempts to violate a security policy — that is, all cases when somebody tries to access a database, a table, or a column that he has no right to. It can be done easily by intercepting the error subclass of events and looking for all error codes that can be used to deny access to a resource:

```
static void securlog_log(MYSQL_THD thd,
                         const struct mysql_event *ev)
{
  struct tm t;
  const struct mysql_event_general *event = ev;
  switch (event->general_error_code) {
  case ER_ACCESS_DENIED_ERROR:
  case ER_DBACCESS_DENIED_ERROR:
```

```
case ER_TABLEACCESS_DENIED_ERROR:
case ER_COLUMNACCESS_DENIED_ERROR:
  localtime_r(&event->general_time, &t);
  fprintf(stderr, "%04d-%02d-%02d %2d:%02d:%02d "
                  "[%s] ERROR %d: %s\n",
          t.tm_year + 1900, t.tm_mon + 1,
          t.tm_mday, t.tm_hour, t.tm_min, t.tm_sec,
          event->general_user, event->general_error_code,
          event->general_command);
  }
}
```

As we can see, it is as simple as it can be—for all matching error codes it prints a log entry with the time of the event, username, the error code, and the error message.

Authentication plugins

Having talked about the features in the MySQL 5.5 branch—both Server Services and the Audit Plugin API are present in the latest MySQL 5.5.4-m3 release—it is time to look into the more distant future. Authentication plugins first appeared in MariaDB—the extended version of MySQL, developed independently as a fork—version 5.2. The code was contributed to MySQL though, and may appear in a post-5.5 release.

How it works

An authentication plugin is specified per user, in the CREATE USER or GRANT statement:

```
CREATE USER serg IDENTIFIED VIA three_attempts USING 'secret';
GRANT USAGE ON *.* TO ''@'%' IDENTIFIED VIA ldap;
```

The second statement specifies a plugin to use for an anonymous user, it means that if the username was not found in the mysql.user table it will be looked up in the LDAP. This allows storage of the list of users in the LDAP without duplicating it in the MariaDB (or MySQL).

Pluggable authentication adds a new concept to the MySQL plugin architecture—client-side plugins. Indeed, an authentication process is a dialog, if the server wants to use, for example, Kerberos, the client needs to support it too. Client-side plugins do just that: they are loadable modules that are loaded into the client by the libmysqlclient library, and provide the client side of the pluggable authentication.

According to a MySQL client-server protocol, on a new connection, the server sends to a client a so called *handshake packet* with the server version and capabilities. The client replies with a packet containing the client capabilities and the username. Both packets carry the authentication data provided by the corresponding plugins. They have to use default plugins, because neither a server nor a client can know what plugin was specified for this user in the `mysql.user` table until the server receives the username from the client. After the server finds out what plugin to use, it switches to the correct plugin and tells the client to do so, as necessary. But the switch happens—if at all—completely transparent for plugins; they do not need to implement anything special to support it.

Now, to get a taste of it, let's write a working plugin that uses USB sticks for logging into the MariaDB server. Sounds cool? A USB mass storage device should (according to the specifications, although not all manufactures adhere to them) have a unique serial number. In Linux, one can easily get serial numbers of all plugged in, even not mounted, USB devices from the `/proc/bus/usb/devices` file. We will use the serial number of a USB device to authenticate a user.

Authentication plugins—server side

A server-side authentication plugin starts by including the necessary API header file:

```
#include <mysql/plugin_auth.h>
```

We also include a few system headers, we will need them:

```
#include <string.h>
#include <fcntl.h>
#include <unistd.h>
```

Just like any other plugin, this needs the usual plugin mumbo-jumbo:

```
mysql_declare_plugin(usbsn)
{
  MYSQL_AUTHENTICATION_PLUGIN,
  &usbsn_handler,
  "usbsn",
  "Sergei Golubchik",
  "USB Serial Number",
  PLUGIN_LICENSE_GPL,
  NULL,
  NULL,
  0x0100,
```

```
    NULL,
    NULL,
    NULL
  }
mysql_declare_plugin_end;
```

We declare an authentication plugin, called *usbsn*, version 1.0. The plugin declaration refers to the authentication plugin handler, which we declare as follows:

```
static struct st_mysql_auth usbsn_handler=
{
  MYSQL_AUTHENTICATION_INTERFACE_VERSION,
  "usbsn",
  usbsn_verify
};
```

This structure contains three members. It starts with the obligatory API version number. Then, it names the client-side plugin that our server-side plugin should work with. It does not need to have the same name as the server plugin. In fact, in many cases, the server plugin only needs to ask the user to enter some information — a password, a key phrase, or a PIN — and MariaDB comes with a useful client-side plugin called *dialog* that can do just that, ask questions as instructed by the server. That is, in many cases a server plugin can simply use the dialog client plugin. In our case, we need a client to retrieve the serial number of a USB device — and this requires us to write a dedicated client-side plugin. For simplicity, we have called it *usbsn* too.

The third member of the `st_mysql_auth` structure is the function that actually performs the authentication. Our authentication function needs to check whether a user — on the client side, not on the server side — has the correct USB stick plugged in. This is not too complex. We will let the client-side authentication plugin read the complete `/proc/bus/usb/devices` file and send it to the server. The server-side plugin will then see if it contains the serial number that is needed for a given user.

```
static int usbsn_verify(MYSQL_PLUGIN_VIO *vio,
                        MYSQL_SERVER_AUTH_INFO *info)
```

This is how the authentication function has to be defined. The first argument, `vio` (from "Virtual I/O") structure, provides methods to communicate with the client — the `read_packet()` and `write_packet()` functions. The `info` structure gives us a username, that we should authenticate, and — in the `auth_string` member — the string that was specified in the USING clause of the GRANT or CREATE USER statement. In our case, it will be the serial number of the USB device:

CREATE USER test IDENTIFIED VIA usbsn USING '1A08051410110';

All we need to do is use the `vio->read_packet()` function to read the data that the client plugin has sent, and search it for the serial number, as specified in the `info->auth_string`. The `/proc/bus/usb/devices` file looks like:

```
T:  Bus=01 Lev=01 Prnt=01 Port=06 Cnt=01 Dev#=  4 Spd=480 MxCh= 0
P:  Vendor=0ea0 ProdID=2126 Rev= 2.00
S:  Manufacturer=OTi
S:  Product=USB Multi- Card Reader
S:  SerialNumber=0123456789abcdef
. . . .
```

We better search for the complete line, with the "S: SerialNumber=" prefix, to make sure we did not, accidentally, find a match in the middle of a longer serial number of some other device:

```
{
  unsigned char *pkt;
  int pkt_len;
  size_t buflen=strlen(info->auth_string) + 20;
  char *buf=alloca(buflen);
  my_snprintf(buf, buflen, "S:  SerialNumber=%s\n",
              info->auth_string);
```

First, we allocate a buffer, and create a string to search for. Note that it uses the `my_snprintf()` function, which is exported via the *my_snprintf* service, as explained earlier in this *Appendix*.

```
  if ((pkt_len= vio->read_packet(vio, &pkt)) < 0)
    return CR_ERROR;
```

Now we read the data, as sent by the client. The `vio->read_packet()` function returns the number of bytes read and stores the pointer to the data in `pkt`. The data itself is in the internal buffer of the MySQL network layer, and it will be overwritten on the next I/O operation. In our case it is fine, but if we need the data for a longer time, we will have to copy it.

```
  return strstr(pkt, buf) ? CR_OK : CR_ERROR;
}
```

Done! After reading the data, all we need is one `strstr()` call to determine if any of the connected USB devices, on the client side, has the correct serial number or not.

Now, we need to write the client part of our USB authentication.

Authentication plugins—client side

Similarly, it starts by including the header:

```
#include <mysql/client_plugin.h>
```

Client plugins are much simpler than their server counterparts. They cannot be unloaded at runtime. There can be only one plugin in the .so or .dll file and its name has to match the filename. There is only one structure—not two—that describes the plugin.

```
mysql_declare_client_plugin(AUTHENTICATION)
  "usbsn",
  "Sergei Golubchik",
  "USB Serial Number",
  {0,0,1},
  NULL,
  NULL,
  usbsn_send
mysql_end_client_plugin;
```

The client plugin declaration starts with mysql_declare_client_plugin() with the argument being the plugin type. It is followed by the plugin name, plugin author, plugin description, plugin version (an array of three integers), and three function pointers—for the initialization, de-initialization, and authentication functions. Only the last function is required, the others are optional, and our plugin does not need and does not provide them.

The authentication function of the client plugin has a prototype similar to its server-side partner:

```
static int usbsn_send(MYSQL_PLUGIN_VIO *vio,
                      struct st_mysql *mysql)
```

It also takes two arguments—the vio structure and the informational structure with the password in the username. The information structure in the client case is the st_mysql (better known as MYSQL) structure used everywhere in the MySQL client C API.

```
{
  int len, res, fd;
  char buf[10240];

  fd=open("/proc/bus/usb/devices", O_RDONLY);
  if (fd == -1)
```

```
      return CR_ERROR;

  len=read(fd, buf, sizeof(buf)-1);
  close(fd);
  if (len == 0)
    return CR_ERROR;

  buf[len++]=0;

  res=vio->write_packet(vio, buf, len);

  return res ? CR_ERROR : CR_OK;
}
```

The function itself is very simple, it only reads the file and sends it to the server.

This is all. When this plugin is built and loaded we can try it out. Plug any USB stick into the computer and look up its serial number in the /proc/bus/usb/devices file. For my Sony Micro Vault Tiny 8GB, it is 1A08051410110. Now, I can create a test user with:

```
CREATE USER test IDENTIFIED VIA usbsn USING '1A08051410110';
```

After that I can connect to the MariaDB server as this user only if my Micro Vault stick is plugged in—plugged in the computer where I start the command line client, not in the computer that runs the server. Congratulations, it works!

SQL extension by Storage Engine plugins

This is another new feature that is at the moment only available in MariaDB 5.2. In various storage engines, tables, fields, and indexes often have properties that a user may want to tune, but has no way of doing it. There is only a fixed set of attributes accessible from SQL such as MAX_ROWS, AVG_ROW_LENGTH, INSERT_METHOD, CONNECTION, KEY_BLOCK_SIZE, ROW_FORMAT, PACK_KEYS, and so on. Lucky engine authors, who had access to the MySQL source code, could modify the parser to add support for new attributes—such as InnoDB or MyISAM-specific values of ROW_FORMAT, MERGE-specific parameter INSERT_METHOD, or Federated only attribute CONNECTION. Other engines had to use the COMMENT field, as in the following:

```
CREATE TABLE ugly (
  a INT
) ENGINE=unlucky COMMENT='count=1200:mode="wrap"'
```

This has limited functionality, prevents the user from using the table comment for its original purpose, forces every engine to implement the same code of parsing of the comment string, and simply looks unprofessional from the end user point of view.

The new extension of the Storage Engine API allows engines to provide a list of attributes that will be supported in the CREATE TABLE and ALTER TABLE statements. For example:

```
CREATE TABLE data (
  name VARCHAR(255) APPROVED=YES,
  cv BLOB AVG_SIZE=2048,
  UNIQUE (name) BUCKET=adaptive
) ENGINE=hypothetical TAGS="data,name,CV" TRAIL=ON;
ALTER TABLE data COMPRESSION=gzip LEVEL=9;
```

These statements show that tables in some hypothetical engine may have four additional attributes — TAGS, which takes a string, TRAIL, which is a Boolean attribute and can be on or off, COMPRESSION, that takes not an arbitrary string, but a value from a predefined set, similar to the ENUM column type in SQL, and, lastly, LEVEL, which is a numeric attribute. Also, we see two field attributes — APPROVED and AVG_SIZE, and one index attribute — BUCKET.

This hypothetical engine only needs to declare these attributes, parsing and saving them in the .frm file would be done by the server. In this example, there are four table attributes — one string, one number, one enumeration, and one Boolean. First, the engine declares a structure to store them:

```
struct ha_table_option_struct
{
  char      *tags;
  ulonglong comp_level;
  uint      compr;
  bool      is_trailed;
};
```

This is the structure that stores the values of the attributes. The only detail worth noting is that it uses unsigned int for the enumeration, not C enum type. The size, in bytes, of the enum type can depend on the compiler and compilation options, and this structure should only use stable types that have the same size in the server and in the loadable engine.

Now, having the structure, we can map it to the SQL attribute names:

```
ha_create_table_option table_option_list[]=
{
  HA_TOPTION_STRING("tags", tags),
  HA_TOPTION_BOOL("trail", is_trailed, false),
  HA_TOPTION_ENUM("compression", compr, "none,gzip,bzip2", 0),
  HA_TOPTION_NUMBER("level", comp_level, 4, 0, 9, 1),
  HA_TOPTION_END
};
```

This is all. The array declares four table options (`HA_TOPTION_*`):

- `TAGS`: accepts a string as a value and stores it in the `tags` member of the structure
- `TRAIL`: accepts a Boolean value (that is, one of `ON`, `OFF`, `YES`, `NO`, `1`, `0`) with the default being `false`, and stores it in the `is_trailed` member of the structure
- `COMPRESSION`: accepts one of `NONE`, `GZIP`, `BZIP2` with the default being `NONE`, and stores the *ordinal number of the value* in the `compr` member of the structure
- `LEVEL`: accepts a number from 0 to 9 with the step 1 and the default 4, which is stored in the `comp_level` member of the `ha_table_option_struct` structure.

Field and index attributes are declared similarly using `HA_FOPTION_*` and `HA_IOPTION_*` macros.

Putting it to use

We could have used this feature in the book, for example with our HTML engine:

```
create table test (
  a int,
  b timestamp,
  c varchar(50)
) engine=html style='border:1; color:#001177';
```

We could also use it with the TOCAB engine (with the option names and values as documented in the Tokyo Cabinet manual):

```
create table t (
  a int primary key,
  b int,
  c int,
  d int,
  e blob,
  key bcd_key (b,c,d)
) engine=tocab lmemb=64 nmemb=128 bnum=32767 apow=6 fpow=8;
```

Let's try to implement the second example. To add support for table attributes to our TOCAB engine, we need to start with the Tokyo Cabinet manual. The function `tcbdbtune()` takes a closed database handle and six tuning parameters:

lmemb	Number of elements in the leaf page; the default is 128.
nmemb	Number of elements in the node page; the default is 256.
bnum	Number of elements in the bucket array; the default is 16381.
apow	Record alignment. The record will be aligned by the 2^{apow} bytes. The default is 8, which means the alignment at the 256-byte boundary.
fpow	Maximum number of elements in the free block pool. Again, the actual value will be 2^{fpow}. The default is 10, that is 1024 elements.
opts	Bitwise OR of flags BDBTLARGE (the file can be larger than 2GB), BDBTDEFLATE, BDBTBZIP, BDBTTCBS (what compression algorithm to use).

To map them to SQL, we can create five numeric attributes, one Boolean—for BDBTLARGE—and one enumeration:

```
struct ha_table_option_struct
{
  ulonglong lmemb, nmemb, bnum, apow, fpow;
  bool large;
  uint compression;
};

ha_create_table_option table_option_list[]=
{
  HA_TOPTION_NUMBER("lmemb", lmemb,   128, 1, 65535, 1),
  HA_TOPTION_NUMBER("nmemb", nmemb,   256, 1, 65535, 1),
  HA_TOPTION_NUMBER("bnum",  bnum, 16381, 1, 65535, 1),
  HA_TOPTION_NUMBER("apow",  apow,     8, 0, 256, 1),
  HA_TOPTION_NUMBER("fpow",  fpow,    10, 0, 256, 1),
  HA_TOPTION_BOOL("large",   large, false),
  HA_TOPTION_ENUM("compression", compression,
                  "none,deflate,bzip2,tcbs", 0),
  HA_TOPTION_END
};
```

Now, we need to tell the server about these attributes by setting the `handlerton` appropriately:

```
static int tocab_init(void *p)
{
  handlerton *tocab_hton = (handlerton *)p;
  tocab_hton->create = tocab_create_handler;
  tocab_hton->table_options = table_option_list;
  return 0;
}
```

It is the same `tocab_init()` function as before, with one new, highlighted line. We have told the server about new table attributes; the server will handle the rest. The only thing that the server cannot do is to use them. Indeed, the job of calling `tcbdbtune()` is ours. But the server makes it easy, by giving us a `ha_table_option_struct` structure filled with values:

```
static TCBDB *open_tcdb(const char *name, TABLE *table,
                        int *error)
{
  char fname[FN_REFLEN+10];
  strcpy(fname, name);
  strcat(fname, ".tocab");
  *error = 0;
  TCBDB *dbh = tcbdbnew();
  if (!dbh) {
    *error = HA_ERR_OUT_OF_MEM;
    return 0;
  }
}
```

So far, it is the same `open_tcdb()` function as in the last chapter. Now, we can add a few more lines to it:

```
ha_table_option_struct *opts=
      (ha_table_option_struct*)table->s->option_struct;
```

We take the structure, `table->s->option_struct`, and cast it from the generic `void*` to a pointer to our table option structure. We call `tcbdbtune()` with all of the tuning parameters:

```
if (tcbdbsetmutex(dbh) &&
    tcbdbtune(dbh, opts->lmemb, opts->nmemb, opts->bnum,
              opts->apow, opts->fpow,
              (opts->large ? BDBTLARGE : 0) |
              (opts->compression == 1 ? BDBTDEFLATE : 0) |
              (opts->compression == 2 ? BDBTBZIP : 0) |
```

```
            (opts->compression == 3 ? BDBTTCBS : 0)) &&
    tcbdbsetcmpfunc(dbh, tocab_compare, table->s) &&
    tcbdbopen(dbh, fname, BDBOWRITER|BDBOCREAT))
  return dbh;
*error = tc_error(dbh);
tcbdbdel(dbh);
return 0;
}
```

As usual, the added lines are highlighted. Done. The server ensures that all members of the structure get the values—as specified by the user or defaults—and that these values are valid, within the ranges that we specified. The server stores the values in the `.frm` file and gives them to us both when a table is created and every time it is opened—which is important, as `open_tcdb()` is called both from `ha_tocab::create()` and `ha_tocab::open()`, and both times it needs to know the values of the tuning parameters.

Test drive

We can create a table and see how options are recognized by the server:

```
mysql> create table t ( a int primary key, b int, c int, d int, e blob,
key bcd_key (b,c,d)) engine=tocab lmemb=64 nmemb=128 bnum=32767 apow=6
fpow=8 compression=tcbs large=yes;
Query OK, 0 rows affected (0.01 sec)
```

Looking in the debugger, you would have noticed that `tcbdbtune()` is correctly called with these values. The server takes care of showing them too:

```
mysql> set sql_quote_show_create=0;
Query OK, 0 rows affected (0.00 sec)

mysql> show create table t\G
*************************** 1. row ***************************
      Table: t
Create Table: CREATE TABLE t (
  a int(11) NOT NULL,
  b int(11) DEFAULT NULL,
  c int(11) DEFAULT NULL,
  d int(11) DEFAULT NULL,
  e blob,
  PRIMARY KEY (a),
  KEY bcd_key (b,c,d)
) ENGINE=TOCAB DEFAULT CHARSET=latin1 lmemb=64 nmemb=128 bnum=32767
apow=6 fpow=8 compression=tcbs large=yes

1 row in set (0.00 sec)
```

Note that invalid values are not accepted:

```
mysql> create table t1 (a int primary key) engine=tocab compression=gzip;
ERROR 1651 (HY000): Incorrect value 'gzip' for option 'compression'
```

Summary

MySQL 5.1 has been released and new features are being added to MySQL 5.5 and later versions, and to independently developed MariaDB—a backward compatible fork of MySQL with additional features. Plugin API is being changed and extended too. In the Appendix, we have seen a few large features that are already implemented and available, but which did not make it to MySQL 5.1. Of course, there are numerous smaller changes of differing importance both in MySQL and MariaDB—this Appendix simply cannot cover them all. And surely even more features are planned or being developed as you read these lines.

Good luck in your plugin development adventure, and have fun!

Index

Symbols

$varvar 135
$while 130
--disable-plugin-my-plugin command 52
.dll extension 27
-lexif 145
-ourplugin-log-size 64
-ourplugin-mode command-line option 64
--plugin-my-plugin=OFF command 52
__reserved1 member 56
--skip-grant-tables option 31
@@static_text_rows 162, 164
@@static_text_text 164
@@static_text_text variable 162
@@static_text_varchar variable 176

A

aggregate UDFs 25, 46-49
analyze() 194
apow parameter 255
arg_count member 34
args array member 35
args member 34
arg_type member 34, 35
arguments() method 104
attribute_lengths member 35
attributes member 34, 35
audit plugins
    about 244
    example 245
authentication plugin
    about 247
    client side 251, 252
    dialog 249

handshake packet 248
libmysqlclient library 247
my_snprintf() function 250
read_packet() function 249
server side 248-250
st_mysql_auth structure 249
strstr() call 250
vio->read_packet() function 250
vio structure 251
working 247, 248
write_packet() function 249
author 55
AUTO_INCREMENT field 191

B

bas_ext method 166
bas_ext() method 209
BDBCUR cursor handle 215
Binary Logs Information Schema plugin
    about 115-118
    get_index_file() method 116
    index_file 116
    LOG_INFO structure 116
    SHOW BINARY LOGS command 115
    show_binlogs() function 115
blk parameter 62
BLOB field content 224
BLOBs 183
bnum parameter 255
boolean full-text parser 139-144
boolean parsers 137, 139
B-tree library
    about 203, 204
    storage, types 204

C

D

WHERE clause 103
WHERE condition 103
Windows
  plugin libraries 16-18
  UDF libraries 10, 12-14
write_html() function 185
write_packet() function 249
write_row() function 224
write_row() method 162, 190, 191, 193, 232, 234

write_set bitmap 189

Y

yesno element 129
yesno property 140

Z

zero-terminated array 59

Thank you for buying
MySQL 5.1 Plugin Development

About Packt Publishing

Packt, pronounced 'packed', published its first book "*Mastering phpMyAdmin for Effective MySQL Management*" in April 2004 and subsequently continued to specialize in publishing highly focused books on specific technologies and solutions.

Our books and publications share the experiences of your fellow IT professionals in adapting and customizing today's systems, applications, and frameworks. Our solution based books give you the knowledge and power to customize the software and technologies you're using to get the job done. Packt books are more specific and less general than the IT books you have seen in the past. Our unique business model allows us to bring you more focused information, giving you more of what you need to know, and less of what you don't.

Packt is a modern, yet unique publishing company, which focuses on producing quality, cutting-edge books for communities of developers, administrators, and newbies alike. For more information, please visit our website: www.packtpub.com.

About Packt Open Source

In 2010, Packt launched two new brands, Packt Open Source and Packt Enterprise, in order to continue its focus on specialization. This book is part of the Packt Open Source brand, home to books published on software built around Open Source licences, and offering information to anybody from advanced developers to budding web designers. The Open Source brand also runs Packt's Open Source Royalty Scheme, by which Packt gives a royalty to each Open Source project about whose software a book is sold.

Writing for Packt

We welcome all inquiries from people who are interested in authoring. Book proposals should be sent to author@packtpub.com. If your book idea is still at an early stage and you would like to discuss it first before writing a formal book proposal, contact us; one of our commissioning editors will get in touch with you.

We're not just looking for published authors; if you have strong technical skills but no writing experience, our experienced editors can help you develop a writing career, or simply get some additional reward for your expertise.

open source
community experience distilled

Building Websites with e107

Building Websites with e107

A step-by-step tutorial to getting your e107 website up and running fast

Theodore S Boomer

PACKT

Building Websites with e107

ISBN: 978-1-904811-31-2   Paperback: 260 pages

A step by step tutorial to getting your e107 website up and running fast

1. Get your e107 website up fast

2. Simple and practical guide to mastering e107

3. Customize and extend your e107 site with new templates and the CMS plug-in

Learning Joomla! 1.5
Extension Development

A practical tutorial on creating Joomla! 1.5 extensions with PHP, written and tested against the final release of Joomla! 1.5

Joseph L. LeBlanc

PACKT

Learning Joomla! 1.5 Extension Development

ISBN: 978-1-847196-20-0   Paperback: 284 pages

A practical tutorial for creating your first Joomla! 1.5 extensions with PHP, written and tested against the final release of Joomla! 1.5

1. Program your own Joomla! extensions

2. Master Model-View-Controller design

3. Build configurable site modules to show information on every page

4. Use built-in HTML and JavaScript functions

Please check **www.PacktPub.com** for information on our titles

www.ingramcontent.com/pod-product-compliance
Lightning Source LLC
Chambersburg PA
CBHW060523060326
40690CB00017B/3362